HEATH SCIENCE

HEATH SCIENCE

Authors **James P. Barufaldi**
Associate Professor of Science Education
University of Texas, Austin

George T. Ladd
Professor of Science Education
Boston College

Alice Johnson Moses
Elementary Science Teacher
University of Chicago Laboratory School

Consulting Authors **Herman and Nina Schneider**
Science Educators and Authors of
Numerous Children's Science Books

Special Needs Consultant Rodger Bybee
Assistant Professor of Education
Carleton College, Northfield, Minnesota

Elementary Curriculum Consultant Phyllis Perry
Education Center
Boulder Valley Schools, Boulder, Colorado

Content Consultants Rolland B. Bartholomew
Associate Professor of Science Education
  and Geological Sciences
University of Texas, Austin

Joan G. Creager
Associate Professor of Biology
Northern Virginia Community College,
  Alexandria
Editor, American Biology Teacher

Joseph E. Davis, Jr.
Chairman, Science Department
Campolindo High School, Moraga,
  California

Mario Iona
Professor of Physics
University of Denver

 D.C. Heath and Company
Lexington, Massachusetts   Toronto

Editorial Development

Harley R. Mutzfeld, *Executive Editor*

Ellen T. Woodberry, *Editor*
Linda Z. Reddy, *Editor*
Dorothy P. Burstein, *Editor*
Leona W. Martin, *Editor*

Design Development

William Tenney, *Senior Designer*

Ann Marie Turley, *Design Assistant*
A. James Casner, III, *Design Assistant*
Pamela J. Daly, *Design Assistant*

Reading Level Consultant

Milton D. Jacobson
Professor of Educational Research
University of Virginia, Charlottesville

Educational Consultants

Sister Marie Andre Guay, RSM
Catholic School Office
Providence, Rhode Island

Elaine S. Barrett
Science Project Teacher
Bellevue School District, Washington

Harriett Brookman
Elementary Teacher
Miami, Florida

Napoleon Bryant, Jr.
Professor of Education
Xavier University, Cincinnati, Ohio

Jerry Hayes
Elementary Science Supervisor
Chicago, Illinois

David Lawrence
District Chairperson Science
Hartford, Connecticut

Richard Merrill
Curriculum Specialist
Mt. Diablo Unified School District, Concord, California

Constance Tate
Coordinator, Office of Science
Baltimore, Maryland

Roger Van Bever
Supervisor of Elementary Science
Detroit, Michigan

Mary Ellen Wandel
Supervisory Instructional Specialist
Pittsburgh, Pennsylvania

Edwin P. White
School of Education
University of South Carolina, Spartanburg

Field Test Teachers

Grateful acknowledgment is given to the teachers and students who participated in field tests of Heath Science.

Phoenix, ARIZONA
Lookout Mountain School, Barbara Semmens
Acacia School, Rebecca Walker

Louisville, COLORADO
Louisville Elementary School, Dorothy Pecina, Cheryl Turvey

Boulder, COLORADO
Bear Creek Elementary School, Barbara Puzio, Beverly Vance, Virginia Holland

Merritt Island, FLORIDA
Audubon Elementary School, Sue Colley, Natalie Jerkins, Peggy Graham, Ann Ehren

Satellite Beach, FLORIDA
Surfside Elementary School, Crystal Otto, Judith Cordrey, Sue Wisler

Atlanta, GEORGIA
E. Rivers School, Lillie Thompson, Virginia Robb, Cecelia J. Thomas, Sandra L. Black

Lexington, MASSACHUSETTS
Bowman Elementary School, Maureen Sullivan
Maria Hastings School, Alice F. Baylies

Maynard, MASSACHUSETTS
Coolidge School, Ellen Holway, Elizabeth Niland
Green Meadow School, Daria Benham, Pamela Tiramani

Newton, MASSACHUSETTS
Oak Hill School, Francis R. Stec, Dorothy Mims

Brooklyn, NEW YORK
Blessed Sacrament School, Marilyn Robinson
St. Jerome School, Sr. Patricia Brennan, R.S.M.

Plainview, NEW YORK
Parkway School, Edna Publicker, Shirley Grant
Pasadena School, Muriel Phillips, Suzanne Freund

Norfolk, VIRGINIA
Mary Calcott Elementary School, Barbara Wright
Ocean Air School, Yolanda Hill
Engleside School, Naomi Bethea
Poplar Halls School, Christine Crouch

Cover and Frontispiece photo: Photo voltaic cells generating electricity; Paul E. Johnson
Photo illustration credits appear on page 371.

TABLE OF CONTENTS

Unit 1

Plants and Animals on Our Planet

Classifying Animals with Backbones

1

There are millions of different kinds of living things in the world. Some of these things are so small that they can't be seen without a microscope. There may be hundreds of living things in a drop of pond water! Other living things are very large. Some blue whales are more than 30 meters long and weigh over 135 tons.

People discover new kinds of plants and animals every year. The world is filled with so many different living things that no one can be familiar with all of them. But people who study living things try to name them and put them in some kind of order.

It is not so easy to find the kind of order that is most useful. Living things are so different from each other in so many ways. But people try to find ways in which they are alike. They study one living thing and try to find what other living things it is *most* like. The living thing is then **classified**—put in the group to which it belongs.

3

Alive and Not Alive

How is a newly discovered thing classified? The first question that is asked may seem very simple, almost silly. Is it alive?

Nobody would have any trouble deciding that robins or dogs are living things. Both eat, move around, and make noise. From what you already know, you would say that plants, too, are living things. What are some things that you know about plants that show they are living?

It is not always so simple, however. Look at the shelled snail in the picture. It is a living thing. It looks much like the stone near it. The white matter that spoils the shoe is a living thing. The rust that spoils the knife seems to live and grow. But it really is not alive. How would you decide whether or not a thing is alive?

Living things may be different in many ways, but they are alike in these important ways:

1. Living things come from other living things of the same kind. A snail's parents are snails, and so are its young. The plant on the shoe came from another plant of the same kind.

2. Most living things are made of cells. Inside each cell is living matter called **protoplasm** [PROH-tuh-plaz-uhm]. Protoplasm is a semiliquid much like the white of an egg.

3. Living things grow and change. A young living thing is smaller than the fully grown living thing that it came from. Living things grow by adding new cells or by adding to the amount of protoplasm.

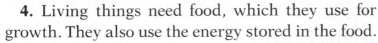

left to right: Infant, 1½ months old; Two-year-old child; Five-year-old child; Ten-year-old child

4. Living things need food, which they use for growth. They also use the energy stored in the food.

5. Living things need oxygen. Most living things take oxygen from the atmosphere, but some take it from the water in which they live. Oxygen is used by the cells in getting energy from food.

6. Living things can move. The energy to move comes from within the living thing. It comes from food that has become part of the living thing. Things that are not alive can move, too. A can may roll down a hill, or the wind may blow it. But the energy to move comes from outside the can.

Living things can also change direction as they move. Some living things move toward bright light. Other living things may move away from light. What animals have you seen that act this way? What did these animals do? How do plants act toward light?

Copy this chart on a sheet of paper. Make a check in one or all of the first four columns. Do this for each heading that describes the thing listed. Then, on the basis of the columns that you have checked, decide if the thing is alive or not. Show this by writing a letter A for *alive* or NA for *not alive* in the last column. Compare your chart with those made by others in the classroom. Do you agree with how others classified each thing?

	Moves by Itself	Needs Food and Oxygen	Grows	Acts Toward or Away From	Alive or Not Alive
1. jumprope					
2. desk					
3. bird					
4. rose bush					
5. chalk					
6. maple tree					
7. rabbit					
8. wind					
9. chair made of maple wood					
10. water					

Animals and Plants

After it is decided that a thing is living, it is usually classified as an animal or a plant. Plants are like animals in many ways, but they are different in these important ways:

1. Most plant cells have a thick wall around them. Look at the pictures of different cells. Which of them have cell walls?

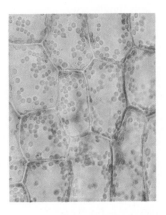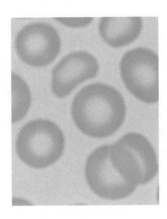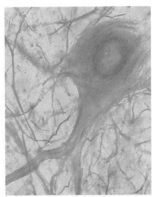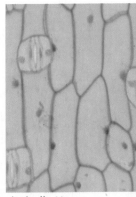

left to right: Elodea leaf cells; Human red blood cells; Nerve cell of human brain; Spiderwort leaf cells

2. Green plants can make food out of materials that are not food. You have learned that green plants in sunlight use carbon dioxide and water to make food.
3. Most plants do not move very much or very fast, compared to animals. Plants move when they grow. Stems grow and move up; roots grow and move down. Petals move as flowers open and close.

Look back at your chart of living things. Classify them in two columns:

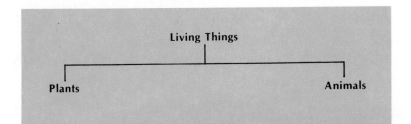

Living Things

Plants

Animals

How Are Animals Classified?

Suppose you have decided that you are looking at a living animal. You aren't sure exactly what it is, and you want to know the group to which it belongs. How are animals classified into groups?

Here are three animals whose shapes are alike. Yet people who study animals do not classify them in the same group. They are too different in ways other than shape. How are they different?

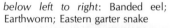

below left to right: Banded eel; Earthworm; Eastern garter snake

Here are two animals that are alike in two ways. They both hatch from eggs, and they both spend part of their time in water. Would you classify them in the same group? Of course not. They are too different in other important ways.

You are not exactly like your mother or father. You may have different eye or hair coloring. You may have curlier hair, or you may even be taller than your mother or father. But you are like them and all people in important ways. You have a heart, lungs, arms, legs, and so on. You are made of the same kinds of parts as other people. The parts do the same kinds of work. You have the same **structure** [STRUHK-chuhr] as other people.

People who study animals classify them by structure. They classify animals into groups by the kinds of parts they have and how they are put together. If you could look inside animals, you would see that some have structures with backbones and some do not. All the different kinds of animals in the world can be classified into two large groups:

1. Animals with backbones, called **vertebrates** [VUR-tuh-brayts]
2. Animals without backbones, called **invertebrates** [ihn-VUR-tuh-brayts]

This is the first big grouping that is used. Of course, this is only the beginning of classifying. There are five groups of animals with backbones in their bodies: **fish, amphibians, reptiles, birds,** and **mammals.**

Fish

How many fish do you see in the pictures? The answer is five! All of these animals are fish. They certainly are very different in shape and color. Yet they are alike in structure. Have you ever caught and cleaned a fish? Then you know some things about its structure.

clockwise, beginning at upper left: Lesser electric ray; Blue ribbon eel; Pipefish, Sea horse; Ornamental butterfly fish

Fish have backbones inside their bodies. Many other bones in the fish are fastened to the backbone. The bones make up the skeleton of the fish.

Most fish are covered from head to tail with hard **scales** that protect the fish. Scales are smooth and slimy. As the fish moves forward, the water slips smoothly over the scales. What would happen if the scales faced the other way? You can sometimes tell how old a fish is by looking at its scales. A ring is added to the scales each year they grow.

Get some large fish scales and a hand lens. Look at the fish scales with the lens and draw a few of them. Which way do the free ends of the scales face? How many rings can you see on the scales? The number of rings is a clue to the age of the fish. How old is the fish from which these scales came?

Fish get their oxygen by means of **gills.** They take in water through their mouths and let it out through slits. Oxygen in the water passes into thin blood vessels in the gills. At the same time, carbon dioxide passes out of the thin blood vessels into the water. Have you ever seen a fish that looks as if it were swallowing water? The fish is not drinking. It is breathing.

11

Look at a goldfish in a fish tank. Watch how the gills move. Look at the slit on either side of the fish's body. Does it close before or after the fish opens its mouth? Or does the slit close at the same time the fish opens its mouth? How does the water move through the gills?

Fish have **fins.** A fish steers itself through the water by moving its fins. The back fin, or tail, moves the fish forward.

Fish are **cold-blooded** animals. The temperature of their blood is about the same as the temperature of the water. If the water is cold, the fish's blood is cold. If the water is warm, the blood is warm.

Certain fish have long thin bodies, round mouths, and no jaws. They have skeletons made of matter that is softer than bone. These fish live by attacking other fish. Their mouths fasten against the sides of other fish. The insides of their round mouths are filled with small curved teeth. With these teeth, the fish cut holes in other fishes' bodies. They suck the soft body parts and blood out of the holes.

below left: Lamprey; *right*: Lamprey mouth, with suckers and tooth-like parts

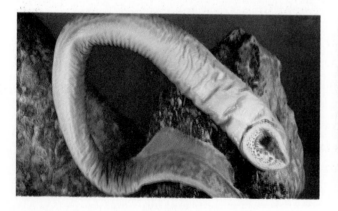

Why are sharks, such as this sand shark, feared so much?

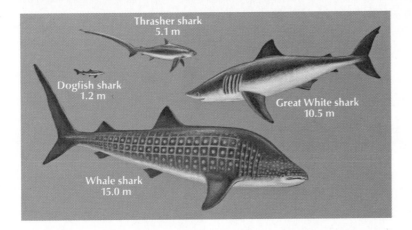

Thrasher shark
5.1 m

Dogfish shark
1.2 m

Great White shark
10.5 m

Whale shark
15.0 m

There is another group of fish whose skeletons are made of matter softer than bone. The ones that you know best are the **sharks.** Sharks have several rows of flat teeth with sharp edges. They are hunters, feeding upon other fish. Some are fairly small, while others are very large. The whale shark is the largest of all fish. It grows to a length of 20 m or more.

Fish lay their eggs in a soft, jellied mass.

Most fish lay soft eggs in the water. Young fish hatch from the eggs. Since most fish lay thousands or even millions of eggs at a time, why aren't the waters crowded with fish?

Amphibians

Frogs, toads, and salamanders belong to the amphibian group. They are cold-blooded animals of the shores, ponds, swamps, and low meadows. Amphibians are often better able to live in these places than other vertebrates. As adults, they have legs and lungs. Because of these structures, they are able to go on land and breathe air. Since their skin loses water quickly, most amphibians must live in damp or wet places. The amphibians then return to the water to produce their young.

The name *amphibian* is fitting for these animals because it means "having two lives." Most amphibians live part of their lives in water and part of their lives on land. A few that spend all their lives in water keep their gills.

clockwise, beginning at far left: Great Plains toad; Zigzag salamander; Fowler's toad; Green tree frog; Wood frog; Marbled salamander

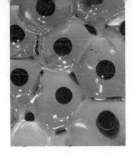

Four stages in the development of the European grass frog

Have you ever gathered up frogs' or toads' eggs in a pond? Maybe you have seen tadpoles hatch out of these eggs. They are the young of frogs and toads. Like fish, they get oxygen from the water through gills. As the tadpoles grow, legs appear and they lose their gills. They are able to take oxygen from the water through their thin, smooth skins. Lungs grow inside their bodies. In this way, they can also get oxygen from the air.

Coelacanth: Until a few years ago, this creature was thought to be extinct. Only a few specimens of it have been found.

This strange-looking animal has scales, fins, and gills. Could it be a fish? But the fins are short like feet. The animal has lungs as well as gills. Could it be an amphibian?

The answer is not clear. This animal is thought of as a kind of in-between animal. It has some of the structures of fish and some of the structures of amphibians. However, people who study animals think it is more like a fish. So they classify it with fish.

Reptiles

Here's a chance for you to do a little detective work. If you found these two animals outdoors, could you tell which one is an amphibian? They both look very much alike, and shape is no help. Both of them have lungs and breathe air. Both are cold-blooded. If you touch them, there is something about their skins that might give you a hint.

The salamander has a smooth, damp skin without scales. Is this true for most amphibians? The lizard has a dry skin with scales. It is a reptile.

Western fence lizard

Tiger salamander

clockwise, beginning at upper left: Emerald lizard; Scarlet king snake; Alligator; Nile crocodile; Florida turtle

Other reptiles are snakes, turtles, crocodiles, and alligators. These animals look quite different from each other. Yet they are very much alike in structure.

Reptiles are cold-blooded. Because of this, no reptiles can live in the very coldest parts of the earth. Some reptiles can live in the hottest deserts, though. When the temperature is high, they can dig in the sand. Or they can hide under the shade of a rock. Reptiles' scales protect them from drying out. That is why some of them can live in very dry places.

Reptiles breathe air. They are born with lungs. How is this different from amphibians? Some reptiles live near or in the water. But even reptiles that live in water must come up to breathe.

Sand lizards hatching

All reptiles are hatched from eggs. The eggs are protected by leathery shells. A reptile lays eggs on land. The shells keep the eggs from drying out. Reptiles lay fewer eggs than fish or amphibians, but their eggs have a better chance of hatching. Some kinds of snake eggs are kept inside the mother's body until they hatch.

Reptile eggs are bigger than fish or amphibian eggs. They have the food and water needed by the young inside. The young don't go through different stages like the tadpole.

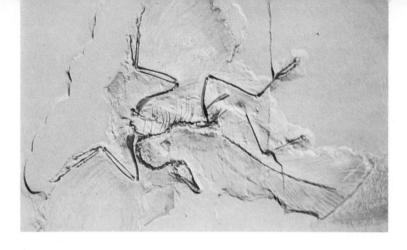

Archeopteryx

Birds

Here is a picture of an animal that lived 150 million years ago. Nobody has ever seen such an animal. But a record in rock like the one you see here has been found. What kind of animal do you think it was? Why do you think so?

Suppose someone brought you an animal covered with feathers. You would know it was a bird. Birds are the only animals that have feathers.

A bird has different kinds of feathers for different uses. You can get some feathers at a place where chickens are prepared for market.

Notice how the wing feathers are broad and flat. They push against the air when the chicken is flying. Look at the down feathers, which serve as a warm blanket. Find the little dark pinfeathers, which are new feathers about to unfold and grow.

These kinds of feathers have different sizes and colors on different birds. You may wish to mount several different kinds of feathers on a chart. Next to each feather, write its use.

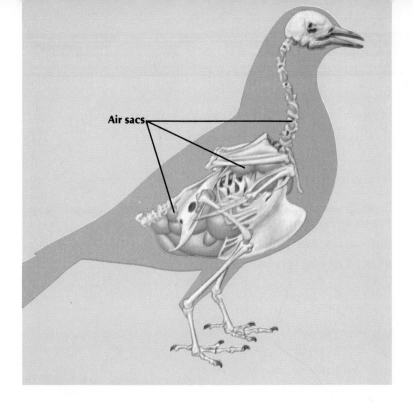

Air sacs

Birds breathe air through lungs. A bird's lungs branch into hollow spaces called **air sacs** in many parts of a bird's body. Air from the lungs is pumped down through the air sacs. In some birds the air sacs even reach into the bones of the toes.

All birds are **warm-blooded.** On warm days and cold days, in the air and in the water, a bird's blood stays at the same temperature. How is this different from cold-blooded animals? Birds can live in cold places and in hot places. Their bodies stay at the same temperature, no matter what the temperature is outside.

When a bird needs more heat, oxygen for getting energy from food can quickly reach its cells through the hollow sacs. When the temperature is too high, fresh, cool air can flow through the sacs. Water from the body cells can leave through the sacs. How does this cool the bird?

Feathers also help birds keep the same body temperature. A blanket keeps you warm because it traps air in its spaces. Your body gives off heat that warms the air in these spaces. A bird's feathers trap air in their spaces, too. This cuts down on the loss of body heat.

Birds hatch out of eggs with hard shells. What other animals hatch from eggs with shells? How are their shells different from bird egg shells? The yolk of the egg has food that the young bird inside needs until it is ready to hatch. The shell protects the young bird from drying out.

Most birds build some kind of nest. Some of these nests are only a few twigs piled together, or a grass-lined hollow in the ground. Birds protect and care for their young in the nests. What are some other ways that birds care for their young?

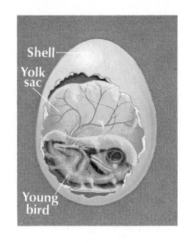

Nests of the sun bittern (*left*), cliff swallow (*center*), and whiskered tern (*right*)

Some birds can fly thousands of miles without stopping. Some are good for only a short hop. But most birds can fly and their structure shows it. Bird bones are very light, and some are hollow. Even a chicken, which doesn't fly very well, has some hollow bones. In what other ways are hollow bones helpful to birds?

20

Save some turkey or chicken bones the next time you have turkey or chicken for dinner. Clean them and let them dry. Save or get a bone from a ham (pig's leg) or a bone from a leg of lamb.

Ask your teacher to saw these bones in two the long way. Do you find that the bird bones are quite thin and that some have air spaces? How are the bird bones different from the ham bone or lamb bone?

Birds have two legs. Different birds have different kinds of feet depending on where they live and how they move about. Some feet are best for sitting on branches, some for holding, and some for swimming.

left to right to bottom: Bald eagle; American sparrow hawk; Grebe; Evening grosbeak; Pileated woodpecker; Brown pelican

Birds have no teeth. Instead of teeth, they have bills that are used for getting food. The size and shape of the bill can help you learn about the different foods a bird may eat. Some bills are good for cracking and opening seeds, some for digging insects out of tree bark, some for catching fish. When you watch a bird eating, notice its bill and its food.

21

Mammals

You have a backbone. How would you classify yourself?

Look closely at your arms. Feel the top of your head. You have a body covering of hair. This is one of the things that make you a mammal.

All mammals have hair. Some, such as bears, may be covered with hair from head to toe. Others, like the whale, have just a few hairs. A sheep's hair is thick and curly. Some of a porcupine's hair is in the form of thick, sharp needles! Hair can be different in many ways, but all mammals have some kind of hair.

Mammals are warm-blooded. Because of this, mammals can live almost anywhere on the earth. The temperature of a mammal's blood does not change with the changes in the outside temperature. Whether it is very cold or very hot outside, the body temperature stays the same.

Mammals have lungs and breathe air. All of them, even the ones that live in the sea, must have air to breathe. Air comes in through their noses and flows into two lungs. Here oxygen in the air passes into the blood. The blood carries the oxygen to all parts of the body.

Even though dolphins are mammals that live in the sea, they must come to the surface of the water in order to breathe. They nurse their young, just as land mammals do.

Mammal mothers can feed their young with milk from their bodies. While many other animal mothers also take care of their young and feed them, only mammals can make milk.

Most mammals give birth to live young. The young stay inside the bodies of their mothers until they are fully formed. Soon after they are born, some can walk or run. Others—like humans—need to be protected and cared for a long time after they are born.

However, there are two groups of mammals whose structures are slightly different from the rest. Instead of giving birth to live young, one of the two groups lays eggs. Once the eggs are laid, they are kept warm by the mother. What other vertebrate group keeps their eggs warm in this way? When the eggs hatch, the young get milk from their mothers, the same as other mammals.

above: Anteater; *left*: Duckbill platypus and young

The other group of mammals have a sack where the young are kept for some time after birth. Here are some of them. At birth, each young mammal is small enough to rest in a teaspoon! It crawls up to the sack on the mother's body. There it stays and drinks the mother's milk. After several months, the young mammal may leave the sack, but it will return to feed.

below, left to right: Opossum carrying young; Young opossums in sack; Kangaroo and young

In deciding how to classify animals, we look at their body structures. Simply looking alike is not enough. A small kind of whale and a large fish may live in the same ocean. They may look a lot alike. But a study of their inside structures shows that they are different. The whale is a warm-blooded mammal that breathes air. The fish is cold-blooded and uses gills to get oxygen from the water.

On the other hand, think about a prairie dog and a horse. The prairie dog is small and the horse is large. The prairie dog has short, strong front limbs with claws that are used in digging. The horse has long front limbs with single toes that have hoofs. These legs look different, but if you were to study them, you would find that their skeletons are alike. Also, both animals are warm-blooded. Both make milk and give birth to live young. Both breathe air. In fact, because of these things, the prairie dog and the horse are both classified as mammals. Since their structures are the same, they are put in the same group.

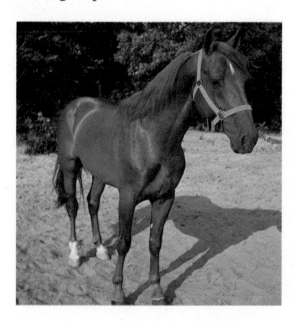

What Did You Learn?

- Most things can be classified as alive or not alive, plant or animal.
- Animals can be classified by their structure into two large groups: vertebrates and invertebrates.
- Fish have a skeleton, fins, and scales. They breathe through gills and are cold-blooded.
- Amphibians have skins without scales and are cold-blooded. When they are young, they have gills and get oxygen from the water. As adults, they have lungs and get oxygen from the air.
- Reptiles have scaly skins, have lungs, breathe air, and are cold-blooded.
- Birds have feathers, are warm-blooded, have lungs, and breathe air. Birds also have bills but no teeth, have two wings and two feet, and hatch out of eggs.
- Mammals have hair on their bodies, have lungs and breathe air, and are warm-blooded. The mothers can also make milk with which to feed their young.

Career

Zookeeper

A zoo is a place where many living things from all over the world are brought to live together. Maybe you have visited one. The zoo is also a place for scientists to study these animals.

Many people work at the zoo to help see that these animals get what they need to stay healthy and alive. Claudia Collier is one of these people. She is a senior zookeeper in charge of the children's zoo and baby animal nursery at the Los Angeles Zoo.

Claudia started as a tour guide answering questions and talking with groups of children about zoo animals. From this experience, she became even more interested in animal life and decided to make a career out of zoo work. She worked with an animal doctor for six months in an animal hospital. After that, she was hired by the zoo as a zoo attendant and later became a keeper.

There is no such thing as a typical day for a zookeeper. The work is always different. Since you can't always tell what an animal is going to do next, a keeper has to think quickly. A keeper must also use care in handling the animals.

Claudia enjoys her zoo work. She plans to go back to school to find out more about animals and how to manage a zoo.

TO THINK ABOUT AND DO

WORD FUN

On a piece of paper copy the names of the animals in columns A through E. In each column cross out the name of the animal that does not belong with the rest. At the top of each column write the name of the vertebrate group to which the remaining animals belong.

A	B	C	D	E
human	bat	snake	salamander	frog
whale	robin	alligator	lizard	shark
penguin	owl	eel	toad	sea horse

WHAT DO YOU REMEMBER?

Copy each sentence on a piece of paper. Write **T** beside the sentences that are true and **F** beside those that are false. Rewrite any sentence that is false to make it true.

1. Each living thing on Earth comes from another living thing of the same kind.
2. Animals are classified by structure.
3. Animals that have backbones are called invertebrates.
4. Fish have fins and scales, and breathe through gills.
5. Amphibians breathe through lungs when they are young and through gills when they are adults.
6. Reptiles have scaly skins, breathe air through lungs, lay eggs with leathery shells, and are cold-blooded.
7. Birds have feathers, breathe air through lungs, are warm-blooded, and have bills, two wings, and two feet.
8. Mammals are cold-blooded, breathe through lungs, and feed their young with milk.

Use books from your classroom or library to help you answer these questions.

1. Find out the following information about vertebrates:
   a. Which is the largest? Which is the smallest?
   b. Which takes the longest amount of time to become full grown?
2. How can birds without teeth grind up hard seeds? The word "gizzard" should help you.
3. How have John Audubon and Carolus Linnaeus added to our knowledge of animals?
4. Find out how snakes can swallow animals that are larger around than they are.

TRY TO CLASSIFY

1. How would you classify this dinosaur? Write at least three reasons why you placed the dinosaur in a certain group.

2. You will need a partner. Describe an animal that you learned about in the chapter, but do not name it. Describe its structure very carefully so your partner can classify and name it. Now it's your turn to classify and name an animal from your partner's description.

Classifying Animals Without Backbones

2

All the animals you have studied so far are alike in one important way. They are all vertebrates, because they all have backbones. Many other animals —in fact, most of the animals of the world—don't have backbones. They are invertebrates.

Jointed-Legged Animals

The word **arthropod** [AHR-thruh-pahd] means "jointed foot." The arthropods are a group of animals all of which have jointed legs. If you have seen a spider, a grasshopper, a crab, or a lobster, you probably noticed their jointed legs. Arthropods are the only invertebrates that have such jointed legs.

Perhaps you have looked closely at these arthropods. If so, you have seen the strong, light covering that serves as an outside skeleton. This outer covering is called an **exoskeleton** [EHK-soh-skehl-uh-tuhn]. It follows the outline of the animal's body, and it has joints that allow the body to bend and move. How is this kind of skeleton different from yours? Which seems better for moving around rapidly? Many arthropods live on land. The exoskeleton keeps their soft bodies from drying out.

The bodies of arthropods are divided into separate parts. Look closely at the picture of the ant. Notice that its body is divided into three parts.

Grasshopper

Wasp

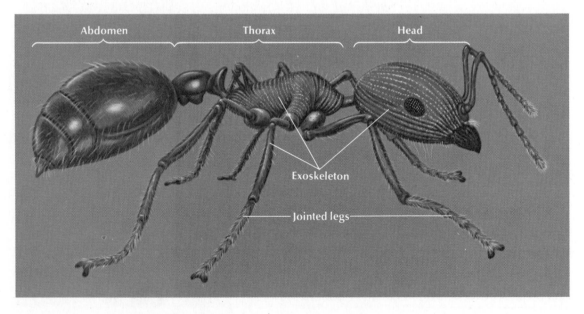
Abdomen Thorax Head

Exoskeleton

Jointed legs

The arthropods are the largest group of animals in the world. In fact, there are more kinds of arthropods than all the other animal groups combined. Arthropods can be found on land, in the air, in the soil, and in water.

The arthropods in the pictures have many legs. One of the arthropods has a single pair of legs on each body segment. The other, often called a "thousand legs," has two pairs of legs on each segment.

These arthropods live in the water. Look at their jointed legs, outer coverings, and segmented bodies. Notice that these animals have long antennae [an-TEHN-ee] on their heads. They use the antennae for finding food and sensing enemies. Some arthropods have large claws for catching food.

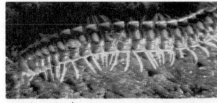

Wood centipede

Millipede

clockwise from left: Lobster; Gooseneck barnacles; Crayfish; Hermit crab

Here's a way to look at arthropod structures. Go out to the woods and turn over a rock or an old log. You will surely find an arthropod called a pill bug under the rock or log. When you pick up the bug, what does it do? Why is the name pill bug a good name? How do the body structures of the pill bug help it to live on land?

Now get some pond water from a nearby pond. Be sure that your pond water has at least one water flea called **daphnia** [DAF-nee-uh] in it. It is large enough for you to see without a hand lens. Yet it is small enough to study under a microscope. In order to study the structures of your daphnia, you will need a dropper, a slide, a cover glass, and a microscope.

Take up a daphnia in a dropper and place it in a drop of water on a slide. Cover the drop with a cover glass. Place the slide under a microscope and watch the daphnia carefully. Note its moving parts. Try to find the structures that you see in the picture.

Notice how the antennae and legs move now and then. How many legs are there? Carefully look at the head and eyes. Notice that each eye is made of many smaller eyes. Each little eye records a separate picture. A slight change in one or more of the eyes is enough to help the animal see an enemy moving.

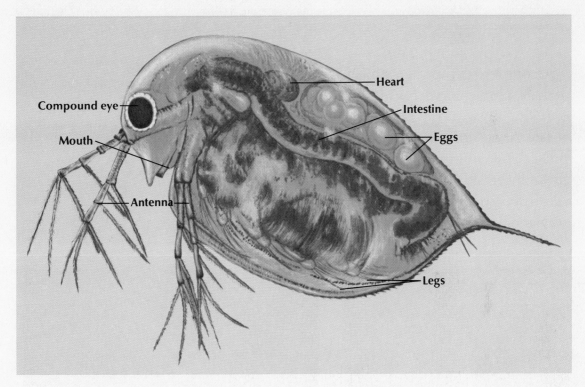

Look again at the head; the mouth parts move every now and then. You may also see the intestine squeeze and become smaller. Inside the intestine you may see some bits of green plants. These bits are food that is being broken down.

Look for the beating heart. The beat is very fast—about 120 beats per minute. Does a daphnia's heart beat faster or slower than yours?

All of the arthropods in this group have four pairs of legs. Some have two body parts. Others have only one body part.

The insect group is the largest group of arthropods. How many legs can you count on each of these insects? All insects have six legs when they are fully grown. Most insects go through several stages of growth before they reach this stage.

left to right: Velvet water mite; Castor bean tick after eating; Black and yellow garden spider; Barn scorpion

left to right: Blister beetle; Walking stick; Praying mantis; *bottom*: Grasshopper

You can also tell insects by their body structure. Six legs, three body parts, two antennae, and two rows of breathing holes—these are the structures of an insect. How are insects like other arthropods?

36

The Soft-Bodied and Spiny-Skinned Invertebrates

On many ocean beaches and in water near the shore, you may find animals with shells. All of these invertebrates have soft bodies. The name of this group, **mollusk** [MAHL-uhsk], means "soft." Their soft bodies are often covered by hard shells. Mollusks are often called shellfish. Can you tell why they are not fish?

Octopus

Brief squid

Moon snail

Whelk

Scallop

Chiton

Some mollusks have a shell in two parts that opens and closes by muscles. Others live in a one-piece shell. Classify these mollusks into groups by the kind of shell they have. Some have no covering shells. Which are these?

Mollusks do not have legs. Most kinds move about on a "foot." If you live near the ocean, you may find a clam buried in the sand. Have you ever dug it out of the sand? If you have, you know the shells open and the clam uses the "foot" to dig quickly back into the sand.

If you watch a clam in sea water, you will see two tubes coming out of one end. One tube takes in water, along with food and oxygen. The food is taken in by the mouth and the oxygen is taken in by the gills. The gills of mollusks work very much like those of fish. They get rid of carbon dioxide and take in oxygen. When this is finished, the water is sent out by the other tube.

Many kinds of mollusks also have a sharp tongue that is covered with teeth. When eating, the animal pushes the tongue out of its mouth and uses it to tear food apart.

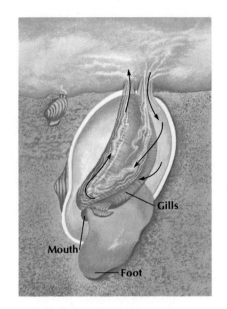

Gills

Mouth

Foot

ACTIVITY

You can look at one kind of mollusk, the snail. Look closely at a snail as it moves on its "foot" along the glass of a fish tank. Sometimes you can see a slimy liquid flowing from a gland at the front of the snail's foot. The snail can move forward on this slimy path.

Snails feed on tiny green plants. In the fish tank, they keep the glass clean by eating these plants. Carefully look at the snail feeding. How does it scrape its food off the glass?

Take a snail out of the fish tank. What happens when you lightly touch the snail's head? What does the shell feel like? How does the snail's shell protect its soft body? Be sure to wash your hands with soap and water after handling the snail.

Starfish and other members of this group live in the sea. Many of these animals have sharp spines sticking through their skin. They are called **echinoderms,** [ih-KY-nuh-durmz] which means "spiny-skinned."

In a saltwater tank, a starfish will soon begin to move on the glass. It is interesting to watch, for the starfish moves as no other animal does. If you look under one of its "arms," you will see thousands of tubes. When they are filled with water, the tubes act like little holders. These holders stick to the surface on which the starfish moves. They are called tube feet because they help the starfish move.

Notice the tube feet on the underside of the starfish.

ACTIVITY

Here's a way to see how a starfish's tube feet work. You will need a dropper with a rubber bulb, a piece of glass, a glass dish, and some water.

Take the bulb from the dropper and fill it with water. Place the bulb against some glass under water. Squeeze out the water by pressing on the bulb, and then let go. Why does the bulb stick to the glass? Where is the pressure greater, on the inside or on the outside of the bulb?

Tube feet can also stick to mollusk shells. A starfish moves over the shell of another animal and fastens its tube feet to it. Slowly the tube feet pull the shell apart as the muscles of the animal get tired from holding its shell closed. Then the starfish can eat the soft animal inside the shell.

clockwise from upper left: Sea urchin; Sea fan; Sea cucumber; Sand dollar; Sun star

Some echinoderms have longer arms and more arms than the starfish. Some have arms that stand out in all directions. Others have arms that wave in the moving water like fans. Some echinoderms are round and covered with spines. They reach out with a five-pointed set of jaws to pull in bits of food. Why do you think the echinoderm in the center of the page is called a *sand dollar*? Does the soft, long animal look something like a vegetable to you? In some countries it is used in soups and other dishes.

Worms, Stinging-Celled Animals, and Sponges

Worms have many body parts, such as simple brains and hearts. These body parts are made of many groups of cells that work together.

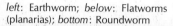

left: Earthworm; *below*: Flatworms (planarias); *bottom*: Roundworm

Find the body parts in the picture of the earthworm. It doesn't have a head, although most other worms do. It has a mouth at the front and another opening at the back. The front, like a head, always points forward as the earthworm moves.

Earthworms swallow soil at the front. The soil passes through a digestive tube and out the back of the body. The soil has in it plant and animal matter that is food for the earthworm. The food is broken down as it passes through the worm.

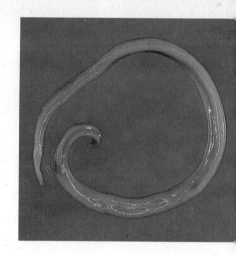

Most worms are alike in these ways:

1. They are invertebrates.
2. They have groups of muscle cells.
3. The digestive tube has an opening at the front and at the rear.
4. They have a head end.
5. They have body parts that do certain jobs.

Jellyfish and corals belong to another group of invertebrates. Their bodies are like empty bags with one open end. Food enters through this open end and wastes leave through it. Around it are a number of armlike parts. They trap food and carry it to the open end. There are many stinging cells on these parts. When an animal touches an "arm," the stinging cells shoot out tiny threads. These threads stick into the animal and give off poison. The animal gets trapped in the threads, and the poison stops the animal from moving. Then the "arms" move the trapped animal into the open end, where it is eaten.

Jellyfish

clockwise from left: Sea anemone; Pillar coral; Sausage coral; Another variety of sea anemone; *Dendrophyllia* coral

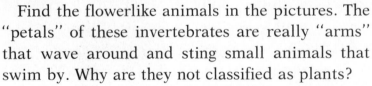

Find the flowerlike animals in the pictures. The "petals" of these invertebrates are really "arms" that wave around and sting small animals that swim by. Why are they not classified as plants?

An interesting and valuable stinging-celled animal is the coral that forms a hard cup around its body. The animal is protected when it darts into the cup. From the cup, it can also reach out its "arms" for food. The corals live in large groups, with their cups all connected together.

42

You may be surprised to learn that sponges are animals. For many years they were thought to be plants. They grow fastened to something and do not move from place to place. They live in salt or fresh water. A sponge's body is hollow, with one open end at the top. The bottom is fastened to something, like a rock. A closer look shows that there are many holes through the wall of the sponge.

left to right: Pink-vase sponge; Hard-head sponge; *Microciona* sponge; Colony of vase sponges

If you drop ink into the water next to a sponge, you will find that the sponge is pumping water. The water with ink would be seen going in through the tiny holes and out through the top. The water that the sponge takes in through these holes brings in oxygen and food. A layer of cells on the inside of the sponge's body breaks down the food.

The outer layer of cells contains matter that makes up the skeleton. The sponge skeleton supports and protects it, just as your skeleton supports and protects you. The sponges that are useful to us all have soft skeletons. The soft skeleton is the part we use. Don't mistake a real sponge for a factory-made one, though it may be used for the same home-cleaning jobs.

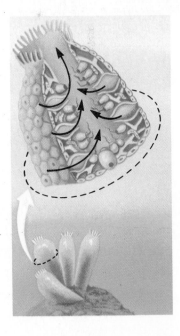

The One-Celled Living Things

For many years most people thought that every living thing was either a plant or an animal. Then the microscope was made and people could see things they had never seen before. This idea changed.

Some living things seemed to have characteristics of both animals and plants. These tiny things did not seem to belong in either the animal group or the plant group. They were placed in a third group called **protists** [PROH-tihsts].

Most protists are just one cell. Even though some may form long chains or large groups, each cell is a separate living thing. Each cell can live without the other cells. Just like all living things, protists get the food they need to live and grow. They also get rid of wastes and produce more of their own kind.

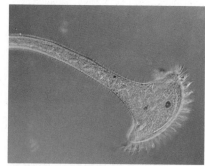
Stentor

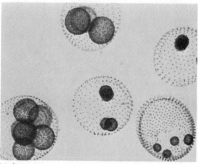
Volvox

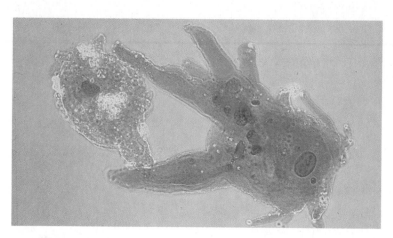
Amoeba

In any pond you are likely to find many protists that act like animals. They are classified by the way they move. One kind of protist moves by a flowing of its protoplasm. The protoplasm flows away from the cell on one side. Then the rest of the protoplasm flows into the new space.

Another kind of protist has a large number of short threads of protoplasm on the outside of its cell. The short threads beat the water like little boat oars, sending the protist through the water.

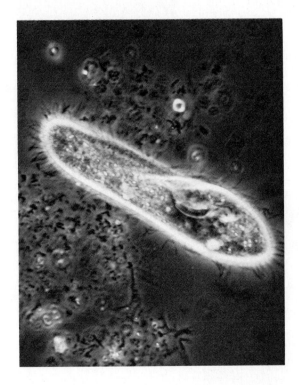

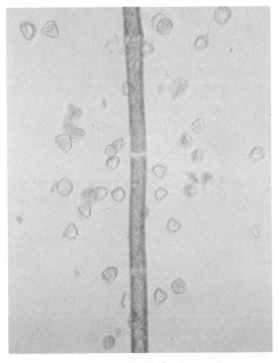

A third kind of protist is both like an animal and like a plant. It has a long body with a thread of protoplasm at the front end. This protist swims through the water by rapidly shaking this thread back and forth. In this way it behaves like an animal. It also takes food into its cell in the way animal protists do. And yet this protist is able to make its own food. In this way, it is like a green plant.

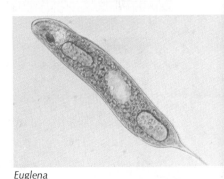

Euglena

The fourth kind of protist has no means of its own for moving about. It may be carried along in water. All members of this group live in or on other living things.

You can find some protists and look at them. Get some water from a pond or fish tank. Put a drop of water on a slide and place the slide under a microscope. If you don't see protists in the first sample, keep trying until you do.

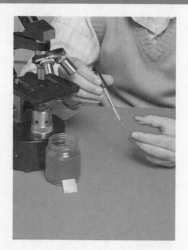

Describe how they move. If a protist comes across a bit of food, describe how it takes the food into its body.

If you are lucky, you will see a protist dividing in two. This is how it gives rise to other living things of the same kind. Each of the two parts can grow, change, and become full-sized.

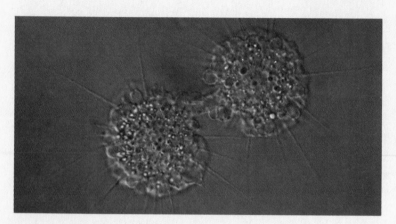

Since **bacteria** [bak-TIHR-ee-uh] provide another puzzle in classification, they are grouped as protists. These living things of just one cell are very small—the largest is about $\frac{1}{1000}$ cm long. The smallest is so tiny that you could put 250,000 in a row on this line _____. Bacteria cells are like plant cells in that both have cell walls. Some kinds move by themselves. They move by whipping a thread of protoplasm from side to side.

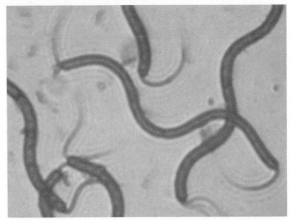

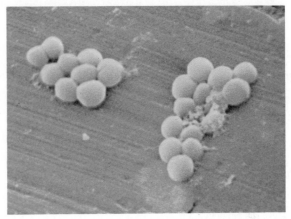

clockwise from left: Bar-shaped salmonella; Threadlike spirilla; Spherical staphylococci

The many kinds of bacteria have different ways of getting food. A few kinds can make their own food, just as plants do. Some live inside living plants and animals, including you, in order to get food. Many, however, use dead plants and animals as food. Even though there are many different kinds of bacteria, they have three common shapes. Some of them are round, some are bar-shaped, and some are spiral.

There are bacteria everywhere—in the air, in the soil, in lakes, ponds, streams, and oceans. They are on floors, walls, ceilings, and furniture. They are on your skin, in your mouth, and in your intestines.

What Did You Learn?

- Most of the animals in the world are invertebrates.
- All arthropods have jointed legs, exoskeletons, and bodies that have separate parts.
- Most mollusks live in water, move about by means of a "foot," and have a shell. Most also have tubes that pass water with food in it over the gills, and some have a sharp tongue that is covered with teeth.
- The starfish and most other echinoderms have spiny skins and move by means of tube feet.
- Three lower groups of invertebrates that live mostly in water are worms, stinging-celled animals, and sponges.
- The protists are living things that sometimes seem to be like animals and sometimes seem to be like plants. Most protists have just one cell.

Biography

Dr. Dixie Lee Ray (1914–   )

Animals are found everywhere on Earth. You can find them in the air, on the ground, under the ground, and in the water. Sometimes when you walk along a shore, you may see the shells of some animals without backbones.

Things that live in the ocean are studied by biologists [by-AHL-uh-jihsts]. Dr. Dixie Lee Ray is such a biologist who has studied some animals without backbones. She has shown special interest in water fleas, lobsters, and crabs. She has also studied and reported on the small ocean animals that destroy the wood in docks and boats.

Dr. Ray was once director of the Pacific Science Center in Seattle. She helped to make the museum a learning place for everyone.

Before she became the governor of the state of Washington, Dr. Ray was the chairperson of the Atomic Energy Commission in Washington, D.C. She worked with energy producers to make sure they didn't harm places where plants and animals live.

Dr. Ray feels that science should not be just for scientists. She says, "It is too wonderful a world to leave to the specialists."

TO THINK ABOUT AND DO

Copy these sentences on a piece of paper. Use the new words that you learned in this chapter to fill in the blanks.

1. The largest group of animals in the world is the _____ group.

2. Animals without backbones whose bodies are soft and often covered by hard shells are _____.

3. The only animals without backbones that have jointed legs are the _____.

4. Living things that sometimes seem to be like animals and sometimes seem to be like plants are called _____.

5. The major parts of an insect's body are the _____, _____, _____.

6. Animals with spiny skins are called _____.

7. Simple animals that were thought to be plants because they don't move from place to place are _____.

8. Most arthropods have strong, light coverings on their bodies called _____.

9. Animals that shoot out tiny threads that give off poison are called _____ animals.

10. One-celled living things that have different ways of getting food and are found everywhere are _____.

Each of these animals is a member of a group of invertebrates. Make a chart on a piece of paper. Use these headings in your chart:

1. Animal
2. Type of Body
3. How It Gets Food
4. Where It Lives
5. Two Other Members in the Same Group

Amoeba

Ant

Starfish

Jellyfish

Sponge

Crab

Clam

Earthworm

1. Find out what a coral reef is and how it is formed. Also find out what effect a coral reef may have on sea animals and people.
2. Find out the name and size of the largest invertebrate.
3. Mollusks are very important to us. Find out several ways in which people use them.
4. Find out two ways that bacteria help people and two ways that bacteria harm them.

Classifying Plants

3

What are they? What are these plants, with their strange shapes and colors? There are so many thousands of plants that no one can know even a fourth of them. Yet a person who studies plants can look at a strange plant and tell what group it belongs to.

How is a plant classified? The same way animals are—by structure. People who study plants look at the parts of a plant and how they are put together. They study the structure of the stem, the leaves, the flowers, and the roots, and they find hints in each. When all the hints are put together, they decide which group the plant belongs to.

Seeds in Flowers

The first step in classifying a plant is to put the plant into one of these two big groups:

1. Plants that make seeds
2. Plants that do not make seeds

If you find cones or flowers, seed holders or seeds on the plant, you know which of the two big plant groups it belongs in—the seed makers. This chart makes a beginning toward classifying plants. Most of the plants that you see around you belong to the group that makes seeds in flowers.

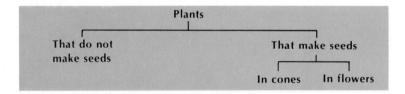

Flowering plants may look very different. Their stems may be long or short, woody or soft. Their roots may be big or little, grow deep in the soil or near the surface. Their leaves may be of different shapes and sizes. But all flowering plants make seeds in the same way.

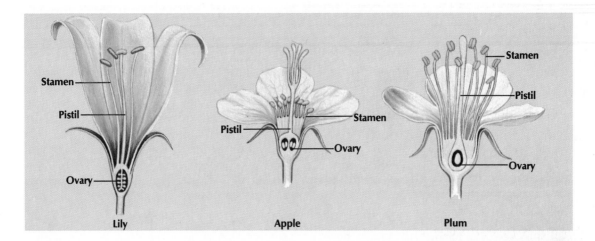

Stamen

Pistil

Ovary

Lily

Pistil

Stamen

Ovary

Apple

Stamen

Pistil

Ovary

Plum

A flower has certain parts for making seeds. Find the thin "stems" in the middle of the flower that you see in the picture. The **pistil** [PIHS-tl] is the largest "stem" in the center. At the bottom of it is a ball-shaped part called the **ovary** [OH-vuhr-ee]. There are hollow spaces inside the ovary that have small round **ovules** [OH-vyoolz] inside. The ovules will become seeds. Each of these future seeds is made of many cells. But one cell on the inside is the egg cell.

The thin stems around the pistil are the **stamens** [STAY-muhnz]. Each stamen is shaped like a thin stem with a little knob at one end. Inside the knob, the tiny grains of **pollen** [PAHL-uhn] are made. These grains contain the sperm nuclei. When a sperm nucleus joins with an egg nucleus in the ovule, **fertilization** [fur-tl-uh-ZAY-shuhn] takes place. The fertilized egg that you know as the seed has a tiny plant inside. If it has everything it needs, this tiny plant may in time become a large, full-grown plant.

All flowering plants make seeds in ovaries. Together the ovules and ovaries grow and ripen into fruits. Cherries, peaches, apples, grapes, and pears are all fruits of flowering plants.

During pollination, pollen cells travel from the stamens to the pistil of a flower. As soon as a pollen cell sticks to the pistil, the cell begins to form a long pollen tube, which extends through the pistil to the ovary. Fertilization occurs when the nucleus of the pollen cell unites with the nucleus of an ovule.

Here's a way to look at the seed-making parts in a flower. You will need a flower, a hand lens, a piece of dark paper, and a straight pin.

Carefully remove the petals from the flower. How many stamens does your flower have? Look closely at them to find the thin "stems" and the little knobs. Gently touch the tip of each knob. What is now on the tips of your fingers?

Sprinkle some pollen grains on the piece of dark paper. Look at them carefully with the hand lens. What is the shape of the grains?

Next, study the pistil, the large "stem" in the center of the flower. With the straight pin, carefully cut the ovary and look inside for one or more ovules.

Make drawings of the pistil and the stamens and write these names next to their parts. Share your drawings with others in the class.

Classifying by Seeds

A new plant is started when an egg cell is fertilized by a sperm cell. The fertilized egg cell then begins to grow and divide to form more cells. After the egg cell has divided many times, the cells form a tiny young plant. At the same time, certain other cells in the ovule are also growing and dividing. These cells make the other parts of the seed.

Each seed has three parts. There is a tiny young plant and stored food in one or two seed leaves. There is also a seed coat that protects the young plant and its food.

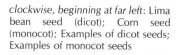

clockwise, beginning at far left: Lima bean seed (dicot); Corn seed (monocot); Examples of dicot seeds; Examples of monocot seeds

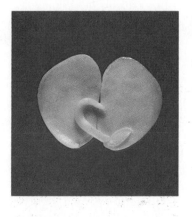

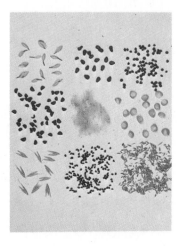

The number of seed leaves helps in classifying seeds into one of two groups:

1. Seeds that have two separate food parts.
2. Seeds that have only one food part.

A seed leaf is called a **cotyledon** [kaht-l-EED-n]. It is the part of the seed where food is stored for the growing young plant. Seeds with two food parts are called **dicotyledons** [dy-kaht-l-EED-nz], or dicots for short. Seeds with only one food part are called **monocotyledons** [mahn-uh-kaht-l-EED-nz], or monocots for short.

57

Most of the fruits, flowers, and nuts we see come from plants that are dicotyledons. You can see these food parts for yourself. You will need a few beans, peas, and peanuts, a dish, and some water. You will also need a few paper towels, a hand lens, and a small knife.

Place the seeds in the dish. Soak them in water for several hours. Then put each seed on the paper towels. With your fingers, carefully remove the seed coat. With the small knife, carefully separate the two parts of the bean, the pea, and the peanut. Look at the seeds under the hand lens.

Each half is a cotyledon. Fastened to one half are the tiny stem and root of the young plant. Make a drawing of the parts of the seed and write the name next to each part.

The other large group of flowering plants make seeds that have only one food part. The members of this group give us most of the world's food. Corn, wheat, and rice are monocots.

left to right: Corn; Wheat; Rice

ACTIVITY

You will need some corn seeds, a dish, some water, a paper towel, and a hand lens.

Put the corn seeds in the dish. Soak them in water for several hours. Did you know that each bit of corn on a cob is a seed?

Place the corn seeds on the paper towel. Look at the corn seeds under a hand lens. Can a corn seed be separated into two parts like the bean seed? Use the picture to help you find the young plant. Also use the picture to find the seed leaf, the new stem, and the new root.

59

Classifying by Leaves, Stems, and Flowers

The leaf is the major food-making part of the plant. The leaves and the other green parts make the food that feeds the whole plant.

You know that leaves have veins with little tubes inside. Some of these tubes carry water and minerals to the green cells of the leaf. Others carry the food down to the rest of the stem and to the root. The way in which these veins are arranged gives another helpful hint in classifying a plant.

The leaves of most seed-making plants can be divided into two groups. Dicots have leaves with the veins arranged in a netlike fashion. Monocots have leaves with veins that do not touch or cross. Look at these leaves carefully. Which of them are dicot leaves and which of them are monocot leaves?

The stem is the major food-carrying part of the plant. Some of the tubes in the stem carry water and minerals from the roots to the leaves. There are other tubes that carry food from the leaves to the rest of the plant. Both kinds are mostly found together in bundles in the stem. Look at the stems in these pictures. The stems have been cut across. All of them are full of tubes. What are the two different ways they are arranged?

In a dicot stem the bundles of tubes are arranged in a ring near the outside of the stem. As the dicot stem grows older, it forms a new ring of tubes every year. Dicot trees get thicker each year by adding this new layer of tubes. Some of last year's layer becomes wood. The layers look like rings when the stem is cut across. How can you tell the age of a cut tree?

In a monocot stem the bundles of tubes are scattered through the stem. The bundles stay scattered even when the plant gets older. The tubes get larger, but no new layers are added.

Another way to classify seed-making plants is by counting the number of parts in the flowers. Flowers that have their petals and stamens in groups of 4 or 5 are dicots. Monocot flowers have their petals and stamens in groups of 3, 6, or 9.

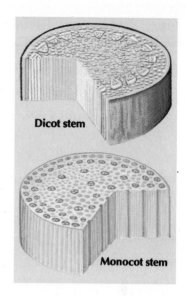

Dicot stem

Monocot stem

Based on the number of stamens and petals, which of the plants below are dicots, and which are monocots?

You can classify seed-making plants as monocots or dicots. You will need some plants with flowers and leaves, a hand lens, and several pieces of paper. Also get red ink, some cups, and a small knife.

Put each plant on a piece of paper. With the hand lens, look at each plant's leaves and flowers. How do the leaves and flowers help you classify the plants?

With the knife, cut a stem, complete with its flowers or leaves, from each plant. How do you think you will find the bundles arranged inside the stem? To see if you are right, put each stem in a separate cup. Pour in some red ink and let the stems stand overnight. The next day, cut off the stem and look at the bundles with your hand lens. Does what you see agree with what you expected?

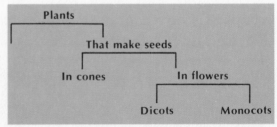

Now look at our chart and copy it on a piece of paper. Fill in the chart by listing the names of your plants under the correct columns.

Dicots and monocots are large groups of plants. In these groups are many different kinds of plants. To classify plants more exactly, these groups are divided into smaller groups called families. On this page are some families of plants and their members. Look at the flower parts in each family. Notice that those plants whose flower parts are alike are grouped in the same family. Which are dicots? Which are monocots?

Seeds in Cones

Plants that make seeds in cones are called **conifers** [KAHN-uh-fuhrz]. It is thought that conifers lived on Earth long before flowering plants. Plants with flowers may have come from conifers. Some pine trees, which are conifers, are almost 5000 years old!

Conifers do not have flowers or flower parts. Their seeds are in cones instead of inside ovaries. Most conifers have two kinds of cones. In one kind of cone, pollen is formed. Wind carries it from this kind of cone to another larger kind of cone. In the larger cone ovules grow. This cone is turned upward when it is young. When the sperm cells in the pollen fertilize the egg cells in the ovules, seeds are formed.

When the seeds are ripe, the upward-growing cone turns down. The seeds drop from the cone and fall to the ground.

In what way is seed making in conifers the same as in flowering plants? In what way is it different?

Bristlecone pines in California are some of the oldest trees in this country.

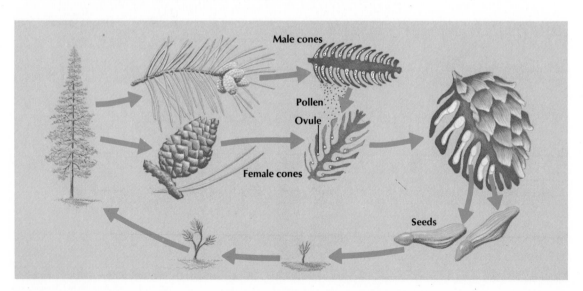

Male cones

Pollen

Ovule

Female cones

Seeds

64

Most conifers are trees or bushes, with stems, roots, and leaves. Their leaves are needle-shaped and stay green all year round. Look at the conifers in the picture. Can you tell two ways to classify them into smaller groups?

Plants That Do Not Make Seeds

Plants that make seeds are one group. The second big group of plants are all those that do not make seeds. There are many, many different plants in this group. Some of them look very much like seed-making plants. Some do not. Some have leaves, roots, and stems. Some do not. Some are green; some are not.

Ferns

Ferns look very much like seed-making plants. They are green, and have roots, stems, and leaves. Ferns have tubes that run through these parts, carrying water, food, and minerals. Most of the fern plant that you see is made of leaves. The stem grows under the ground and the roots grow from this stem.

below: Interrupted fern; *bottom left to right*: Cinnamon fern; Spleenwort fern; New York fern

If you look closely on the underside of a fern leaf, you may see rows of brown dots. If you break these open, a brown powder comes out. The powder is made of very tiny bits called **spores.** If spores fall in a wet place, they grow into thin green plants that don't look like ferns. These plants make sperm and egg cells. The sperm cells must swim in water to reach the egg cells. When the sperm cells fertilize the egg cells, new fern plants begin to grow.

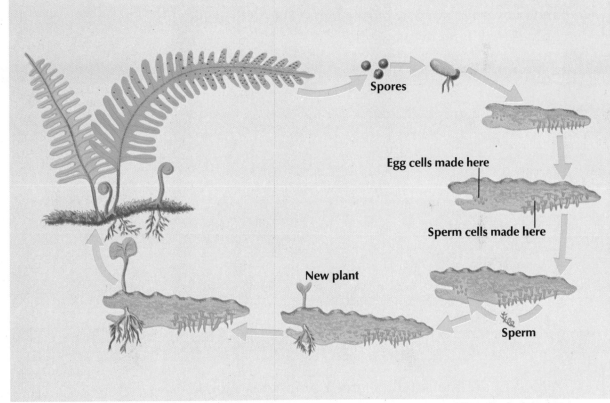

Life cycle of a fern plant

Some ferns are very tiny and grow to a height of just a few centimeters. Most grow to a height of at least 20 cm. However, there are some that grow as tall as trees. But whether a fern is short or tall, it must live in a wet place. Why is this so?

67

Mosses

Mosses, like ferns, are green plants that make spores. Before spores can grow, however, some other things must happen. Sperm and egg cells form near the top of a moss plant. A sperm cell moves through dew on the moss plant and joins with an egg cell. The fertilized egg cell then gives rise to a long stem. This stem makes the spores in a case at its tip. They fall out of the case like salt from a salt shaker. Spores are carried by the wind and may grow into new moss plants. They will grow only if they land on wet soil.

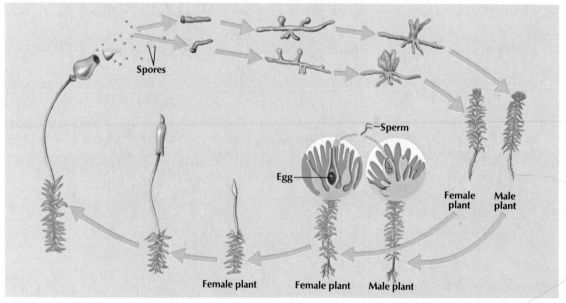

Spores

Sperm

Egg

Female plant   Male plant

Female plant   Female plant   Male plant

Life cycle of a moss plant

Mosses are the smallest green plants that grow on land. The tallest moss plants are only a few centimeters high. Unlike ferns, they do not have true stems and roots. They have parts that look like stems and roots, but there are no tubes inside. Soil, water, and minerals cannot flow up easily. They have to soak their way up from cell to cell.

Tundra moss

Haircap moss

Several mosses growing together

Moss on log

You may wish to go on a walk through a park or woods, looking for mosses. Where do you find them? Chances are you will not find a single moss plant growing by itself. Moss plants usually grow in clumps in wet, shady places.

Compare mosses with seed-makers. You remember that a seed has a tiny plant inside, together with its food. The seed has a seed coat that protects the young plant. Seeds can live through cold, dry times.

The Lower Plants

There is another group of plants that do not make seeds. These plants are called "lower plants" because they are simple in structure. The lower plants do not have roots, stems, or leaves. The lower plants are divided into two groups:

1. Those that have the green coloring **chlorophyll** [KLAWR-uh-fihl] are called **algae** [AL-jee].
2. Most of those that have no chlorophyll are called **fungi** [FUHN-jy].

Algae

Algae are found in puddles, streams, ponds, oceans, and in all the wet places of the world. Have you ever been swimming in a pond or stream? The water's surface sometimes looks like a green meadow. This "meadow" is algae. Bubbles of oxygen catch in the algae and keep them floating. Where do these bubbles come from? You may also find algae as a green fuzz on damp soil or on rock. Or you may find them on the shady side of a tree trunk.

left: Algae in a freshwater pond; *right*: Algae on rocks along the seacoast

Some algae have other colored materials besides chlorophyll. These colors hide the green chlorophyll and make the algae look brown, yellow, or red. But because algae have chlorophyll, they can make their own food. The differences in color are often used to classify them into groups.

clockwise, beginning at upper left: Corallina, a kind of algae; Giant kelp, a kind of brown algae; Chondrus, a kind of red algae; Rockweed, a kind of brown algae

Algae vary greatly in size. Some of them are one-celled. Others live as chains of cells in fresh and salt water. Besides these, some very large, many-celled algae live in the sea. They have plant parts that look like stems and leaves, and they may grow to a length of 60 m.

Here's a way to look at some algae. You will need a microscope, a glass slide, and a cover glass. Also get a small dish and some algae.

In a fish tank, look for a green film on the glass. You may also find algae as a green fuzz on a rock or on damp soil. Or you may find them on the bark of trees.

Scrape some of the algae you find into a small dish of water. Place a drop of this water on a clean slide. Use the microscope to look at the drop.

Do you see algae made of one cell? Do you see long threads or chains? Make drawings of what you see. Compare your drawings with others in the class.

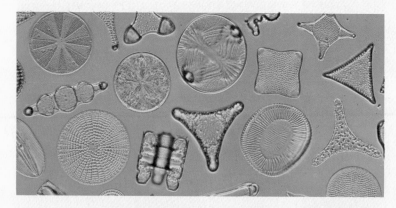

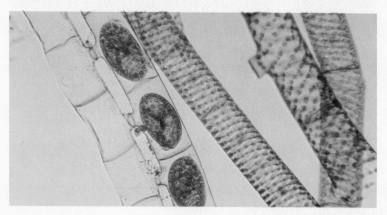

Fungi

Have you ever seen mold growing on a piece of bread, fruit, or cheese? Do you like to eat mushrooms? Mushrooms and molds are fungi. They are lower plants, too. Some fungi make spores that grow into new plants. Other fungi divide in two, and each part grows into a new plant.

Like algae, fungi do not have roots, stems, or leaves. Unlike algae, they do not have chlorophyll. They live in or on other living things, or on things that were once alive. They get their energy from the food stored in these things. The fungi that live on dead plants and animals help break them down. Dead plants and animals become food for other plants and animals. Or they become part of the soil.

Mushrooms produce spores on the undersides of their round caps. When the spores are ripe, they fall from the caps.

top: Penicillium mold
bottom: Edible mushrooms

ACTIVITY

You can see spores. You will need a mushroom, a small knife, a piece of light-colored paper, and a dish.

With a knife, cut off the mushroom cap. Place it gently underside down, on the piece of light-colored paper. Cover the cap with a dish and leave it for a day.

Gently lift the dish and the cap. This is what you may see. This is a spore print. It was made by the thousands of spores that fell from beneath the cap.

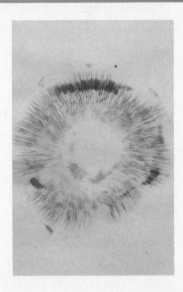

Some mushrooms are very good to eat. Others have a poison in them. Only people who have studied mushrooms for many years can safely tell the difference. And even they have a hard time telling them apart. The mushrooms that you buy from a store are a kind that are known to be safe to eat.

The word *mold* is used for any fungi that grow by forming threads. When they grow on bread or any other starch food, they look fuzzy. Bread mold grows from spores that float in the air. If a spore falls on damp bread, it grows by sending out branching threads. These threads grow down into the bread. They give off a chemical that breaks down the bread. Then the mold uses this bread for food.

At the same time, other threads of the mold spread across the surface of the bread. At their ends, new sets of branching threads grow down into the bread. Some threads grow up into the air. Cells at the tops of these threads produce thousands of tiny spores. They are then carried by the air and may land where they can grow.

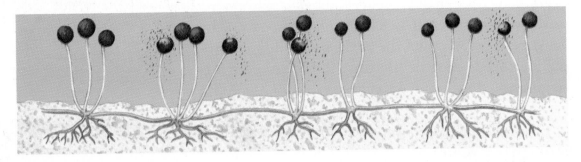

ACTIVITY

You can look at new mold plants by getting bread for spores to grow in. You will need a slice of bread, some water, and a jar or dish with a cover. You will also need a toothpick, some slides, and a microscope.

Put the bread into the open jar or dish and leave it for an hour or two. Sprinkle a few drops of water on the bread. Cover the wet bread and put the jar or dish in a warm, dark place. Look at the bread two days later. What has happened to the bread? Leave it in the warm, dark place for another day or two. Leave the bread there until you see a "fuzz" on it.

Put a drop of water in the center of a slide. With the toothpick, pick up a tiny bit of bread mold. Then stir it gently into the center of the drop on the slide.

Look at your slide under the microscope. Find the branching threads and the spores. Draw what you see.

Yeasts are another group of fungi. They are each made of one cell. Each cell can grow a little bump called a bud. These buds break off and become new yeast cells.

The main energy food of yeasts is sugar. When yeasts break down sugar, they produce energy, carbon dioxide, and alcohol.

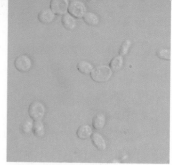

Budding yeast cells

When a baker makes bread, the baker adds yeast to the dough. Then it is left in a warm place. The yeast cells break down the sugar in the dough, producing carbon dioxide. Because the bread dough is so gummy, the carbon dioxide gas cannot escape. It gathers in bubbles, causing the dough to swell up, or "rise." The dough is baked in this puffed-up form. What would bread be like if it did not rise before being baked?

Bread dough before rising

Bread dough after rising

ACTIVITY

You can see why yeasts are useful in making bread. You will need $\frac{1}{2}$ teaspoon of dried yeast, 1 cup of flour, and some warm water. You will also need two small mixing bowls and a spoon.

Put 5 teaspoons of warm water into each of the bowls. Stir the dried yeast into just one of the bowls until the water becomes milky. Add $\frac{1}{2}$ cup of flour, a little at a time, to each of the bowls. Mix well until a ball of dough is formed in each bowl.

Let the two balls of dough stand. Look at them every 15 minutes. At the end of two hours, what do you see? What is the difference between the two balls?

The alcohol made by yeast plants may be used either in industry or as a drink. Alcohol is made by allowing yeasts to feed on the sugar in some plants.

Fungi that use living plants or animals for food can be very harmful. Here are some of the harmful kinds. Most fungi are not harmful to us, and some are very useful. Which of these have you seen before?

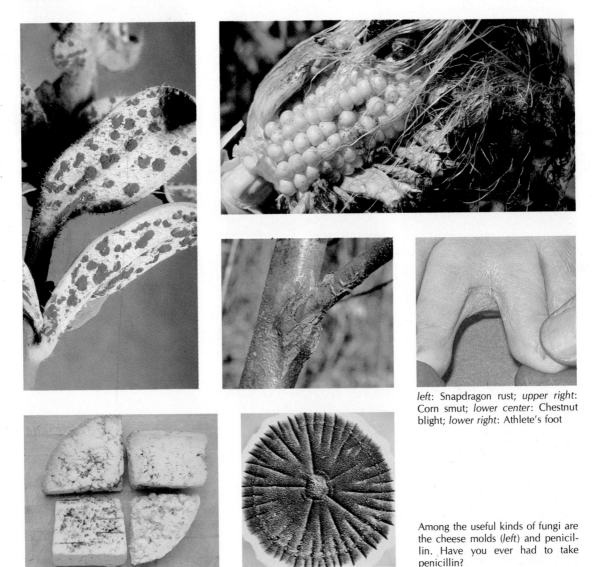

left: Snapdragon rust; *upper right*: Corn smut; *lower center*: Chestnut blight; *lower right*: Athlete's foot

Among the useful kinds of fungi are the cheese molds (*left*) and penicillin. Have you ever had to take penicillin?

Plant Puzzles

There are many puzzles in the plant world. Many plants are not easy to classify into groups. Let's look at a few that are classified as "in-betweens."

These plants are found on rocks and on the bark of trees. They can grow in very cold places where hardly any other living thing can grow. Look closely at them. You can see that they are really clumps of two kinds of plants—algae and fungi. The algae with their green chlorophyll make food. The fungi provide minerals and water which the algae need to make food. Do you think either kind of plant could live alone? Why is it hard to classify these plants as a group?

These lichens, made of algae and fungi, break down soil to create a suitable habitat for plants such as mosses.

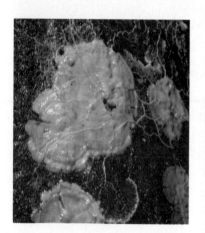

In what ways are theses slime molds like animals? In what ways are they like plants?

These are very simple living things. They flow over food and take the bits of food into themselves. Because they move in this way, they appear to be very simple animals.

During part of their life, these living things divide into thousands of single cells. Some of the cells make spores that grow into new plants.

Should they be classified as plants or animals? Or should there be a third group, the "in-betweens"?

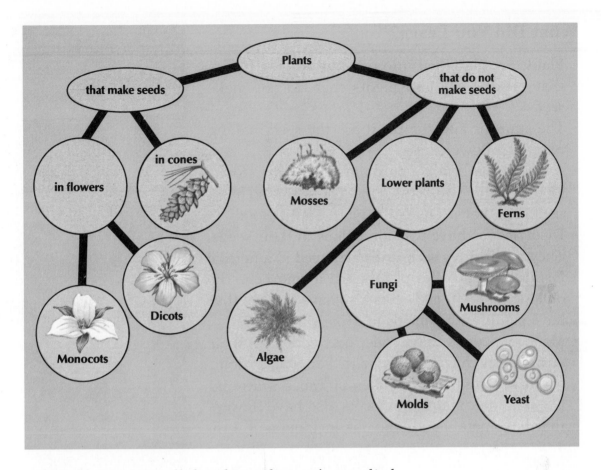

Let's look at how all the plants that we've studied fit into a large chart. Start at the bottom of the chart and trace the history of plants on the earth. It is believed that the earliest plants lived in water. Later some of them may have changed in ways that helped them live on land. Some algae that lived in water may have developed ways of living on wet land. They may have given rise to today's mosses.

Mosses spread on the land, and later may have given rise to ferns. Ferns, with their roots, stems, and leaves, could grow even farther away from water than mosses could. Conifers may have come from ferns. And, as we said earlier, some people think that plants with flowers came from conifers.

What Did You Learn?

- Plants are classified into two big groups: plants that make seeds and plants that do not make seeds.
- The stamens and the pistil are the seed-making parts of a flower.
- A seed has a tiny young plant inside and stored food in one or two cotyledons. The seed also has a seed coat that protects the plant and its food.
- Dicotyledons have two cotyledons in their seeds. They have leaves with veins arranged in a netlike fashion and bundles of tubes in a ring near the outside of the stem. Dicots also have flowers that have petals and stamens in groups of 4 or 5.
- Monocotyledons have one cotyledon in their seeds. They have leaves with veins that don't touch or cross and bundles of tubes scattered through their stems. Monocots also have flowers that have petals and stamens in groups of 3, 6, or 9.
- Plants that make seeds in cones are called conifers.
- Ferns are green plants that have roots, stems, and leaves. They make spores instead of seeds.
- Mosses are green plants that make spores and do not have true stems and roots.
- The lower plants are a group of simple plants that do not make seeds and have no roots, stems, or leaves. Those with chlorophyll are the algae and those without chlorophyll are the fungi.
- "In-betweens," which are somewhat like plants and somewhat like animals, are not easy to classify into groups.

Career

Botanists

Most life on earth depends on plants. Why is this so? Plants are different from all other living things because they can make their own food. No animals, including humans, can do this.

Plants have been interesting to scientists for many years. Theophrastus, a Greek who lived over 2000 years ago, was one of the first to group plants. He is known as "the father of botany." He studied the parts of plants and how they are put together, and he wrote many books about them.

Plant scientists called botanists (BAHT-n-ihsts) study plants in the same way. From its structure, they can usually classify a plant, placing it in the group to which it belongs.

It would be difficult for one person to know everything there is to know about plant life. Because of this, there are several branches of botany. Visit your library to learn more about the science of botany. Maybe you can visit a botanical garden. Botanical gardens are large beautiful parks where flowers, trees, herbs, and shrubs are planted. These gardens are grown for botanists who are studying plants. At the same time, the public can enjoy them.

TO THINK ABOUT AND DO

Copy this puzzle on to a piece of paper. Use the words in the columns to help you fill in the puzzle boxes.

fertilization   cones
ovary   stamen
ovule   pistil
flower   fruit
seed   pollen

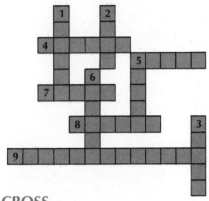

ACROSS

4. carried by wind or insects from flower to flower

5. part of a flower in which seeds grow, also called "fruit"

7. the part of flower you eat

8. pollen grows on this flower part

9. what happens when a sperm cell joins with an egg cell

DOWN

1. pretty part of a plant

2. grows inside the ovary

3. seeds that are not inside ovaries can be seen in these

5. becomes a seed after fertilization

6. when pollen reaches it, a tube begins to form

Copy each sentence on a piece of paper. Write **T** beside the sentences that are true and **F** beside those that are false.

1. Plants are classified by whether or not they make seeds.

2. The part of the seed where food is stored is called the cotyledon.

3. Plants that make seeds in cones are called ferns.
4. Spores are different from seeds in that they don't have a baby plant in them.
5. Mosses, like ferns, have roots, stems, and leaves.
6. Algae are simple plants that depend on other plants or animals for food.
7. Certain kinds of fungi are helpful to bread and cheese makers.
8. Most conifers have needle-shaped leaves that stay green all year round.

MONOCOTS AND DICOTS

Copy these sentences on a piece of paper. Notice that each picture has a number next to it. After looking at each picture, complete the sentence that has the same number.

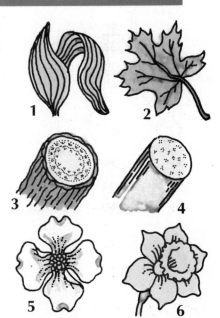

1. This leaf has _____ veins.
2. This leaf has _____ veins.
3. The tubes in this stem are arranged in _____.
4. The tubes in this stem are arranged in _____.
5. Since this flower has four petals and stamens, it is a _____.
6. Since this flower has six petals and stamens, it is a _____.

THINGS TO FIND OUT

1. Mushroom growers do not plant mushroom spores. Find out how they get new mushroom plants.
2. *Venus-flytrap* is the name of a certain plant. Find out what kind of plant it is and what other plants are like it.
3. The navel orange has no seeds. Find out how new navel orange trees are grown.

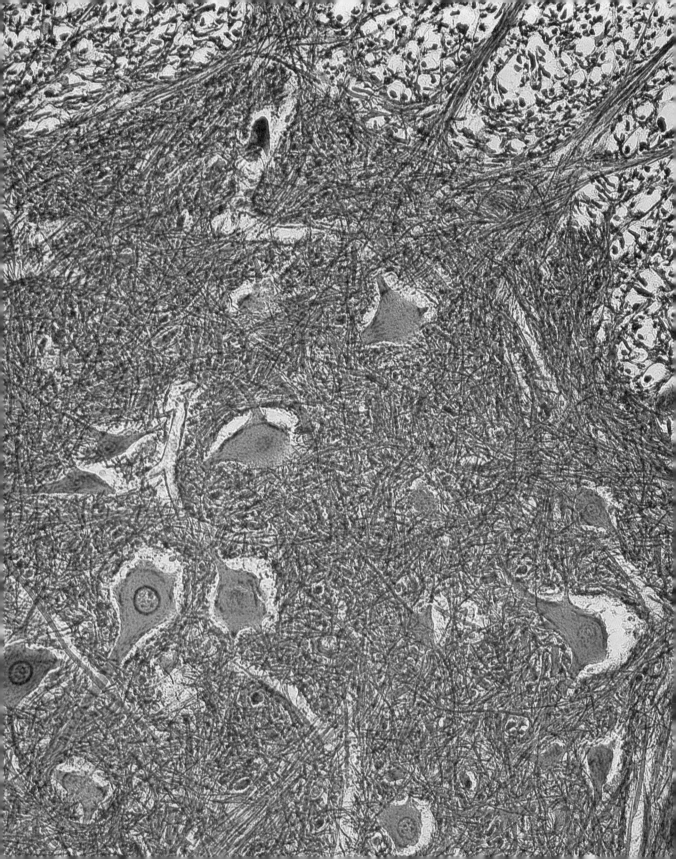

Life Cycles

4

Suppose that after a long journey, a spaceship brings back some strange new matter from a far-away place. The scientists are quite excited. They think the matter *might* be alive. It moves a little from time to time. At times it acts as though it is eating some bits of food. The scientists study the matter carefully. They want to know if it is alive or not.

Suppose you were one of the scientists. What kinds of questions would you ask to find out if the matter is living?

One important question you might ask is, "Can the matter grow and change?" Another question is, "Can it make more of its own kind?" What other questions would you ask? How would you go about trying to find out answers to your questions?

Life Cycles

How do we know if something is living or not? We know that living things need food, react to what is around them, grow, and change. They also **reproduce** [ree-pruh-DOOS]. This means that they make more of their own kind. The changes that each living thing goes through during its life are called a **life cycle.** Can you name the changes people go through in their life cycle?

A life cycle is a pattern that is repeated again and again. Starting with one cell or a group of cells, a living thing grows and changes, becomes an **adult,** [uh-DUHLT] and later dies. Before they die, some of the adults have young. Then the cycle repeats itself.

What parts of the life cycle are shown here?

All living things change as they grow. Some change more than others. Many baby mammals look much like their parents. These young animals have changed and grown inside the bodies of their mothers. After birth, they are taken care of by the adults. The mothers make milk to feed them. They also protect the young ones from harm. Taking care of the young is an important part of the life cycle of mammals.

Musk ox and calf

86

Many insects, such as butterflies, have four parts or **stages** in their life cycles. The egg hatches into a **larva,** a young form of the animal. It is very different from the adult. You may have seen a caterpillar crawling along a leaf. A caterpillar is the larva of a butterfly. This is the feeding and growing part of its life cycle. The caterpillar eats and grows. At times it will shed the outside layer of its skin.

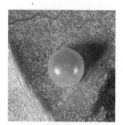
Tiger swallowtail egg

Larva

Pupa

Adult butterfly

When the larva has finished growing, it becomes a **pupa.** The pupa has an outside covering that protects it while it is changing into an adult butterfly. Wings, legs, and mouthparts grow and change. When the changes are finished, the butterfly breaks through the covering. Soon it is ready to fly away. Later, the female butterfly lays the eggs that were fertilized by the male. What happens at the end of the adult stage in the butterfly's life cycle?

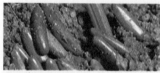
Grasshopper eggs

Some insects, such as grasshoppers, have three stages in their life cycles. The female grasshopper lays eggs in the soil. **Nymphs** hatch from the eggs. The nymphs look like small forms of the adult insects, but they have no wings. The young grasshopper nymphs eat and grow. When they become too big for their skins, they shed them. In time they become adults. The adult grasshoppers lay eggs. Later the adult grasshoppers will die, but the life cycle will repeat itself.

Nymph shedding its skin

Adult grasshopper

You can find out about the stages in a mealworm's life cycle. You will need a mealworm, some cereal, a piece of apple, and a hand lens. You will also need a metric ruler, some paper towels, and a jar with a lid.

Put the mealworm on a paper towel. Look at it with the hand lens. Measure it. How many body parts does it have? Does it have legs? Write what you see on a sheet of paper. Make a drawing of it.

Put the mealworm in a jar with some cereal and a piece of apple. Make a few air holes in the jar lid and put it on the jar. Look at the mealworm at least once a week. Measure it each time. Record what you see. Note any changes. What happens to it?

The mealworm is a larva. It grows from an egg, which is the first stage in its life cycle. The larva is the second stage. What other stages do you notice as it grows? Make a drawing of the life cycle of your mealworm.

Growth and Development

You are growing and changing all the time. Most likely, you are a little taller than you were last year. Even after you stop growing in height, you will still be replacing parts of your body. If you happen to cut yourself, new skin grows as the cut heals. How are you able to do these things?

How has your body changed in the past three years? How may it change in the next three years?

You are making new cells all the time. New cells are needed for growing and for taking the place of damaged or worn-out cells. You may have noticed dead skin cells that rub off as you dry yourself with a towel. The old skin cells are replaced by new ones that are growing under them. From time to time you have to trim your nails and cut your hair. Your hair and nails come from skin cells. They will grow all through your life. What changes take place in the hair color of people as they go through their life cycle?

As you grow, new cells must be added. This is also true of plants and animals. New cells are made by **cell division** [sehl duh-VIHZH-uhn]. During cell division one cell divides and becomes two new cells that are exactly the same.

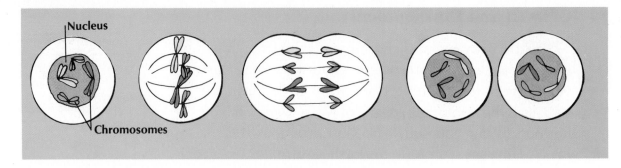

Look at the pictures of a cell during cell division. Notice the round part called the **nucleus** [NOO-klee-uhs]. When a cell is ready to divide, many changes take place inside the nucleus. Study each picture. Look at what happens to the different parts of a cell as it divides.

Notice the **chromosomes** [KROH-muh-sohms] inside the nucleus. They are the parts that look like threads. Chromosomes control the growth and activities of the cell. Most of your body cells have 46 chromosomes. Each kind of plant or animal has a certain number of them. Look at the chart. It shows the number of chromosomes in the body cells of different plants and animals.

During cell division, chromosomes make exact copies of themselves. This means that there are two matching sets of chromosomes. Each new cell gets a set like the set of the cell from which it came. Each new cell is complete and able to carry on its different activities.

Human	46	Corn	20	Garden peas	14
Mouse	40	Fox	34	Tomato	24
Rat	42	Rabbit	44	Red clover	14

New Living Things from One Parent

In living things with many cells, new cells are needed for growth and for replacing injured or worn-out cells. However, for one-celled plants and animals, cell division is a way of reproducing.

This animal, made of only one cell, lives in fresh water. It feeds on small plants and animals. When this animal is fully grown, it reproduces. It divides into two new living things.

A one-celled amoeba dividing to form two new cells

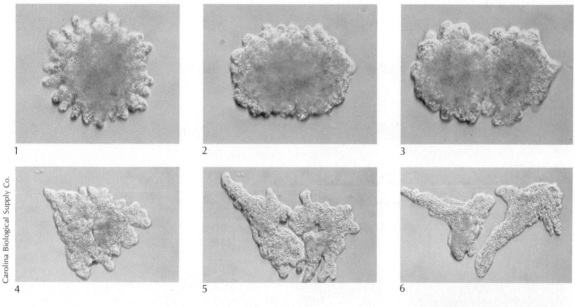

1 2 3

4 5 6

Bacteria make more of their own kind in this way, also. Look at the picture of the bacteria. Some kinds divide into new cells every 20 minutes. Starting with one cell, after 40 minutes there will be four cells. After one hour, there will be eight cells. After three hours there will be 512 bacteria cells!

It is important to remember that new cells can come only from living cells. This is true whether the living thing is reproducing or growing or replacing body cells.

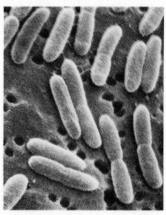

You can find out if plants and animals of just one cell make more of their own kind. You will need a handful of dry hay or grass, a microscope, a glass slide, and a cover glass. You will also need an eyedropper, a jar, and some water from a fish tank or pond.

Put a handful of hay into a jar of water and wait one day. Using an eyedropper, place a drop of water from the jar on a glass slide. Place a cover glass on the slide. Then look at the slide under a microscope. How many plants and animals do you see in the drop of water? Write down the number that you counted.

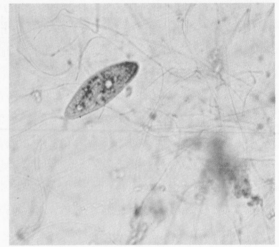

Put the jar in a warm place. Wait one week, and then look at another drop of water from the jar. Are there more plants and animals in one drop of water than before? What do you think happened?

Draw pictures of some of the plants and animals. Show your pictures to others in the classroom. Did any of your classmates find plants and animals that looked exactly like the ones you found?

Look at the small water animal in the picture. It is an animal with very simple body parts. Inside it is a hollow sac lined with cells. The opening at one end of the sac is its mouth. The mouth has long parts around it that look like threads. These parts can catch food and move the food into the mouth. The food is then digested inside the sac.

Every so often, a group of cells begins to grow on one side of the adult animal. The cells form a small clump. The clump of cells grows and changes until it becomes a new animal. The new animal then breaks away from the old one. The new animal is able to live on its own. This way of making new animals is called **budding.** During budding, a new animal grows out of the cells of an older animal. The new animal is like the old animal. At the end of the adult stage of its life cycle, the old animal will die.

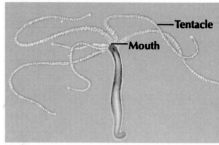

Tentacle
Mouth

Hydra

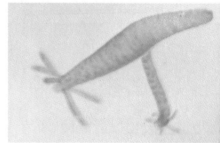

Hydra budding

ACTIVITY

Let's look at some of these animals. Maybe you can find one that is budding. You will need a few of the animals, an eyedropper, a dish, and a hand lens. You will also need some pond or fish-tank water.

With the eyedropper, gently place one of the animals in a dish. Cover the animal with water. Look at the animal with the hand lens.

How many parts that look like threads does it have? Does it have a small animal growing from its body? If it does, look at the new one. Does it look like the older one? Does it have the same kinds of body parts?

Make a drawing of the animal on a sheet of paper. Write about the animal on the paper, too.

Sometimes a whole animal can grow from part of an animal. If an earthworm is cut in two, the head end may grow a new tail end. Sometimes a starfish can grow a whole body from just one of its arms. Tadpoles can grow back missing legs. (But fully grown frogs cannot.) Growing missing parts from the remaining body cells is called **regeneration** [ree-jehn-uh-RAY-shuhn].

Regeneration takes place over a long period of time. *below top*: Sea star regenerating lost arms; *below bottom*: House gecko regenerating tail

A **planarian** [pluh-NAIR-ee-uhn] is a small worm that lives in fresh water. It has a flat body, two "eyes," and a mouth. On each side of its head, it has small bumps.

What would happen if it were cut in half? The head end could grow a new tail. The tail end could grow a new head. These worms can regenerate missing body parts.

What would happen if this animal were cut into three pieces? The middle piece could grow a head and tail. What do you think would happen to the head and tail pieces? A planarian is able to grow two heads. How is this possible?

Planarian

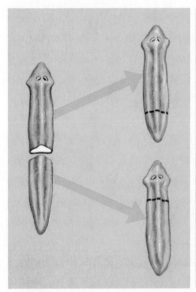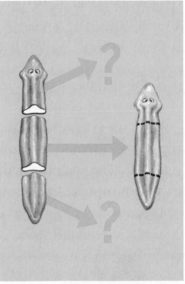

More complex animals are less able to regenerate. A crab can grow a new claw. But a claw from the animal will not grow into a new crab. Higher forms of animals, such as mammals and birds, can grow back some tissues, but not whole body parts. Can a dog grow a new tail? Can you grow a new arm or leg?

New Animals from Two Parents

In the spring many female frogs lay their eggs. Each egg looks like a small black spot. The eggs are covered with a matter that looks like jelly. This matter protects them. As the female lays the eggs, the male frog covers them with sperm cells. When a sperm cell joins with an egg cell, fertilization takes place. Large groups of eggs may be found in ponds, near the top of the water.

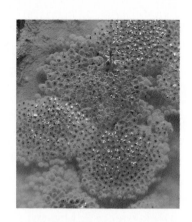

Look at the cell in the picture. It is a fertilized frog's egg. When an egg is fertilized, many things happen. At first it is only one cell. Then it divides into two new cells. Each of these two new cells divides, forming four cells. The cells divide again and again. Cell division goes on and on until there are thousands of cells. The cells stay together, forming a ball.

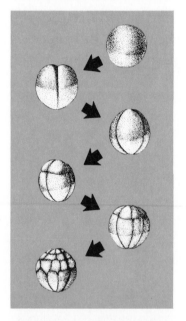

Now the ball of cells forms the different parts of a tadpole's body. Some of the cells become skin tissue. Others form bone, blood, nerve, and other tissue. Finally a living tadpole is formed. It has grown from one fertilized egg cell. The tadpole will become an adult frog. What will happen at the end of its life cycle?

You can watch how frog's eggs grow and change. You will need some fertilized frog's eggs, a dish, some pond water, a fish tank, and a hand lens. Later, you will also need some lettuce and cooked liver.

Place the frog's eggs in a dish of pond or aged water. Look at the eggs with a hand lens. Find the black spot in each egg. Draw pictures of the eggs. Then place the eggs in a fish tank filled with pond or aged water.

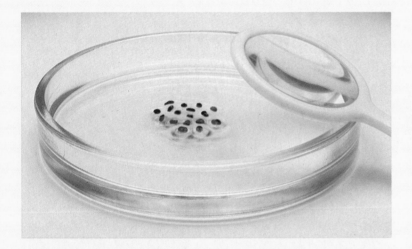

Look at the eggs every day. What happens to them? What changes do you see in the black spots? How long does it take for tadpoles to form from the eggs? Make drawings of what you see.

Tadpoles can be fed lettuce and tiny bits of cooked liver. But keep the water clean. After 30 minutes, re-move the food that has not been eaten. Add more aged water to the fish tank if it is needed.

How many days did it take for the tadpoles to hatch from eggs? When did you first notice legs on your tad-poles? How many days did it take for them to grow and change into frogs?

Egg cells and sperm cells are different from body cells. Each has half the number of chromosomes that most body cells have. In one kind of frog, body cells have 26 chromosomes (in 13 pairs). Its egg cells and sperm cells each have 13 chromosomes.

Egg cells and sperm cells are made by a certain kind of cell division called **meiosis** [my-OH-sihs]. During meiosis, each new cell receives only one chromosome from each pair of chromosomes. Why is this important? When the egg cell and sperm cell join together, the new cell will have the full number of chromosomes. The new frog will have 26 chromosomes in its body cells, just as its parents have.

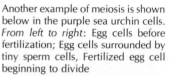

Another example of meiosis is shown below in the purple sea urchin cells. *From left to right*: Egg cells before fertilization; Egg cells surrounded by tiny sperm cells, Fertilized egg cell beginning to divide

 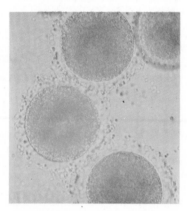 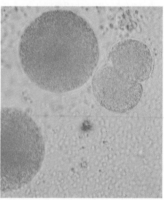

Look at the pictures of a chicken's egg. The egg was fertilized by the rooster, a male chicken. When the female chicken, a hen, lays a fertilized egg, many changes have already taken place. The egg cell has already begun to divide into many cells. The heart is formed and is pumping blood only four days after fertilization has taken place. Legs and wings begin to form by the 9th day. What happens on the 15th day? By the 19th day, the young chick is almost fully formed. After about 21 days, the chick will peck its way out of the egg.

facing page: Stages of a chick's growth—3 days, 9 days, 15 days, 19 days, 22 days

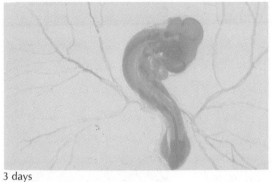
3 days

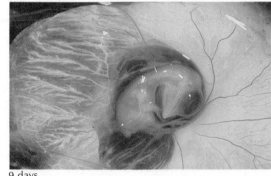
9 days

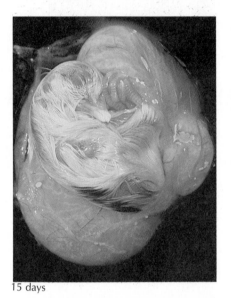
15 days

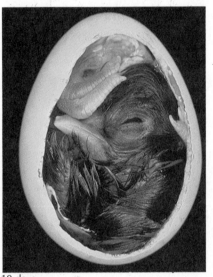
19 days

22 days

As you may remember, flowering plants also grow from fertilized eggs. How do sperm cells reach the egg cell in flowering plants? After sperm cells fertilize the egg cells, each fertilized egg develops into a seed. Can you describe the life cycle of flowering plants?

Many plants and animals are made of millions of cells. However, a great number of these living things each grew from one fertilized egg cell. These plants and animals have chromosomes from both parents. Therefore, they are like both parents in different ways.

Magnolia tree in flower

Parents Pass On Some Traits
When They Reproduce

When you see a duck sitting on a nest, what would you expect to hatch from the eggs? You would be surprised if a young swan were hatched. That kind of thing happens only in fairy tales. Baby ducks always hatch from duck eggs. Each kind of living thing produces its own kind of young.

Among individuals of the same kind of living thing, there are many differences. Look at the dogs in the picture. These dogs have many different fur colors, ear lengths, tail shapes, and nose shapes. Each of these things is a **trait.** Each dog has many traits, but none of these dogs has exactly the same traits. That is why they do not look exactly alike.

In what ways are these dogs alike? In what ways do they look different?

Has anyone ever told you that you have your mother's eyes or your father's nose? What they may mean to say is that the color of your eyes is like your mother's. They may also mean that your nose has the same shape as your father's. You have **inherited** these traits from your parents. Information about these traits was passed on in the chromosomes from your parents to you.

If you look at a family, you can see that different members look the same in some ways but not in others. How can we explain why family members share some, but not all, traits?

In what ways do these people look alike? In what ways do they look different?

The chromosomes in a fertilized egg cell have all the information that is needed to form a new living thing. One-half of the chromosomes came from each parent. During the many cell divisions that follow, each new body cell receives exact copies of the chromosomes in the fertilized cell. Certain places on the chromosomes carry the information needed to form each trait. These places are called **genes** [jeenz]. Genes control hair color, eye color, height, and all of the other inherited traits. There are two genes for almost every trait—one from each parent.

Sometimes the new living thing has traits that seem to be in between the traits of its parents. Let's look at morning glory flowers. Suppose one parent has red flowers and one parent has white flowers. The young plants will all have pink flowers. In the next generation, different plants will have either red, pink, or white flowers.

Sometimes only one of two different traits can be seen in the new living thing. Let's look at the seeds of pea plants. Suppose one parent has two genes for yellow seeds and the other parent has two genes for green seeds. The new plants will all have yellow seeds. The gene for green seeds is still there, but the trait can't be seen. Traits that can't be seen are called hidden traits. The genes for both yellow and green will be passed on when the new plants reproduce. Some of the pea plants in the next generation may have green seeds. In this way some traits seem to skip generations.

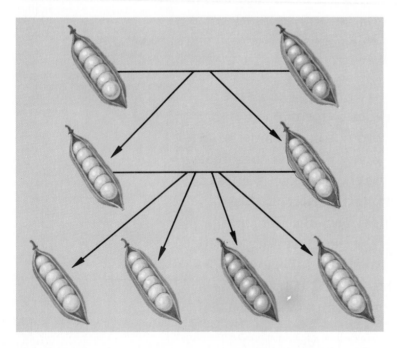

Let's find out about some of the traits you and your classmates have. Copy the chart on a sheet of paper. Look at your classmates to find different traits. How many of your classmates have blue eyes? How many have brown eyes? How many have brown, black, blond, or red hair? Do more students in your class have straight hair or curly hair? Look at the ears in the pictures. How many of your classmates have ears like the one in the first picture? How many have ears like the one in the second picture?

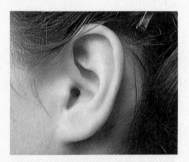 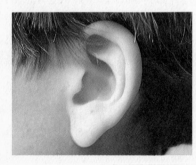

Characteristics	How Many?
Eyes:	
Blue	
Brown	
Black	
Green	
Hair Color:	
Brown	
Black	
Blonde	
Red	
Straight or Curly Hair:	
Curly	
Straight	
Earlobes:	
Attached	
Detached	

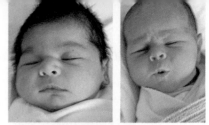

The genes in your chromosomes control the traits of eye color, hair color, and curly or straight hair. What other traits do your genes control?

You began your life as one cell. Half of your chromosomes came from your mother and the other half from your father. At this time you looked very much like any first human cell. When you were born, you already looked different from other human babies. Your traits are from your parents. Yet you have traits that are different from each of your parents and your friends. You are like other people in many ways, but you are also very different.

ACTIVITY

You can find out about other differences between you and your classmates. You will need a sheet of paper, a piece of string, and a meterstick. Copy this chart on the paper. Measure your head size by wrapping the string once around your head above your eyes. Then place the piece of string along your meterstick. This will show your head size. Fill in the chart by measuring your height, arm, foot, and wrist sizes. Compare your measurements with others in the classroom. Are yours exactly like those of your classmates?

Body Part	Size in Centimeters
Head size	
Height	
Arm size	
Foot size	
Wrist size	

All people are the same in many ways. Yet they are very different in others. Differences in traits are called **variations** [vehr-ee-AY-shuhns]. Variation is found in all living things.

Variations can be seen in the height, weight, and hair coloring of the people in your class. Let's find out about another kind of variation among you and your classmates.

ACTIVITY

This picture shows you how to roll your tongue. Try to roll your tongue in the same way. Use a mirror to see if you can do it. Try this again and again. Were you able to do it? Can your classmates roll their tongues? Record how many can and how many cannot. Can people be taught how to roll their tongues? Find out how many members of your family can roll their tongues.

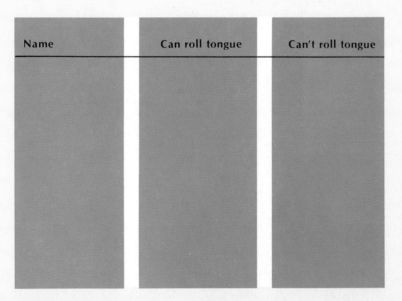

Name	Can roll tongue	Can't roll tongue

The children in the first picture have the same parents. Yet they are not exact copies of their parents or of each other. Identical twins are the only people who have inherited exactly the same genes. These flowers are the same kind of flower. They are all moss roses. Yet none of these is exactly like any of the others. How are they different?

Is there variation among radish seeds, too? Here is a way to find out. You will need a sponge, some radish seeds, and a bowl.

Wash the sponge several times with water. Then place it in a bowl and soak it with water. Sprinkle some radish seeds on top of the sponge. Make sure that it stays wet during the next few days. When the seeds begin to grow, look at the young plants. Are any two plants *exactly* alike? Are they the same height? Are some greener than others? How are they different?

Variation is found in radishes and other plants. Can you describe the variations in the vegetables and fruits that you eat?

What Did You Learn?

- The stages a living thing goes through as it grows and changes make up its life cycle.
- New cells are needed for growing or for taking the place of worn-out or damaged cells.
- During cell division one cell becomes two new cells.
- Each cell has chromosomes, which have information to help it grow and change.
- New animals can form by cell division, budding, and regeneration.
- Many living things grow from a fertilized egg.
- Half of your chromosomes came from your father and half came from your mother.
- The genes in your chromosomes control your traits.
- Variation is found in all living things.

Career

Geneticist

Scientists called geneticists [juh-NEHT-uh-sihsts] study how and why living things inherit looks and traits from their parents. They try to find ways in which traits are passed from one generation to the next. They may also study inherited illnesses.

Dr. Frank C. Dukepoo is a geneticist who works for the National Cancer Institute. He has taught genetics at many schools and colleges, and he has made several scientific studies. For five years, he was part of a team studying unusual growths in fruit flies for the Atomic Energy Commission.

Frank Dukepoo was born on the Mohave Indian Reservation in Arizona. He later moved to Phoenix, where he attended public school. In about the fifth grade he decided that he wanted to become a doctor of medicine. His college grades were not high enough for him to enter a school of medicine. He did not give up. He went on with his studies and became a scientist working in the field of genetics.

Dr. Dukepoo's interest in science and people has taken him to many places. He has gone into communities in California and Arizona to study the problems of aging. Now he travels around the country for the National Cancer Institute, visiting cancer study centers.

Dr. Dukepoo has been honored in many ways for the work he has done.

TO THINK ABOUT AND DO

Read the sentences. Arrange these letters so that they form words that will complete the sentences. Write the completed sentences on a piece of paper.

1. Many insects have four _____ in their life cycle.

2. Growing a new body part is called _____.   arlva

3. _____ is a certain kind of cell division by which   ulsadt
egg cells and sperm cells are made.   tiongenreaer

4. Many living things grow to be _____.   apup

5. The young form of some insects is a _____.   phnym

6. A _____ is a young insect that looks like the adult.   seagst

7. Eggs that are _____ can make new life.   msisoie

8. The stage after the larva is the _____.   lizerefidt

Copy each sentence on a piece of paper. Write **T** beside the sentences that are true and **F** beside those that are false. Rewrite any sentence that is false to make it true.

1. Living things make the same kind of living thing.

2. Life cycles are stages that living things go through during their lives.

3. Genes look like tiny threads and are found in the nucleus.

4. Your traits are controlled by genes in your chromosomes.

5. Variations are found among most living things.

6. Budding and cell division are the only ways that animals can be formed.

1. Make a list of traits that change as you grow. What traits do not change as you grow?
2. Find out how the work of Gregor Mendel, an Austrian monk, is important in understanding inherited traits.

3. Try to find the average life span of several different animals. Compare these with the average life span of humans. Make a bar graph to show your findings.
4. An amoeba, a one-celled animal, takes about an hour to reach full growth and divide in two. This happens only if the surroundings are just right. Starting with one amoeba, how many amoebas will there be at the end of five hours?

Unit II

Energy for Now and the Future

Elements and Compounds

5

In a way, you do some important science every day of your life! If you drank milk for breakfast, some of it is already being changed to another kind of matter—the cells of your bones. If you ate an egg this morning, you separated the protein that you received into another kind of matter. This matter will soon be on its way to becoming muscle cells. Your body is always causing changes in matter.

Scientists also cause changes in matter. The kinds of matter that they study are everywhere and in everything. Everything on Earth is interesting to them. Out of a mold on rotting fruit they make some drugs that could save your life. Out of waste matter they make fertilizers and fuels. Out of tiny bits of sand they make shining glass.

Most likely, you have many questions about matter. Of what is matter made? How does it change? What happens when different kinds of matter are mixed together? Let's get some answers.

Building Blocks of Matter

How many stone blocks were used to build the Washington Monument? Certainly, thousands of the cut stones must have been used.

In one way, all matter is like this monument. Just as it is made of thousands of smaller pieces, all matter is made of many smaller parts. We call these smaller parts **atoms** [AT-uhmz].

Atoms are such tiny parts that you cannot see or feel them. They are too tiny to see even with the most powerful microscope. They are so tiny, in fact, that there are many more of them in this letter— O—than there are people in the world. Yes, really! Yet some of the things that these tiny atoms do have been measured. Atoms have even been torn apart and put together again!

But how can you talk about something that you can neither see nor feel? For years people have used their fancies to try to explain things that they could not see directly. They have made **models** to describe the way they supposed something looked or behaved. A model may be a drawing that you make or an object that you find. It may even be a picture that you form in your mind.

No one could see the atom. For this reason, the models were based on what people believed about how the atom "looks" and behaves.

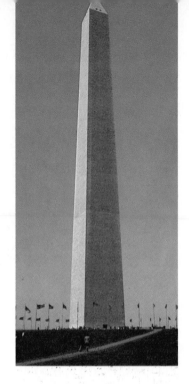

left to right: Billiard ball model; Plum pudding model; Rutherford's model: a nucleus surrounded by rapidly moving electrons

Today we know that each of these models is only partly correct. In fact, we now have a model that is, in some ways, the simplest of all. It is mostly empty space!

Think about blowing up an atom so that it is the size of your classroom. The **nucleus** [NOO-klee-uhs], or central part of this atom, would be the size of a tiny bit of dust. It would be found close to the middle of your room. Particles called **protons** [PROH-tahnz] and **neutrons** [NOO-trahnz] are inside the nucleus. They make up most of the mass of the atom.

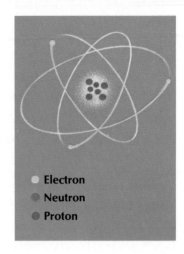

● Electron
● Neutron
● Proton

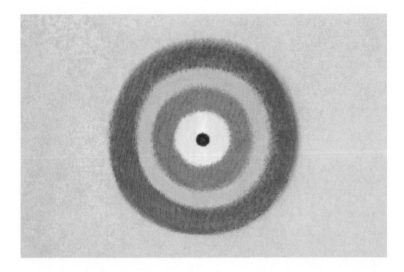

Electron cloud model

Surrounding the nucleus and taking up a space as large as your classroom is the rest of the atom. In our model, this space looks like a huge cloud.

Have you ever seen a rapidly spinning toy top or a whirling paper windmill? You may have noticed that after a while the spinning part looked blurred. As particles called **electrons** [ih-LEHK-trahnz] move around the nucleus, something similar happens. We imagine they make the space around the nucleus appear blurred as they move about it.

How is this spinning top like the electron cloud model?

117

How Matter Moves and Changes

You know that every single bit of matter in the world is made of tiny moving parts called atoms. Whether something is a solid, a liquid, or a gas, it is made of atoms. The paper in this book, the air in your classroom, and the pencil in your desk are all made of atoms.

When atoms are joined together in a certain way, a **molecule** [MAHL-uh-kyool] is formed. A molecule of water is the smallest amount of water you can have and still have water. It is made of atoms of hydrogen and oxygen. If these atoms are separated from each other, the bit of matter that was water is no longer water.

When the molecules in matter are held very tightly by forces between them, the matter is a solid. A lump of coal, a bar of chocolate, a piece of ice—all these are solids.

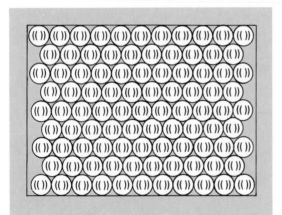 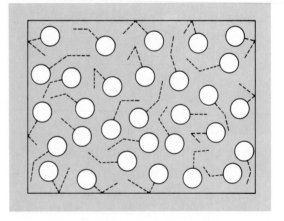

left: Molecular movement in a solid; *right*: Molecular movement in a liquid

Molecules that are close together, but loosely held, slip and slide around each other. They are in a liquid state. Drinking water and melted chocolate are made of molecules that behave this way. They are liquids.

Some molecules bounce far apart whenever they hit each other. When this happens, we say that the matter is a gas. Water vapor is a gas. So is the air you breathe.

When a solid is heated, the molecules begin moving faster and farther apart. As they move farther apart, the forces that cause the molecules to "stick" together become weaker. When this happens, the molecules are able to move more freely about each other. This does not mean that the forces between molecules are no longer present, however. If there were no forces, the molecules of every bit of matter, even you, would fly apart!

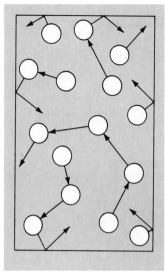

Molecular movement in a gas

What is happening to the molecules in this picture?

When you change the state of matter, you don't change the way the atoms in the molecules are arranged. In a change of state, only the relationship of one molecule to another is changed. A change of state is one kind of **physical change.** Melting, freezing, and boiling are physical changes. You change only the state of the matter. The arrangement of atoms in the molecules remains the same. The molecules in liquid water, frozen water, and water vapor are all water.

There are other kinds of physical changes. Sawing a piece of wood causes a physical change. The size of the piece of wood is changed, but its molecules are not changed. Chopping, cutting, bending, squeezing—these actions change the shape of something and the way it looks. But the makeup of its molecules is not changed.

What physical change is happening to the material in each picture?

When you compare several kinds of matter, you find ways they are like each other and ways they are different. The things you can notice and describe about kinds of matter are called their **properties** [PRAHP-uhr-teez]. Some of the physical properties of matter are color, taste, smell, and touch.

120

Let's compare the physical properties of two different kinds of matter. You will need about one gram each of iron filings and powdered sulfur, a piece of paper, a hand lens, and a magnet.

Put the iron filings and the sulfur next to each other on your paper. Notice the differences between these two kinds of matter. What color is each? How does each feel?

In some ways the two kinds of matter are alike; in other ways they are different. With the hand lens, look at each kind of matter. Which is made up of larger grains? Which is more shiny?

Now move the two substances farther apart on the paper. Hold the magnet close to the iron. What happens when you do this? Try the same thing with the sulfur.

Mix together the iron filings and the sulfur. What do you think would happen if you mixed the two kinds of matter together and held the magnet close by? Try it.

Mixing Things Together

When iron filings and powdered sulfur are mixed together, their properties are not changed. In most cases, a **mixture** is made when two or more kinds of matter are put together without changing either of them. Think about some of the things around you that are mixtures—the air you breathe and the soil where your food grows. Many of the foods you eat are mixtures too.

Here is a way to see what happens when two kinds of matter are mixed together. You will need a glass of water, a teaspoon, some table salt, a small pan, and a hot plate.

Put two teaspoons of salt in the glass of water. Stir the water with the spoon. Then set the glass down and look for the salt. Do you see the grains of salt? If not, where do you think the grains have gone? Now, taste the water. How can you tell that the salt is still there?

Put the water in the pan. Heat it until all the water has boiled away. Let the pan cool and then taste the white matter that has been left behind. What do you learn from the taste? Where do you think the matter in the pan came from?

When table salt is mixed with water, no new matter is made out of the salt and the water. Even though you can no longer see the salt, it is in the water all the time. We say that the salt has been **dissolved** [dih-ZAHLVD] by the water. When a solid is dissolved in water or in any other liquid, the mixture that is formed is a **solution** [suh-LOO-shuhn].

Not all matter will dissolve in water. Have you ever put some muddy water into a jar? If so, you may have noticed that it is full of tiny pieces of clay or sand. These pieces are not dissolved in the water. Some of the larger pieces settle to the bottom of the jar. What do you think causes this to happen?

Compare the muddy water that has settled for one hour (*left*) with the water that has settled for one day (*right*).

Naming the Atoms

Millions of different combinations of atoms make up all the matter on the earth. Yet there are only 92 kinds of atoms from which these combinations can be made. Each of these different kinds of atoms is an **element** [EHL-uh-muhnt]. An element is any matter that is made of only one kind of atom. This means, then, that iron is an element made only of atoms of iron. Copper is an element made only of copper atoms. Can you name other matter that is made of only one kind of atom?

Fourteen other elements have been made from the 92 atoms that are found naturally on the earth. In all, then, 106 elements are known for sure at the present time.

Copper, iron, lead, tin, and silver are elements that you may already know. In the chart you see the names of the elements most often found in the earth's crust.

Some elements were discovered hundreds of years ago. Others have been made in the laboratory since your parents were born. The names of elements were sometimes chosen by the people who discovered them. Others were named for well-known scientists.

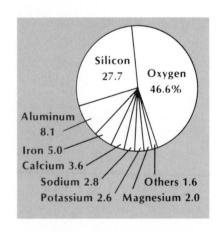

Silicon 27.7
Oxygen 46.6%
Aluminum 8.1
Iron 5.0
Calcium 3.6
Sodium 2.8
Potassium 2.6
Magnesium 2.0
Others 1.6

To make it easier to put the elements into writing, a short form or **symbol** [SIHM-buhl] is used for each element. Scientists the world over have agreed to use a certain symbol to stand for each different element. In other words, the whole world shares the same language when it comes to the elements! The symbol "H" stands for hydrogen, whether you live in the United States, in Brazil, or in France.

Sometimes the names of two or more elements begin with the same letter. Then two letters are used as an element's symbol. Since *S* stands for sulfur, then *Si* stands for silicon, and *Na* stands for sodium. But *N* and *a* are not letters in sodium! Sometimes a symbol is taken from a name in a language other than English. The symbol *Na* is taken from the Latin word *natrium*.

This chart shows most of the known elements. The atomic number of each element stands for the number of protons in the nucleus of that element.

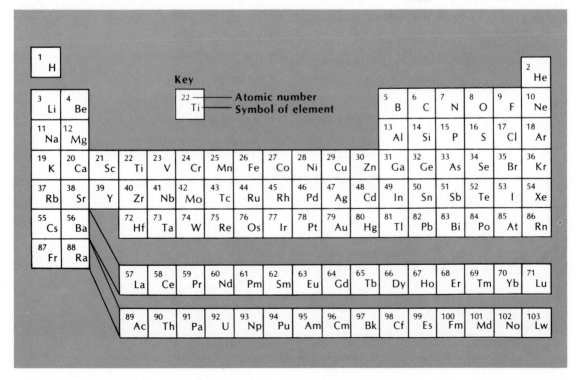

Putting Elements Together

Each kind of matter is made up of at least one kind of atom. Mined gold, as you know, is made only of gold atoms. Silver is made only of silver atoms.

But most things are not single elements made of only one kind of atom. Most matter is made of more than one kind of element. Water is made of two different elements. So is table salt. Sugar is made of three elements—carbon, hydrogen, and oxygen. When two or more elements join together, we say that a **compound** [KAHM-pownd] has been formed.

Here is a way to see how elements fit together to form compounds. You will need a piece of cardboard, a metric ruler, a pair of scissors, and a pencil.

On the cardboard, mark off eight 5-cm squares. Cut them out as shown in the drawing. Then tell what they are by using the names of the elements and their symbols.

How many pieces can you fit together? Are there some pieces that will not fit with another element?

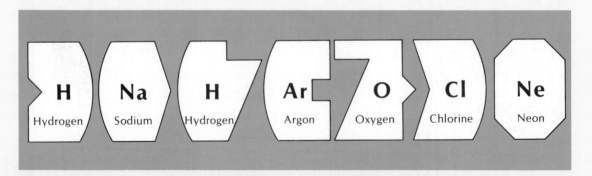

126

You know that not every group of letters will form a word. What can you do with these groups of letters: *xyw* or *srko?* You will find that elements do not always combine, either. It is important to find out which elements will join together and which will not.

In most cases, a compound is quite different from the separate elements of which it is made. Sugar is a compound made of a black solid called carbon and two other elements that are gases. Taken separately, none of these three elements is either white or sweet like sugar.

Each of the elements in a compound is written in the compound's **chemical formula.** From the chemical formula, you can tell what elements are present in a molecule of that compound. You can also find out how many atoms are in the molecule.

Look at the formula for water. If you could look at only one molecule of water, you would find that there are two atoms of hydrogen joined with one atom of oxygen. In a formula, there is no need to write a figure *1* by itself.

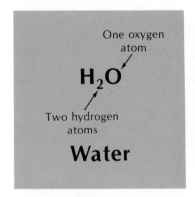

One oxygen atom

H_2O

Two hydrogen atoms

Water

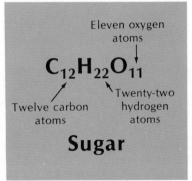

Eleven oxygen atoms

$C_{12}H_{22}O_{11}$

Twelve carbon atoms

Twenty-two hydrogen atoms

Sugar

below: What elements are present in each of these compounds? How many atoms of each element are present?

Vinegar	$C_2H_4O_2$
Baking soda	$NaHCO_3$
Carbon dioxide	CO_2
Lime	CaO
Limestone	$CaCO_3$
Quartz	SiO_2

Cane sugar is $C_{12}H_{22}O_{11}$. This means that there are 12 atoms of carbon, 22 atoms of hydrogen, and 11 atoms of oxygen in one molecule of cane sugar.

Changing One Kind of Matter to Another

The changes that take place in matter are often used to make new substances. To make rayon out of wood, we must first chop the wood into very fine bits. The bits of wood are much smaller than the larger piece of wood from which they were made. But each of the pieces is still wood. What kind of change have we caused in the wood?

In order to make the pieces into rayon, we must rearrange the different kinds of atoms that make up the wood. When we do this, a new kind of matter is formed. The change from one kind of matter to a different kind of matter is known as a **chemical change.**

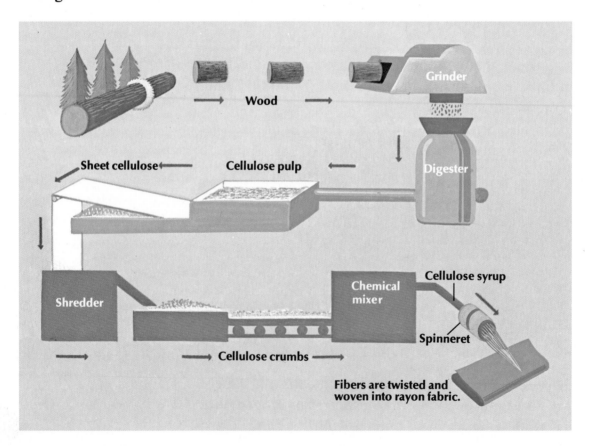

Breaking wood into smaller pieces, melting a stick of butter, allowing perfume to change to a gas —these are physical changes. When wood is burned, however, a chemical change takes place. A completely different kind of matter is formed.

Which of these pictures show physical changes, and which show chemical changes? What change is taking place in each one?

When the elements iron and sulfur are mixed together, neither is changed in any way. When heat is added, however, they combine or **react** [ree-AKT] with each other in a **chemical reaction.** The brown-black matter that forms does not look or act like either iron or sulfur. A new compound has been formed.

The compound iron sulfide (FeS)

Here is a way to find out what happens when two kinds of matter, a liquid and a powder, are mixed. You will need 5 g of baking soda, 5 ml of vinegar, and a glass.

Put the 5 g of baking soda in the glass. Then add the 5 ml of vinegar and watch what happens. How can you tell that a chemical reaction may have taken place?

When baking soda and vinegar react, a gas is made. But neither the baking soda nor the vinegar looks like a gas. One sign that there has been a chemical change is a change in the way something looks. This alone is not enough to tell you that the change has been chemical, however. (After all, water and ice look different.)

In order for some chemical reactions to take place, heat may be needed. But sometimes heat is also given off in a reaction. What happens when a candle burns?

Chemical Sentences

In the reaction between iron and sulfur, a compound called **iron sulfide** [EYE-uhrn SUHL-fyd] is formed. How would you describe what happens in this reaction?

One way would be to use words to tell about what takes place.

"One atom of iron and one atom of sulfur, when heated, form one molecule of iron sulfide."

Or you might draw a picture.

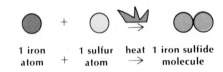

1 iron atom + 1 sulfur atom → heat 1 iron sulfide molecule

To explain what happens in every reaction, many words would be needed. There is a faster and easier way to describe what takes place. You can use chemical symbols and signs:

$$Fe + S \xrightarrow{\Delta} FeS + \Delta$$

The arrow that points toward the right means "makes" or "yields." The Greek letter Δ above the arrow shows that heat is present. The Δ on the far right shows that heat was given off. FeS is the symbol for iron sulfide.

Let's use symbols to show how the gas carbon dioxide is made:

$$C + O_2 \xrightarrow{\Delta} CO_2 \uparrow + \Delta$$

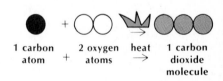

1 carbon atom + 2 oxygen atoms → heat 1 carbon dioxide molecule

What new things do you notice here? First, oxygen is written as O_2 rather than O. This is because there are two atoms in every molecule of oxygen. Oxygen and a few other gases are usually found as molecules of two atoms each.

The second thing you may notice is an arrow that points upward. This arrow shows that a gas, in this case CO_2, is given off.

So far, you have seen how elements may be put together to form compounds. But what happens when a compound is separated into its parts?

On Sunday, August 1, 1774, Joseph Priestley did some tests with mercury, a shiny silver-colored liquid. He began by heating the mercury in air. A brick-red powder—now called **mercuric oxide** [muhr-KYUR-ihk AHK-syd]—began to appear.

Priestley put some of this powder into a test tube and heated it. Shortly, he saw tiny balls of liquid in the top part of the test tube. These were drops of mercury, for sure!

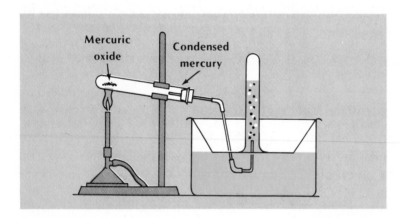

A modern demonstration of Priestley's experiment

But mercury is only one thing that is given off when mercuric oxide is broken down by heat. Can you think what else Priestley might have found?

Priestley believed that he had also found some kind of gas. Even though the gas had no color and he could not see it, he was sure that what had formed was very different from plain air. Why did he think so? Because a glowing piece of wood burst into flame when it was put into the gas! Priestley used a very long name to describe the "new" gas. Later, however, the name of the gas was changed to oxygen.

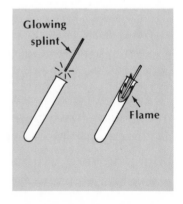

Testing Chemicals

Have you ever owned a chemistry set? Most likely, it is packed with boxes and bottles. Each box or bottle is labeled with the name of the chemical that it holds. For the **chemist**, a person who studies the chemical and physical properties of matter, it is different, however. The chemicals must first be tested to find out what the labels should be. Thousands of different kinds of matter—milk, blood, hair, meat—are tested every day. It is the chemist's job to find out what each is made of.

What is in this person's flasks? It may be any one of several million things! And there are tests for each of them. Let's say we started with tests for a certain substance and kept going until the right one was found. We might be testing for the rest of our lives! Because of this, chemists have come up with the idea of group tests. A group test is used to find out what group the unknown matter belongs to.

You have often used "group tests" yourself, without even knowing it. How? If you see a strange animal on the lawn, you don't ask, "Is it a new kind of grasshopper, or fish, or tiger, or frog?" You see two legs, a bill, and some feathers. You know it is a bird. You have already grouped the new animal. At the same time, you have set aside millions of things that it cannot be. You can do this without even having to think about them. You may still have to find out what kind of bird it is. But you don't have to go through the whole animal kingdom to find out!

How would you find out what this is?

A chemist doesn't have such an easy time of it. Chemicals don't have bills or feathers! Just looking at the matter you are testing is not enough. A white powder may be sugar, starch, or salt. But it so happens that another white powder is a deadly poison. That's a good reason why you should never taste something that is unknown to you. It could harm you, even though it may look like something you have seen before.

SALT
(NaCl)

ARSENIC TRIOXIDE
(As_2O_3)

POISON ☠

CORNSTARCH
($C_6H_{10}O_5)_n$

SUGAR
($C_{12}H_{22}O_{11}$)

But how can you group matter whose name you do not know? One way is to find out how it behaves when it is mixed with matter that you know about.

Describe the taste of each of these foods. Which is the most sour? Which is the least sour? How can you account for the difference?

You may be able to group one kind of matter already. If you have ever eaten a lemon pie or have had some orange juice, you have had a weak **acid.** In most cases, foods that taste sour or sharp have acid in them.

Bases are substances that you or your parents may have used for cleaning your house or baking a cake. In fact, you may have had a base for breakfast. If you had milk, you did! But remember: many bases in jars around your house are poisons. Never eat or drink anything that has no name on it or that you do not know is safe.

How can a group test be done to find out whether something is an acid or a base? **Indicators** [IHN-duh-kay-tuhrz] can be used. Some indicators are pieces of red or blue paper called **litmus** [LIHT-muhs] paper. Red litmus will turn blue if it is touched by a base. Blue litmus will turn red if it is touched by an acid. Sometimes neither the red nor the blue paper changes color when touched to the matter that is being tested. Then we say the matter is **neutral** [NOO-truhl]. In other words, it is not an acid or a base.

below: Examples of bases; *bottom*: Examples of neutral substances

135

You can find out what group a certain kind of matter belongs to. You will need about 5 ml each of vinegar, sugar water, soda water, ammonia, salt water, and milk of magnesia. You will also need several pieces each of blue and red litmus paper. Use a clean plastic cup for each liquid that you test. Have a piece of paper and a pencil ready to record what you see.

Put each of the liquids that you will be testing into a separate cup. Write the name of each liquid on the outside of each cup. Then dip the end of a strip of blue litmus into each cup. Be sure to use a new strip for each test. Did you find that the litmus paper turned red in any of the cups? If so, list the names on these cups under "Acids" on your paper.

With the red litmus, test the group of liquids that are not acids. What two groups might these liquids belong to? Did you find that the litmus paper turned blue in any of the cups? If so, list the names on these cups under "Bases" on your paper. Are any of the liquids you tested neutral?

Aside from grouping different kinds of matter, the chemist is also working to discover ways of making new matter. About a quarter of a million new compounds are developed each year. Can these new compounds make a difference in *your* life? Let's find out about a few of them.

Most likely, some of the foods you eat have been changed by chemicals called **additives** [AD-uh-tihvz]. Small amounts of additives are put into foods to slow down spoiling. For the most part, you cannot tell by the taste or smell that anything has been put into your food. However, it is believed that some additives may harm you. Now a way has been found to bind some additives to other kinds of matter. In this form, the additives are carried right through your body without harming you.

Scientists have also been developing many new plastics, from parts that replace organs of the human body to suits worn by people who work around radioactive materials.

To help stop tooth decay, sweeteners with no sugar have been made. They are made from matter that is found in grapefruit peels!

A compound much like a hormone was taken from the gland of a camel. Chemists were able to make the same kind of matter in their laboratories. Some day you may be given this compound instead of an aspirin!

Scientists have also been concerned about pollution of the earth's atmosphere by harmful chemical compounds. They have developed ways of removing some chemicals from the fuels that we burn.

The chemistry of living things is a field that is beginning to make sense of certain chemical "secrets." These "secrets" happen inside living things, including your own body. The better you understand the things the chemist does, the better you can understand the great secret of life itself. The tests that chemists are doing right at this moment may make a real difference in your health and the way you live.

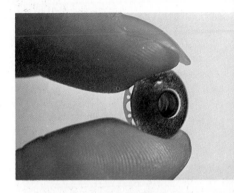

top: Plastic eye cornea for transplant into eye; *above*: How does pollution affect land and water as well as the atmosphere?

What Did You Learn?

- All matter is made of tiny parts called atoms.
- In an atom, protons and neutrons are found in the nucleus, and electrons move around the nucleus.
- Matter may be a solid, a liquid, or a gas, depending on how its molecules behave.
- When a physical change takes place in matter, the way it looks may change. The way its molecules are made is not changed.
- If two or more kinds of matter are not changed when mixed together, we say a mixture has formed. In the mixture, bits of one kind of matter may or may not be dissolved by the other.
- Matter that is made of only one kind of atom is an element.
- When two or more elements join together in molecules, a compound is formed.
- From a chemical formula you can find out the number of atoms and the kinds of elements that are present.
- When a chemical change takes place, one or more different kinds of matter may be formed.
- Group tests can be used to find out whether something is an acid, is a base, or is neutral.
- The new compounds that are being made can make a difference in the way you live.

Biography

Dr. Percy Julian (1898–1975)

There is an important drug that helps many people who have arthritis. This drug is called cortisone [KAWR-tuh-sohn]. Dr. Percy Julian, a famous black chemist, used raw materials found in plants to make this drug.

A compound taken from oxen was already being used to make cortisone for treating arthritis. However, large amounts of this compound were needed to make a very small amount of the drug. It cost a lot to make, and only a few people could be treated. Dr. Julian found that the properties of some substances in soybean oil and yams were similar to those found in oxen. It was possible to make cortisone from these plants in such large amounts that many people could be treated. Cortisone could now be made at a much lower cost.

Dr. Julian and his team made many useful materials from the soybean. They made a chemical to treat an eye disease. They also made a soybean protein that could make paper stiff and cardboard waterproof.

Dr. Julian worked his way through college and finished at the top of his class. He taught for a few years before going to school in Vienna. After working at universities and in laboratories, he decided to form his own company, Julian Laboratories.

Dr. Julian's work earned him many honors for his research and contributions in science.

TO THINK ABOUT AND DO

On a piece of paper copy the headings and numbers in Column A. Then select the phrases from Column B that describe each heading and write them next to the numbers.

Column **A**

Column **B**

Physical Change
1.
2.

sand floating in water

burning wood

squeezing a lemon

iodine dissolved in alcohol

Chemical Change
1.
2.

breaking an egg

tarnishing silver

Mixture
1.
2.

WHAT DO YOU REMEMBER?

1. All matter is made of tiny moving parts called _____ .

2. Most of the mass of an atom is made of _____ and _____ found inside the nucleus.

3. Particles that move rapidly around the nucleus are called _____ .

4. Depending on how its molecules are moving, the state of matter may be a _____ , a _____ , or a _____ .

5. Matter that is made of only one kind of atom is called an _____ .

6. When two or more elements are combined chemically, a _____ is formed.

7. The number of atoms and the kinds of elements that are present in a compound may be found by looking at the compound's _____.

8. We can find out whether something is an acid, a base, or is neutral by doing a _____ test.

Look at the labels on foods in your kitchen or at the grocery store. Find out what additives have been put into the foods and make a list of them.

You can use cabbage leaves to test for both acids and bases. You will need two red cabbage leaves, a small bottle, a wooden spoon, a glass bowl, and an eye dropper. You will also need a cup of boiling water, some vinegar, and some ammonia.

Tear the cabbage leaves into small pieces and put them in the bowl. Then add the boiling water to the leaves.

Crush the leaves with the wooden spoon, squeezing out as much juice as you can. Then let the cabbage water stand until the liquid is deep purple.

Drain some of the purple liquid into the bottle. Drop by drop, add vinegar until you notice a color change. How is the purple liquid acting like litmus paper? Is vinegar an acid or a base?

Now try the test with ammonia. What color changes do you notice? Is ammonia an acid or a base?

Electricity and Magnetism

6

More than likely, you have already heard about how important electricity is in your life. After all, it may have done more to change the way people live than anything else in the last hundred years. Think about the things you can do today that would have been impossible when your grandmother and grandfather were young. You can talk to people in other countries. You can even see a runner win a race on the other side of the world!

But you may wonder what electricity really is. People have been trying to answer this question for quite some time. They have not, as yet, come up with an answer that explains everything. But they have found out a great deal about how electricity behaves. They also know that magnetism has something to do with electricity.

In the next few pages, you will discover some of the things that have already been learned about electricity. You will also learn how electricity makes a difference in the way you live.

Electricity at Rest

How are combs, hair, shoes, and rugs alike? For one thing, each is a kind of matter, which is made of atoms. And an atom is made of three kinds of particles. You remember that the proton and the neutron are found in the nucleus of an atom. The electron moves about the nucleus.

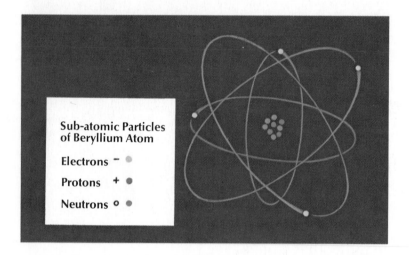

Sub-atomic Particles
of Beryllium Atom

Electrons − ●

Protons   + ●

Neutrons   o ●

In most cases, matter has equal numbers of protons and electrons. Whenever these numbers are not equal, we say that the matter takes on a **charge.** There are two kinds of charge: the **positive** charge carried by protons and the **negative** charge carried by electrons. Neutrons have no charge.

But how can this balance be upset? You yourself can cause this to happen. When you comb your hair, you rub electrons from your hair on to the comb. Your hair, which once had equal numbers of protons and electrons, has lost some of its electrons. Your comb, on the other hand, has gained some electrons. We say that your hair, which now has more protons than electrons, is positively charged. How do you think the comb is charged?

What do charges have to do with electricity anyway? As you comb your hair, electrons are rubbed off your hair and on to the comb where they begin piling up. This pile of electrons, which is not moving, is called **static** electricity.

What happens to the electrons that have piled up? Surely they can't just keep piling up. The girl in the picture decided to find out. First, she made sure her hair was dry. Then she stood in front of a mirror and made the room dark. Next she began combing her hair. Soon she saw little flashes of light and heard several crackling sounds. What had happened? The girl had rubbed electrons off her hair on to the comb until there was a pile of static electricity on it. When the comb became crowded with electrons, the electrons moved swiftly back to her hair. As this happened, little flashes of light appeared and sounds could be heard.

ACTIVITY

What will happen when you cause electrons to pile up on something? To find out, you will need a wool rug. Be sure that you are wearing shoes with soles that are not rubber.

Make the room as dark as you can. Walk across the wool rug, moving your feet back and forth as you go. Then touch a metal doorknob. What happens?

You may have found that static electricity can pile up on you when you walk across some kinds of rugs on dry days. When you walk across a wool rug and touch a metal doorknob, the piled-up electrons move swiftly from your finger to the knob. You may have felt a little shock as the electrons moved off your finger. Did you see or hear anything at the same time?

What use can you make of charge that piles up on things, flows for an instant, and is gone? This kind of charge doesn't seem to be very useful, but let's learn more about it.

Moving Charges

Electrons don't just flow when you say "Please." Somehow they have to be made to move. How can this be done?

The boy and girl in the picture are using two sheets of plastic food wrap to do this. Each sheet is about the size of a page in this book. The boy slipped the end of his sheet into a book and is holding it near the edge of the table. The girl is holding her sheet between the fingers of one hand.

The boy and the girl rub their sheets five times between two fingers of the other hand. As they do this, the electrons are rubbed off their fingers and on to the sheets. Since the sheets gain electrons, each sheet is now charged with static electricity.

Now the two sheets are held a little apart. What is happening to them? We say that electrons **repel** [rih-PEHL] each other. The electrons on one sheet were pushed back by the electrons on the other.

What is happening here? These things seem to be **attracting** each other. They are somehow being pulled together. In order to understand how this happens, let's look at each thing and its charge.

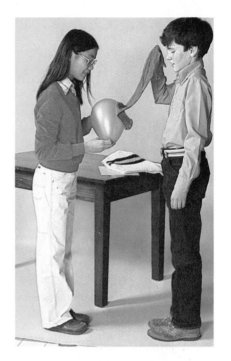

The balloon was rubbed with a piece of wool. As electrons from the wool piled up on the balloon, the balloon became negatively charged. The piece of nylon, on the other hand, lost electrons to the paper on which it was rubbed. What charge did it have then?

When the balloon and the nylon were brought near each other, they quickly moved toward one another. Why do you think this happened? In general, we say that charged things whose charges are alike tend to move away from each other. Charged things whose charges are not alike tend to move toward each other.

ACTIVITY

You can find out what happens when you pile up charges on two things. You'll need a 5-cm square of cardboard, a 5-by-4-cm piece of paper, a straight pin, a piece of wool cloth, and a drinking straw.

Push the pin through the cardboard, up to the head of the pin. Fold the piece of paper the long way, and balance it on the point of the pin.

With the cloth, rub the straw fairly hard for about ten seconds. Then, holding it at one end, bring the other end near the paper. What happens? Move the straw slowly. Does the paper follow right along? From what you have learned, how can you explain why this is happening?

What happens when many more electrons build up on one thing than on the other? The electrons suddenly begin to flow off that thing because they have become crowded. That's when the two things move toward each other. This flow of charge between two things is called an **electric current.** Since their charges were not alike, the two things came together. In this way, they could get an equal number of protons and electrons again, and no longer be charged.

What would happen if you built up a larger charge of static electricity? Suppose it were billions of times larger than the charge you make as you run across a wool rug and touch a metal doorknob. When the charge suddenly flowed off as an electric current, what a huge flash and loud noise it would make!

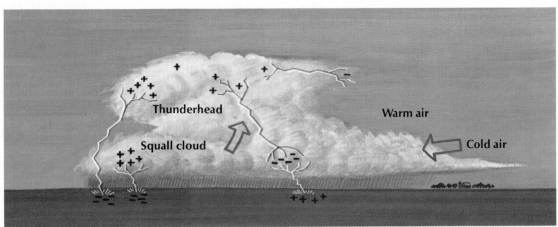

Flashes of lightning occur between a region of positive charge and a region of negative charge.

The earliest known form of electric current was the flash of lightning. What causes lightning? The huge charge that has built up inside a cloud is suddenly given off. It moves as an electric current to another cloud or to the earth. You see the bright lightning and then hear the loud thunder.

But this current, which we see as a giant flash across the sky, lasts for only a part of a second. We have not been able to harness the huge current in a flash of lightning. If we could do this, we would be able to light millions of light bulbs. And it would take only a few flashes!

Benjamin Franklin was the first person to point out the relationship between electric current and lightning. He made a kite out of silk and fastened a sharp-pointed wire near the top. To the lower end of the string holding the kite, he tied an iron key.

From time to time a storm cloud charged with electricity came near the kite. When this happened, Franklin noticed that the loose ends of the string became stiff. When he touched the key on the string, he felt an instant shock. It was lucky for Franklin that he wasn't killed by the shock.

Franklin thought that the electric current moving through the wire was positively charged. We now know that a stream of electrons moved through the wire and along the wet string to the key. What charge was the stream of electrons carrying?

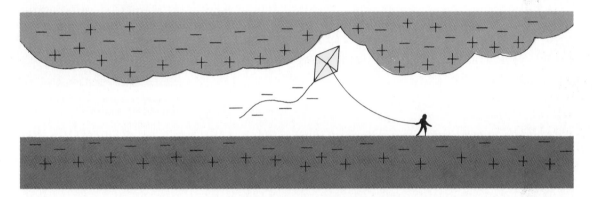

A charge of electricity from lightning is given off as a powerful electric current. But electricity in this form is not useful to us because it comes in a burst, all at once. We need a smooth, even flow of electric current to light our light bulbs and run our machines.

Suppose we had a way of pushing electrons into one end of a wire. As we pushed them in, they would push away their neighboring electrons. These electrons would then push away their neighbors, and this would keep happening through the whole length of the wire. In this way, we would be able to get an even flow of electric current.

Electricity from Magnets

Things that are electrically charged either attract or repel one another. Magnets also do this. Could magnets attract or repel an electric charge? Could an electric charge change a magnet in some way? People wondered about these questions for some time before an answer came—quite by accident.

About 70 years after Franklin's kite experiment, the Danish scientist Hans Christian Oersted was speaking to one of his classes. On a table he placed a cell, some wire, and a compass. To one pole of his cell he connected one end of the wire. To the other pole he connected the other end of the wire. It happened that the needle of the compass was directly beneath the wire.

Oersted accidentally discovered the connection between electric current and magnetism.

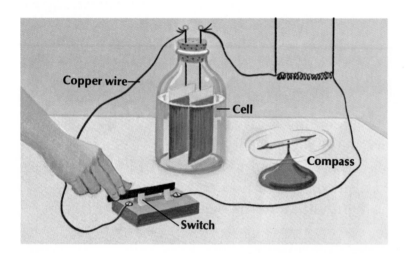

As electric current flowed through the wire, Oersted saw the needle swing around under the wire! Flowing electric current must have a **magnetic field** around it. A magnetic field is the space around a magnet or an electric current where magnetic force is felt.

You can see that a magnetic field forms around an electric current. You will need a piece of cardboard, a dry cell, some iron filings, an iron nail, and a piece of wire about 30 cm long.

Scrape off about 3 cm of the outside cover from each end of the wire. Wind the middle third of the wire around the nail as you see in the picture. Shake the iron filings on to the cardboard. Hold the wire-wrapped nail under the cardboard and lightly tap the cardboard several times. What happens to the filings?

Now connect one end of the wire to one pole of the cell and the other end of the wire to the other pole. Again hold the wire-wrapped nail under the cardboard, and tap the cardboard several times. Describe what happens. Why did the filings behave differently?

From what Oersted discovered, it was found that an electric current could cause magnetism. But was it possible for magnetism to cause an electric current? That was the question that Michael Faraday, an English scientist, asked in the early 1800's.

In 1831, Faraday tried something new. Instead of just setting a magnet inside a loop of copper wire, he pushed the magnet sharply into the loop. As he moved the magnet back and forth through the wire loop, he caused the electrons in the wire to move back and forth, too. He had made a tiny electric current with a magnet!

153

You can see how a magnet can cause a small electric current. You will need a bar magnet, a piece of copper wire about one meter long, and a compass.

Wrap the middle third of the wire around the magnet, so that you have two free ends of about 30 cm each. Wrap these ends around the compass, as you see in the picture.

Now move the magnet back and forth inside the wire. What happens to the compass needle? What, do you think, causes it to move?

Try moving the magnet more rapidly. Now what do you notice about the way the compass needle moves?

Pushing Electrons with Chemicals, Light, and Heat

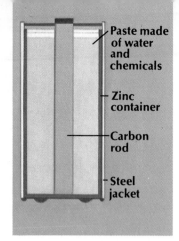

Paste made of water and chemicals

Zinc container

Carbon rod

Steel jacket

What often happens when electrons are crowded into one place? In most cases, they flow toward less crowded places. This is true of the way electrons behave in a **chemical cell.** When the two parts of the cell, the positive and negative poles, are connected to a bulb, electrons begin to flow. They flow away from the crowded part of the cell, through the bulb, and back to the cell.

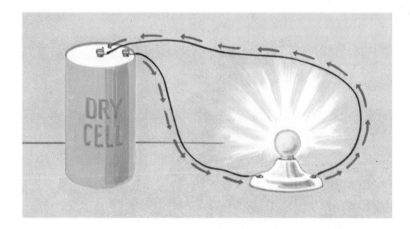

Chemical reactions then cause the current to flow through the cell. What causes the bulb to light? The moving charges cause it.

The chemicals keep crowding electrons over to one part of the cell. When this happens, the electrons are pushed out through the bulb and back into another part of the cell. What happens to the chemicals? As they push electrons through the cell, they change. They become too weak to push electrons. Little by little, the cell loses its power to send out an electric current. Then we say that the cell is dead. What has happened when your flashlight no longer works?

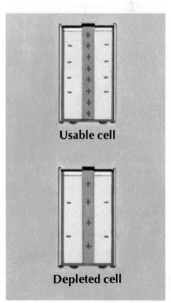

Usable cell

Depleted cell

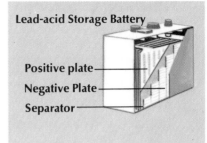

Lead-acid Storage Battery

Positive plate——
Negative Plate——
Separator——

All the things in the picture are used for sending out an electric current. They all make use of chemical energy to do this. Some of the objects are called cells. Others are called **batteries** [BAT-uh-reez]. A battery contains a group of cells. Inside each of these cells there are chemicals that can make an electric current.

Light can also be used to make an electric current in certain kinds of matter. When a ray of light hits some kinds of matter, electrons are given off. As long as light keeps hitting the matter, an electric current is sent out.

Solar cells can be used in this way to change light from the sun to an electric current. Why do you think a solar battery is very well suited for this use?

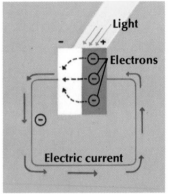

Light

Electrons

Electric current

above: Solar cell; *left*: Spacecraft use panels of solar cells for energy.

You can also get electricity by using heat. If you place together two different metals, such as copper and iron, and heat them, electrons will flow from one metal to the other. If wires are connected to the metals, the electric current can be made to do useful work.

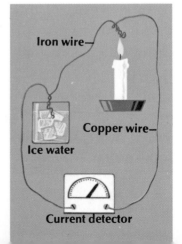

Iron wire——

Ice water

Copper wire——

Current detector

Paths for Electric Current

You know that you cannot use the electricity in lightning. Nor can you use the electricity that you sometimes make when you comb your hair. In order to make electricity that you can use, you must not only have electrons and a way of moving them. You must also have a path over which the electrons can move. Such a path is called a **circuit** [SUR-kiht].

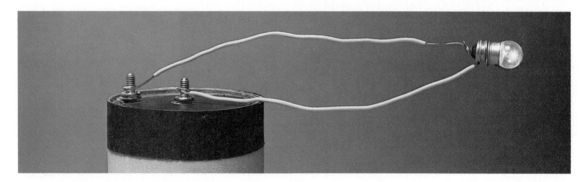

In the picture, two wires, a dry cell, and a bulb have been used to set up a circuit. One of the wires allows the current to flow from the cell to the bulb. The other wire allows the current to flow from the bulb back to the dry cell. Whenever the cell and the bulb are connected in this way, there is a **closed circuit** and the current can flow.

In order to have a steady current, you must have a closed circuit. One of the wires must come from one pole of the dry cell and another must go back to the other pole. Not much will happen until the current is allowed to flow through such a closed circuit. Toast won't pop up from a toaster. Your favorite show won't appear on the screen. You may even be late for school when your electric alarm clock doesn't go off!

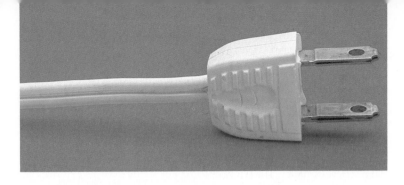

Look at the plug. It has two prongs. Each is connected to a bundle of wires. Now look at the outlet. It has two slots that are connected to wires leading to the powerhouse. What would you do to close the circuit?

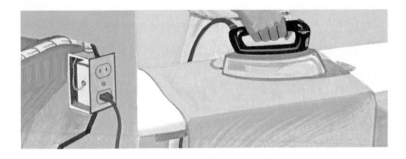

What happens to the iron when the circuit is closed? How can the flow of current be stopped?

As long as the circuit is closed, the current will flow. But this could cause trouble if the flow were through a bell that kept ringing, or a light that kept shining. How can you stop the flow of the current? One way is to use a switch.

Switches come in many shapes and sizes, but they all work in much the same way. In all switches, there is a metal part that can be moved. You move this part by pushing a button, pulling a chain, turning a knob or handle, or moving a lever. When you move the metal part in one direction, it closes the circuit, allowing the current to flow. When you move it in the other direction, the current stops because you have caused a gap in the circuit.

You can find out how a switch works in closing or opening a circuit. You will need a dry cell, a bulb and socket, two pieces of wire each about 30 cm long, one piece of wire about 15 cm long, and a switch.

Scrape off 3 cm of the outside cover from the ends of each of the wires. Connect the cell, socket, and switch as you see in the picture.

Push down the lever in the switch so that the two metal parts touch. What happens? Raise the lever. How can you explain what happens now?

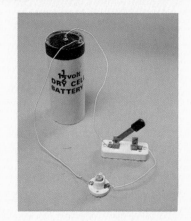

Most switches can be moved back and forth by hand. But some switches move only when there are changes in temperature. These switches are called **thermostats** [THUR-muh-stats]. Are there any thermostats in your school or home? See if you can find one on a wall, in a heater, on an electric blanket, or on an oven.

Most thermostats have a small metal bar. The bar is made of a strip of brass fastened to a strip of iron. When the temperature rises, the bar bends in one direction. When it drops, the bar bends in the other direction.

How does a change in temperature affect the position of the iron bar?

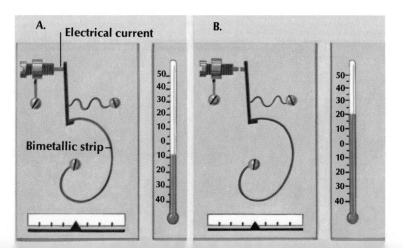

A. Electrical current

Bimetallic strip

B.

159

Electrons Move Through Certain Matter

A good **conductor** of electricity is anything that allows electrons to move smoothly through it. What kinds of matter allow electrons to move in this way? In general, metals allow a smooth flow of electrons and, for this reason, are said to be good conductors. This is why copper wire is used to conduct electricity in your home. Silver and gold are also good conductors; however, they cost far more than copper. Aluminum, though not as good a conductor as copper, is much lighter and stronger. For this reason, it is used for huge power lines.

Here are some things that are very poor conductors: your rubber eraser, the pages of this book, and a rubber balloon.

You can test different things to find out if they are poor conductors or good ones by making a circuit tester. You will need a board, a dry cell, a bulb and socket, two thumb tacks, two 30-cm lengths of copper wire, and one 15-cm length of copper wire. You will also need several things to test. You may use a small piece of bare copper wire, a piece of paper, a comb, a key, and a wooden pencil. You may also use a piece of pencil lead, a paper clip that has been scraped so that it is shiny, and a rubber band.

Scrape off the outside cover on both ends of each wire. Then connect one 30-cm length of wire from one of the screws on the dry cell to the bulb and socket. Fasten the other 30-cm length of wire to the other screw on the dry cell and to one thumb tack. Then fasten the 15-cm length of wire to the light and the other thumb tack.

Push the tacks into the board about 5 cm apart, as shown in the picture. Now you are ready to test the different things to see whether they are good or poor conductors. Lay the piece of bare copper wire on the two tacks. What happens to the light in your tester? Is copper a good conductor? Lay a wooden pencil on the two tacks. What happens to the light? What kind of conductor is the pencil?

One at a time, place the other things on the tacks. How can you decide whether a certain kind of matter is a good conductor or a poor one?

Although poor conductors do not allow much electric current to flow, this doesn't mean that poor conductors are not useful. They are, in fact, very useful. Things that are poor conductors can be used as **insulators** [IHN-suh-lay-tuhrz]. Why are insulators used to cover bare wires that are carrying an electric current? If you touch two points on the circuit of an insulated wire, you do not become part of the circuit. The current cannot flow into you. It remains safely inside the wire.

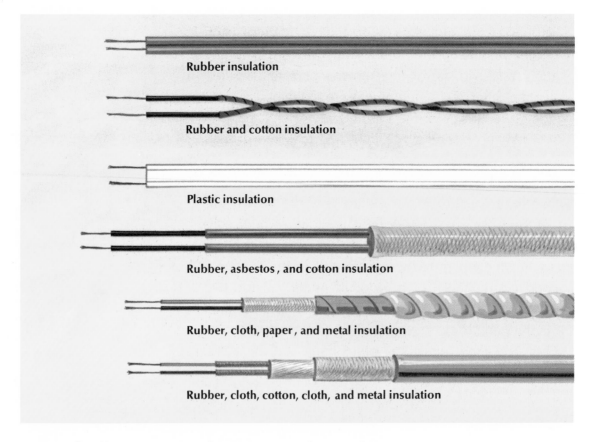

Rubber insulation

Rubber and cotton insulation

Plastic insulation

Rubber, asbestos, and cotton insulation

Rubber, cloth, paper, and metal insulation

Rubber, cloth, cotton, cloth, and metal insulation

Many different kinds of matter can be used as insulators. Some wires are insulated with plastic, others with cloth or rubber. Sometimes several kinds of matter are used together as insulators.

Using Electricity Safely

What happens if the insulation wears off both wires in an electric cord? The wires inside the cord may touch each other. The current can then pass directly from one copper wire to the other. When this happens, we have a **short circuit.**

When electric current flows through a short circuit, the wires can become red hot. For this reason, wires with worn insulation should either be thrown away or properly repaired. Otherwise, they could be the cause of a dangerous fire.

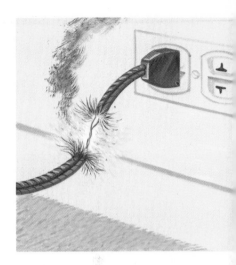

Let's see what happens in a short circuit. You will need a dry cell, a bulb and socket, two 30-cm pieces of insulated wire, and a pencil.

Scrape off the outside cover from the ends and middle part of both wires. Connect the two wires to the cell and the socket so that a closed circuit is made. How do you know that you have made a closed circuit?

Now hold the two wires together at places that are insulated. What happens? With the pencil, push together the two bare parts of the wires. Allow them to touch for a second or so. What happens? Why did the light go out?

With your fingers hold the bare parts of the wires together for only a second. Do the wires become warm? Why should you be careful not to hold the wires together too long?

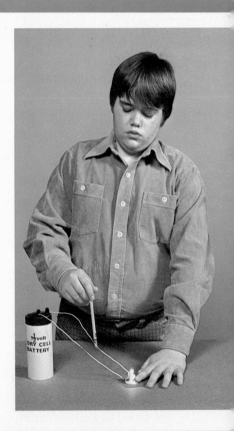

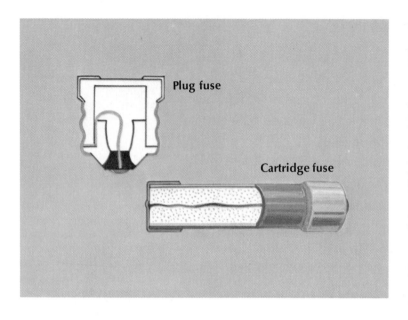

Plug fuse

Cartridge fuse

What has happened to the lower fuse?

Since short circuits can be dangerous, the wires in many houses and other buildings are protected by parts called **fuses.** A fuse is used to break an electric circuit whenever the current becomes too great. It is made of a thin strip of metals that melts quickly when too much current flows through it. When the thin strip melts, the electric circuit is broken. Now the current can no longer flow. Can the wires get hot?

A **circuit breaker** may be used instead of a fuse. It has a part that moves a switch, much as a thermostat does. If too much current moves through this part, the switch is thrown. This opens the circuit and stops the flow of current.

When the cause of the short circuit has been corrected, the circuit breaker can then be switched to close the circuit. In this way, the current is allowed to flow again. Can you think why some people would rather use circuit breakers than fuses?

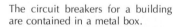

The circuit breakers for a building are contained in a metal box.

Using Electrical Energy

How are an electric clock, a doorbell, and an electric fan alike? They all use energy from electricity to move something. This energy moves the hands of the clock, the hammer of the bell, and the blades of the fan.

How does electrical energy make these parts move? Each part has an **electromagnet** [ih-lehk-troh-MAG-niht]. An electromagnet is made of wire wrapped around a bar of soft iron. This core of iron becomes magnetized whenever the current flows. Electromagnets may be small and simple—a loop of wire wrapped around an iron nail. They may be used to power electric doorbells and buzzers.

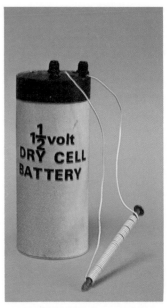

When current flows through the wire, what happens to the nail?

How is the electromagnet being used in this scrapyard?

In an electric gong there are two electromagnets. When the current flows through them, they pull a strip of iron that hits the gong. When the current goes off, they let go. A spring pushes the iron back, ready for the next stroke. Each time the current is turned on, only one ring is heard.

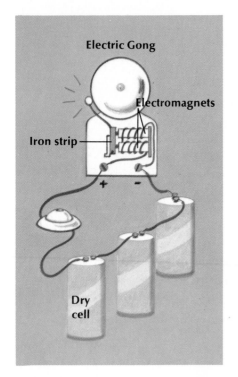

Electric Gong

Electromagnets

Iron strip

+ −

Dry cell

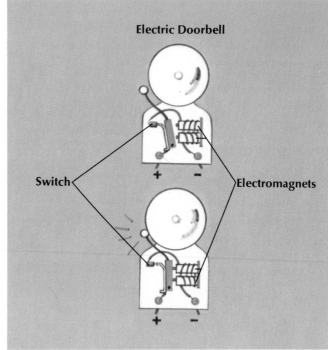

Electric Doorbell

Switch

+ −

Electromagnets

+ −

The kind of doorbell that goes "r-r-r-ring," is really a gong with a switch built into it. This switch turns the current on and off, on and off, very quickly. The strip of iron is also pulled and let go very quickly. The bell rings many times.

In door chimes the iron inside the electromagnet moves forward, hitting a metal bar. In this way a sound is made. An electric fan or clock, on the other hand, has a different kind of electromagnet. This kind of electromagnet causes a metal wheel to whirl around and around.

Most clocks, as well as the other electric things in your home, are built to work on **alternating current** or AC. The current flows in one direction, stops, and then flows in the other direction. This back-and-forth flow takes place 60 times in one second!

In an electric clock, the current flows through the wire loop of the electromagnet. Each time the current changes direction, the magnetism in the arms of the electromagnet is changed. As the magnetism keeps changing, a metal wheel is pulled around and around. This is an electric **motor.** The motor then turns the machine that moves the hands of the clock.

Motors that are powered by batteries use **direct current** or DC. In a direct current, the current flows in only one direction.

AC or DC, there are many different motors doing many different jobs. They range from the tiny electric motor in a watch to the huge motors that power subway trains. How are these motors alike? They are alike in that they all cause electrical energy to be changed to a form of energy that can move things.

Subway trains, like this one in Washington, D.C., usually operate on direct current.

What Did You Learn?

- All matter is made of atoms. Inside the atom there are protons with positive charges, electrons with negative charges, and neutrons with no charge.
- There is static electricity whenever electrons pile up on something and remain there without flowing off.
- Charged things with like charges repel each other. Charged things with unlike charges attract each other.
- The flow of charge between two points is called electric current.
- Electric current has a magnetic field around it where magnetic force is felt.
- An electromagnet is a loop of wire wrapped around a bar of iron. When an electric current flows, the iron becomes magnetized.
- Cells and groups of cells called batteries are used to make an electric current.
- In order for an electric current to flow, it must have a path called a closed circuit. A switch is used to open or close the circuit.
- Things in which electric current flows are called good conductors. Things in which current doesn't flow well are called poor conductors. Poor conductors are useful as insulators.
- A short circuit happens when two bare wires touch and electric current flows through them.
- Fuses and circuit breakers are used to protect against the danger of short circuits.
- Alternating current flows in one direction, stops, then flows in the other direction. Direct current always flows in one direction.

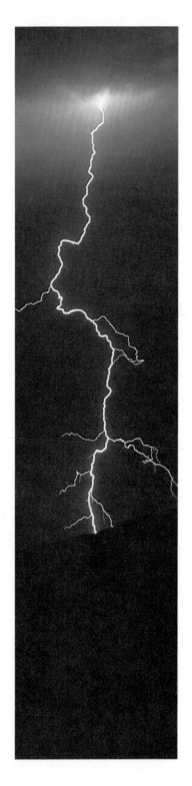

Biography

Michael Faraday (1791–1867)

Before 1831, the only way to produce electric current was by using electric batteries. It would take a lot of batteries for today's electricity needs.

Michael Faraday discovered a way to make electric current. He did this by moving a coil of wire in the magnetic field of a U-shaped magnet. His discoveries in electricity led to the development of electric motors.

Michael Faraday was born in England. He spent very little time in school. In fact, because his family was poor, he went to work in a bookbinder's shop when he was 12. There he developed an interest in science books and learned about electricity and chemistry.

Faraday attended four talks given by a great scientist, Sir Humphry Davy. He took careful notes, bound them into a book, and sent them with a letter to Davy. In his letter, Faraday asked if he could have a job in science. Davy was pleased with the book and, some time later, gave him a job. Faraday became Davy's assistant at the Royal Institution in London.

Michael Faraday started out washing glassware and keeping the laboratory clean. Later he was even given his own laboratory. He worked at the Institution for 54 years. Before he died, he was asked to become its president.

TO THINK ABOUT AND DO

On a piece of paper, write the letters from A to E. Beside each letter write the name of the part that goes with that letter in the picture of the circuit. Then answer the numbered questions.

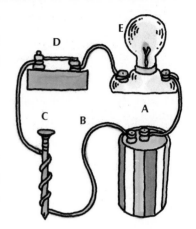

1. Why is the lamp in the circuit lighted?
2. What part does the switch play in the circuit?
3. If the switch were rusty and did not make good contact, what would happen to the brightness of the lamp? What would happen to the strength of the electromagnet?

WHAT DO YOU REMEMBER?

On a piece of paper, copy the numbered terms in Column A. Then match each term with the letter of the clue that describes it from Column B.

Column **A**

1. battery
2. short circuit
3. direct current
4. electric current
5. poor conductor
6. circuit breaker
7. atom
8. magnetic field

Column **B**

a. happens when two bare wires touch and electric current flows through them
b. used as an insulator
c. caused by the flow of charge in a conductor
d. forms around electric current and is felt as a force
e. always flows in one direction
f. group of cells used for making an electric current
g. used to protect against the danger of short circuits
h. makes up all matter and contains protons, electrons, and neutrons

170

1. You are sitting at your desk doing homework. Suddenly the lights in your house go out. Explain what could have happened.
2. Find out several ways in which electromagnets can be used in your home and make a list of them.

ACTIVITY

You can make a current tester. You will need a magnetic compass, a dry cell, and a roll of insulated wire. You will also need a milk carton, some plastic tape, and a pair of scissors.

Cut off the base of the milk carton about 3 cm from the bottom. Then cut a slot in the base, about 6 cm long and 2 cm wide.

Wind 20 turns of wire to make a coil about as large as the compass. Then flatten the coil and attach it to the compass with tape.

Lay the coil and compass over the slot. Let the two ends of the wire come through two holes in the side, as shown in the picture.

To test an electric current, connect one end of the wire to one pole of the dry cell. Then tap the other end of the wire to the other pole. What happens? How does the compass needle show that a current is flowing?

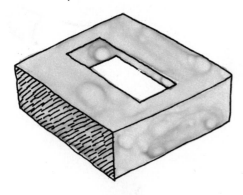 

Sources of Energy

7

There is a lot happening here. Work is being done. Energy is being used.

When you say you feel full of energy, you mean that you feel able to do many things. You have the energy to do work. You could carry a bag of groceries, sweep the steps, wash the dishes, or clean your room.

When you ride a bicycle or throw a ball, you are working, too. In science, swinging a baseball bat is work. Work is making something happen. Energy is needed to do work.

It is important to learn about energy. We use energy to go places and to make the things we need. Will we always have enough energy to use? We need to find out more about different kinds of energy and the ways in which we get energy.

Energy Makes Things Happen

Energy is the ability to do work, to make something move. Nothing can happen without energy. Different forms of energy can be used to do work.

In the pictures you can see different forms of energy being used. Electric motors, lights, and heaters use **electrical energy.** Even the plants near the window use energy. Green plants use **light energy** to make food and to grow. **Heat energy** is often a sign that other kinds of energy are being used. Heat energy is used for cooking and many other kinds of work.

There are other kinds of energy, too. Sometimes when certain kinds of matter are brought together, a chemical change takes place. Energy may be given off. This **chemical energy** can be used to do work. Burning fuel is one way to get chemical energy. When you use your muscles you are also using chemical energy. Chemical changes happen in your cells when you use your muscles.

Wind can push something. We say that it has **kinetic energy** [kih-NEHT-ihk EHN-uhr-jee]. Kinetic energy is energy of motion. If a hammer is raised, it can fall and push something. We therefore say the raised hammer has **potential energy** [puh-TEHN-shuhl EHN-uhr-jee]. A falling hammer has kinetic energy.

Grizzly bear habitat in Yellowstone National Park, Wyoming, shown in New York City's American Museum of Natural History.

No matter how real and alive these things look in the museum, you know they aren't going to move. How do you know? A scientist would say it this way: no **energy transfer** is taking place. Whenever something happens, energy is moved or **transferred** from one thing to another.

Look at the drawing of an invention by Rube Goldberg. He made many other inventions like this one. How does each part move another part? Now trace the transfer of energy. What are some other energy transfers that you have seen?

below: Trace the energy transfer shown in this Rube Goldberg invention:

At last! The great brain of the distinguished man of science gives the world the simple automatic sheet-music turner!

Press left foot (A) on pedal (B), which pulls down handle (C) on tire pump (D) Pressure of air blows whistle (E). Goldfish (F) believes this is dinner signal and starts feeding on worm (G). The pull on string (H) releases brace (I), dropping shelf (J), leaving weight (K) without support. Naturally, hatrack (L) is suddenly extended and boxing glove (M) hits punching bag (N), which in turn is punctured by spike.

Escaping air blows against sail (P), which is attached to page of music (Q), which turns gently and makes way for the next outburst of sweet or sour melody.

Energy That Goes In
Equals Energy That Comes Out

There are different ways to do work. The energy that is put into the handsaw comes from chemical energy from your muscles. But the energy that is put into the power saw comes from electrical energy that turns the motor. Work is being done by both saws. Not all of the energy that was put in is used to saw wood. Some of it is **transformed**, or changed, to heat.

What happened here? The car ran out of fuel. A car engine won't run without the energy of burning fuel. You must put in some energy in order to have energy to do work.

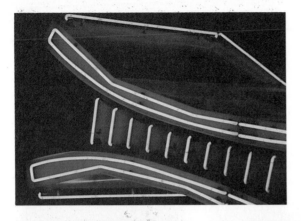

Look at the pictures of different kinds of work. Try to answer these questions about each picture:

1. What work is being done?
2. What kind of energy is put in?
3. What kind of energy comes out?

You can't get more energy out than you put in. The form of energy may be changed, or transformed, but the amount of energy remains the same. The amount of energy that is put in always equals the amount of energy that comes out.

This fact is called the **law of conservation of energy:** "Energy cannot be created or destroyed; it can only be transformed from one form to another."

Here is a way to show conservation of energy. You will need 12 marbles of the same size, a pencil, and two books of the same thickness. You will also need a piece of wood or a book that is about 2.5 cm thick.

Place the books as shown in the picture. Make sure that the grooves in the covers exactly fit one against the other.

Lay eight marbles in the groove of the lower book. Then place a marble at the top of the other groove. Let it roll. When the marble hits the others, how many are knocked out of the row?

Next, place the eight marbles exactly as before. Hold two marbles at the top of the other groove. Let them roll down together. How many marbles are knocked out of the row? Try it again with three marbles and then with four. What do you think will happen?

What will happen if you make the rolling marbles move faster? Place the higher book so that its upper edge is 5 cm high. Notice the number of marbles that are knocked out and their speed.

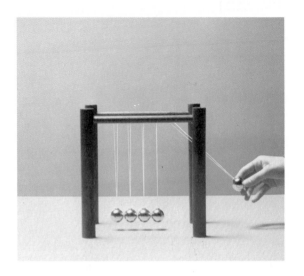 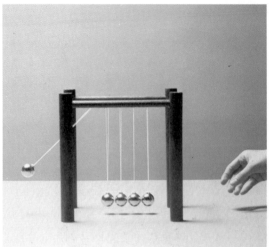

Here is a way to show conservation of energy from one thing to another. In this toy, each ball hangs from two strings. Each ball can swing from side to side. If you lift one ball and let it swing, what happens? It hits the next ball. Then kinetic energy is transferred from one ball to the next. The last ball in line swings out. It swings out to about the same height as the starting place of the first ball. If two balls hit the others, two balls at the other end will move. Each time, the energy that goes in equals the energy that comes out.

The law of conservation of energy is not always easy to prove or to measure. During burning the chemical energy from wood equals the energy that comes out. This energy is in the form of heat and light. The chemical energy put in equals the light and heat energy that is given off.

Matter and Energy

Sometimes you can get huge amounts of energy out of matter. During a display of fireworks, chemical energy is changed into flashes of light, heat, and sound.

Where does chemical energy come from? Energy is stored in **chemical bonds.** Chemical bonds are forces that hold atoms within a molecule together. During a chemical change, bonds can be broken or put together. During a chemical reaction, energy is either taken in or given off.

Iron and oxygen can be joined together very easily. A strong chemical bond forms between them. After they have become a compound called **iron oxide,** it is very hard to separate them. Lots of energy must be added to break the chemical bonds of the iron oxide molecules.

The rust on these chains and the iron ore from this Minnesota mine are both iron oxide.

In iron mines we dig out iron ore, which is mainly iron oxide. But iron oxide itself is useless. It is a reddish, crumbly powder. To change it into useful iron, the oxygen must be separated from the iron. If iron oxide molecules are heated to a very high temperature, they vibrate very rapidly. This rapid vibration breaks the chemical bonds. Other kinds of matter are added to help this happen.

Iron oxide   +   heat   →   iron atoms + oxygen atoms

Lots of heat energy is needed to break the bonds between the atoms of iron and oxygen. What happens when bonds are made between iron and oxygen? Steel wool, which is mostly iron, and oxygen from the air can be used to make iron oxide.

ACTIVITY

You can make iron oxide. You will need a small, narrow jar, and some steel wool. You will also need a large jar that is half filled with water.

Dip the small amount of steel wool into the water. Then push the steel wool into the bottom of the narrow jar. It should fit snugly. Turn the jar upside down and place it in the jar of water. Be careful to keep air inside the narrow jar.

After a day or two, look at the steel wool. What changes do you see?

Some scientists wanted to find out if energy is given off when iron oxide is formed. They placed some steel wool in a special bottle that kept heat from escaping quickly. A little water had been added to the steel wool. They used a thermometer to keep track of the temperature. They found that steel wool became warmer as it rusted. Heat energy was given off.

181

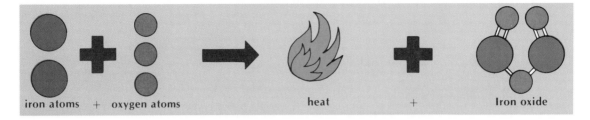

iron atoms + oxygen atoms → heat + Iron oxide

A chemical change in which oxygen is combined with another kind of matter is called **oxidation** [ahk-suh-DAY-shuhn]. During oxidation, the matter bonds readily with oxygen, and heat energy is usually given off.

Oxidation can take place slowly or rapidly. When iron rusts, the oxidation takes place slowly. When wood, coal, and other fuels are burned, oxidation happens rapidly. In an explosion, matter is oxidized almost all at once.

Describe the oxidation shown here.

The faster the oxidation, the more rapidly the heat is given off. Matter that oxidizes rapidly and gives off a lot of energy can be a good fuel to use. When gasoline is mixed with oxygen in the air, a little energy from an electric spark makes the mixture oxidize. When this happens, a lot of heat energy is released, but is controlled. In a car engine, the heat energy is used to do work by making parts of the motor move. Although different, jet engines also use oxidation of fuel to do work.

above: Coal-burning power plant that generates electrical energy

Coal, oil, and natural gas are high-energy fuels. They are called fossil fuels because they were formed millions of years ago. When we burn fossil fuels, we are really using energy from the sun! It was stored by plants that captured the energy from the sun.

Long ago the weather in many places was hot
and wet. There were many large swamps in the
world. Huge ferns grew as large as the trees of
today. These plants and other organisms grew,
died, and sank to the bottom of the swampy waters.
On the bottom of the ocean, the remains of sea organisms were deposited. More and more of this
matter was added every year. This added weight
put pressure on the lower layers. Through the ages,
heat and pressure helped to change the plant and
animal matter into coal, oil, or natural gas.

Fossil fuels are brought to the surface by mining
or drilling. They supply about 91 percent of the energy we use. They have become our major source of
energy because they are high in energy and easy to
use.

This crater was formed by a nuclear explosion. The crater is 100 m deep and 400 m wide. Notice the automobiles on the left. Compare their size with the size of the crater.

Nuclear Energy

How was such a large, round crater formed in the earth? In a special testing place, scientists were learning more about the power of **nuclear energy.** Nuclear energy is the energy present inside atoms. Twelve million tons of earth were moved in the explosion. It all happened in three seconds.

Where does nuclear energy come from? The central part of the atom is called the nucleus. Electrons move in an area around the nucleus. Chemical energy comes from changing the groupings of electrons of one atom with another. Nuclear energy comes from special changes inside the nucleus. The energy inside the nucleus is much greater than the energy of electrons.

About 40 or 50 years ago two scientists brought some neutrons together with **uranium** [yuh-RAY-nee-uhm] atoms. The uranium changed into two different kinds of matter! Two other scientists found a way to explain what happened. A uranium atom can be split into two new atoms, both of different kinds. The scientists called the change **fission** [FISH-uhn]. During fission, the uranium atom can be split in different ways.

185

A slow-moving neutron is absorbed by the uranium nucleus. The nucleus breaks into two smaller nuclei and a few neutrons. These neutrons are free to move to other uranium nuclei and continue the splitting process. The reaction spreads from one atom to the next. Sometimes it can spread to several atoms at once. This reaction is called a chain reaction and it can happen very quickly.

During fission, large amounts of energy are given off. The new nuclei that are produced by the splitting of the uranium nucleus continue to give off radiation. This radiation is what makes nuclear waste harmful.

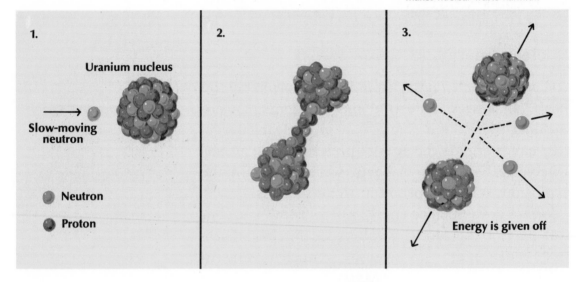

Although the number of protons and neutrons does not usually change, the new atoms and released neutrons lose a little mass. We observe this loss of mass, first as kinetic energy, then as heat.

Albert Einstein predicted in 1905 that what we usually observe as mass could be observed as energy. This was a very new idea and hard to accept. But it has been tested in many ways.

Scientists have found ways that nuclear reactions can be controlled. Certain kinds of matter are used to absorb neutrons and slow down the reaction. **Nuclear reactors** have been built as special places in which these things can happen.

In a nuclear reactor, the splitting process and the release of energy are controlled.

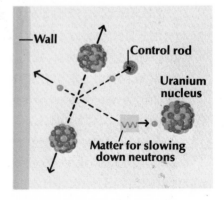

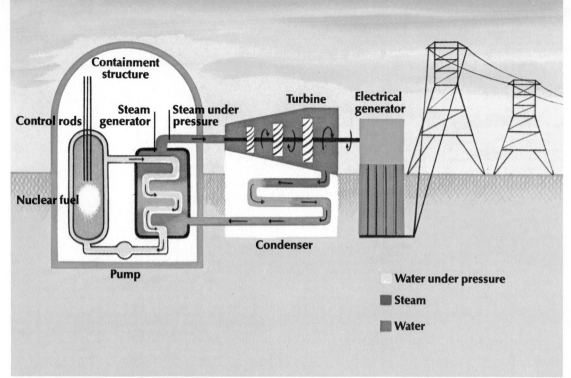

Control rods | Containment structure | Steam generator | Steam under pressure | Turbine | Electrical generator

Nuclear fuel

Pump

Condenser

- Water under pressure
- Steam
- Water

In a nuclear reactor, great amounts of heat from a nuclear fuel are transferred to water under pressure. This water, in turn, heats steam, which turns a turbine. The turbine turns a generator that generates electrical energy.

Nuclear reactors are used to heat water and change it to steam. The steam can be used to generate electrical energy. Smaller reactors are being used to power submarines.

Nuclear power plants have caused a number of problems. Some of these power plants need large amounts of water to cool them. Water is taken from a river. Then the warm water is pumped back into the river. This heating of the river can harm plant and animal life in it.

Nuclear power plants produce matter that gives off radiation. This radiation can harm living things. Damage caused by earthquakes, mechanical problems, and human mistakes could let this harmful matter into the environment. We are still looking for better ways to get rid of nuclear wastes. They can give off dangerous radiation for hundreds of years.

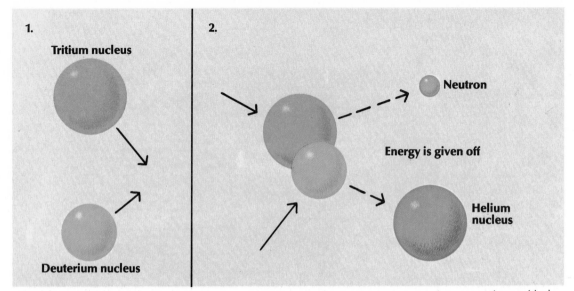

1.

Tritium nucleus

Deuterium nucleus

2.

Neutron

Energy is given off

Helium nucleus

During fusion, two forms of hydrogen (tritium and deuterium) are combined. What happens next?

Scientists have found another way to get energy from atoms. The nuclei of some kinds of atoms can be put together. This is called **fusion** [FYOO-zhuhn]. Certain kinds of hydrogen nuclei can be forced to combine. Larger nuclei are formed. Yet they have less mass than the nuclei that they came from. Something is missing. Both in fission and fusion, mass is transformed into heat, light, and other forms of energy. Scientists are looking for safe ways to use fusion as a source of energy.

Years ago, the law of conservation of energy seemed complete. There was also a law of conservation of mass. Now we recognize that mass and energy describe the same thing in different ways! We observe it as mass or as energy. Since we no longer think of mass and energy as being completely different, we can call it **mass-energy.**

The Law of Conservation of Mass-Energy
Mass-energy can neither be created nor destroyed; it can only be transformed.

More Sources of Energy

We need to find new sources of energy even to keep using the same amount that we are using today. Where will this energy come from? There are no easy answers.

Look at the pie chart that shows the sources of energy that we use. Most of this energy comes from fossil fuels. After fossil fuels are burned, they are gone. They are **nonrenewable resources.** It takes millions of years for new coal, oil, and natural gas to be formed. Some people think that most of the world's oil may be gone in a few years. What changes do you think this would cause?

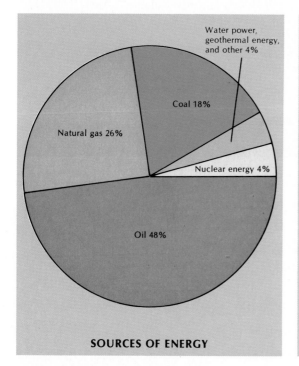

Water power, geothermal energy, and other 4%

Coal 18%

Natural gas 26%

Nuclear energy 4%

Oil 48%

SOURCES OF ENERGY

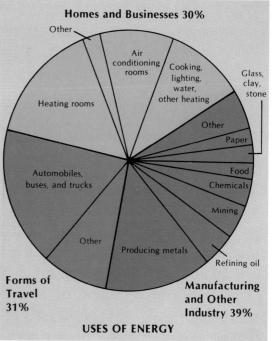

Homes and Businesses 30%

Other

Air conditioning rooms

Cooking, lighting, water, other heating

Heating rooms

Glass, clay, stone

Other

Paper

Automobiles, buses, and trucks

Food

Chemicals

Mining

Other

Producing metals

Refining oil

Forms of Travel 31%

Manufacturing and Other Industry 39%

USES OF ENERGY

Now look at the pie chart of different uses of energy. For what two things do we use the most energy? What would be the easiest ways to cut down our total use of energy?

What is our greatest source of energy? How could we cut down our use of this energy?

In what ways do air pollution and oil spills like this one in the Gulf of Mexico harm the environmment?

When fossil fuels are burned, smoke and gases are given off. These cause air pollution, which can harm living things. Different ways of drilling, mining, transporting these fuels can harm the environment. You remember that there were also a number of problems with nuclear energy.

There are other sources of energy that we can use. Moving water has been used for many years. The axle of a water wheel can transfer energy from the moving water to tools. These tools can do work, such as lifting objects, grinding grain, and sawing wood. Moving water wheels can also be used to generate electrical energy.

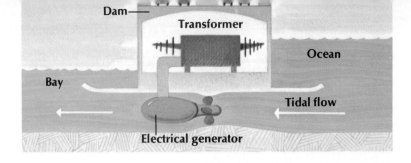

A power plant near Mont-St.-Michel, France, uses the moving water of tides to generate electrical energy. As the tide flows into the bay, the water turns the generators under the dam.

Rivers aren't the only source of moving water. The energy in the ocean tides and waves is great. Over 700 years ago people used tides to turn water wheels. Energy from tides is not being used very much now. But we are learning to use some old ideas in new ways.

Wind energy has been used for thousands of years. What energy source causes the wind to move? Some people are thinking of building long rows of giant windmills to generate electrical energy. Where do you think such rows of windmills would be placed?

left: An old windmill in Holland right: This modern windmill is located near Boone, North Carolina. Its 60-meter blades are turned by the wind to generate electrical energy.

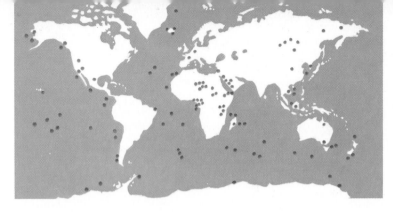

Each dot on this map shows a place where geothermal energy has been found.

Old Faithful, a geyser in Yellowstone National Park, Wyoming

There is a huge amount of heat energy beneath the earth's surface. Within the earth's crust itself, there are places where liquid rock can be found. Sometimes we can find these "hot spots" because we find hot springs and geysers. Heated water comes to the surface. Around the world, **geothermal energy** has been found. Iceland, New Zealand, Mexico, the Soviet Union, Italy, Japan, and the United States all have some geothermal energy. However, there are not enough of these places for them to be a main source of energy.

Long ago the hot water from such places was used for bathing and washing. In time, people learned to drill wells and to control geothermal energy. In some places, geothermal energy provides all of the energy for heat, hot water, and the generating of electrical energy.

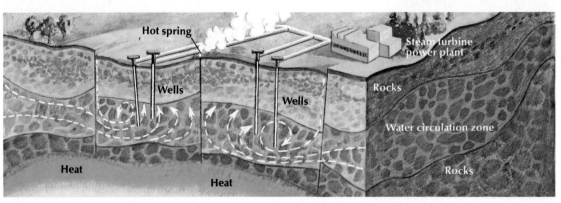

Energy from the Sun

Have you ever stopped to think that much of the energy we use comes from the sun? Solar energy in the form of heat and light is transferred to other forms of energy. The heat from the sun causes the earth's air to move as wind. Water is evaporated and lifted by the heat of the sun. Then it is cooled and it falls to the earth again. Energy from fossil fuels was once solar energy, too.

left: Solar cells on the roof of this building generate electrical energy. Water is also being heated in solar panels in the background. The electrical energy is used by water pumps that pump heated water throughout the building for heat. For a close-up view of solar cells, look at the cover of this book.

right: This music box uses solar energy to run its electric motor.

Can we use the sun directly as an energy source? Maybe you have seen a radio or a watch that gets its energy from **solar cells.** Solar cells change the sun's energy directly into electrical energy. So far, they only generate small amounts of electrical energy. Some day, there may be large power plants using solar cells.

Is there another way that we can use the sun's energy now? Maybe it could be used to heat water and change it to steam. Steam can be used in an engine or to generate electricity. But to change water to steam, its temperature must be raised to 100°C. Can sunlight heat anything to that temperature?

You can find out whether direct sunlight can be used to change water to steam. You will need a thermometer, a hand lens, and a reflector from a flashlight.

Record the temperature shown on the thermometer. Then put it in the sunlight for five minutes. Record the temperature again.

Next, use a hand lens to focus the sunlight to point on the thermometer bulb. Be careful to do this only for a short time or the thermometer may break. What is the temperature this time?

Now hold the reflector so that its shiny side faces the sunlight directly. With your other hand, push the thermometer bulb through the opening. By moving the thermometer up and down, you can find where the light on the bulb is brightest. Hold the thermometer steady for a little while. Watch for changes in temperatures. Record what you find out.

Do you now think that solar energy can be used to make steam?

By directing lots of the sun's energy into a small space, we can get stronger heating from sunlight. Both lenses and reflectors can be used to do this. A large lens for heating water to steam would be very heavy and expensive. Besides that, even a large lens would not focus enough sunlight to be worth bothering about. A curved mirror can be made that is large enough to do the job. A huge mirror reflects sunlight onto a small spot where water is heated until steam is made. The steam is used to generate electrical energy. The electrical energy can be used to move parts in a motor. So far, only a few small solar motors have been built.

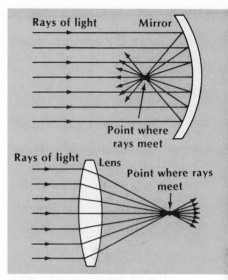

*above:*Focusing the sun's energy with a mirror and with a lens

left: This solar generator in France uses mirrors to focus the sun's energy. At the point where the rays meet, the very high temperature is used to heat water to steam. The steam is used to generate electrical energy.

Scientists have found another way of getting energy directly from sunlight. This depends on what is called the **greenhouse effect.** A greenhouse has glass walls and a glass roof. Sunlight passes through the glass and heats the air inside. The heated air cannot move through the glass. Much of the heat is trapped inside and the greenhouse becomes warmer.

Let's find out more about the greenhouse effect. You will need two thermometers, a box lined with black paper, a sheet of clear plastic large enough to cover the top of the box, and masking tape.

Read and record the temperature of both thermometers. Then put one thermometer inside the box. Put the clear cover on the box, holding it in place with the masking tape. Now set the box out in bright sunlight. Lay the second thermometer on top of the cover.

Leave the box in the sun for several minutes. Then read both thermometers. Which thermometer has had a greater temperature gain? What does this mean?

In the same way, sunlight can be used to heat our homes. Large windows are built on the sunny side of the house. The walls and roof are insulated to keep the heat in. Warmed air is moved to all parts of the house.

The use of large windows to collect the sun's energy is called *passive solar heating*. North of the equator, the south side of a building receives the most sunlight during a day. Large windows on the south side allow sunlight to warm the air in the rooms. Fans can be used to move this warmed air to colder areas in the building.

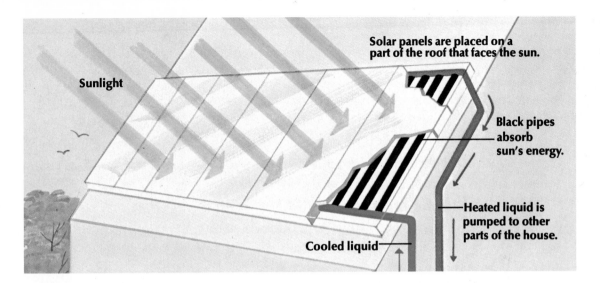

Sunlight

Solar panels are placed on a part of the roof that faces the sun.

Black pipes absorb sun's energy.

Heated liquid is pumped to other parts of the house.

Cooled liquid

We also use solar collectors to heat water for washing, bathing, and home heating. Long boxes are placed on the roofs of many homes and businesses. Inside are black water pipes that absorb energy from the sun. The heated water is moved to a place when it is stored and used when needed.

Solar energy is a very clean and safe energy source. Yet it is still quite expensive. What differences would weather and nighttime make in using solar energy?

There is another way to get solar energy. You remember that plants store energy from sunlight. We can use that stored energy by making fuels from plant matter. Some people are even finding ways to make fuel from garbage!

Maybe the best way to have enough energy is to use less energy. Then we will have more energy to use for the things that we think are important.

By using less of our nonrenewable resources, we can make the supplies last a little longer. This will give us more time to learn how to use renewable resources.

What advantages are there in using waste materials to make fuel?

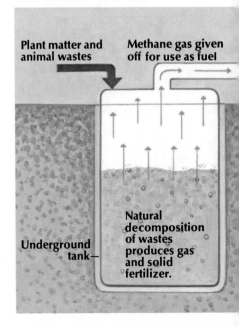

Plant matter and animal wastes

Methane gas given off for use as fuel

Underground tank

Natural decomposition of wastes produces gas and solid fertilizer.

What Did You Learn?

- Energy is the ability to do work, to make something move.
- Whenever something happens, energy is moved or transferred from one thing to another.
- The amount of energy that is put in always equals the energy that comes out.
- There are different forms of energy. Energy can be transformed from one form to another.
- Oxidation is a chemical change in which oxygen is combined with another kind of matter. Heat energy is usually given off.
- Coal, oil, and natural gas are fossil fuels that were formed millions of years ago. They are our major source of energy.
- The fission of atoms can be used in controlled nuclear reactors to heat water to generate electrical energy.
- The law of conservation of mass-energy can be stated as: "Mass-energy can be neither created nor destroyed; it can only be transformed."
- Wind, tides, geothermal energy, and solar energy are ways that we can get more energy to use.
- By using less of our nonrenewable resources, we can have more time to learn how to use renewable resources.

Biography

Albert Einstein (1879–1955)

Albert Einstein was a famous physicist. A physicist [FIHZ-uh-sihst] is a scientist who studies both matter and energy and how they are related.

Through his work, Einstein tried to explain how such things as light, space, time, matter, gravitation, and energy are related in the universe. Even though his ideas seemed strange at first, scientists in later years were able to prove that they were correct. What we know of nuclear energy within matter came from one of Einstein's ideas.

Einstein was born in Germany. As a child, he seemed slow to learn. But Einstein was interested in many things. At the age of five, his father gave him a compass. He began to wonder why the compass needle always pointed north. After he grew up, he found out about magnetic forces through his studies.

When he lived in Switzerland, he went to work in a patent office. He enjoyed this job because it left him with more time to think about the universe. Later, he went to the Institute for Advanced Study in Princeton, New Jersey. There he was able to study and teach in a way that suited him.

Einstein was one of the greatest scientists of all time. Still, he was a simple man who cared little about money and owning things. He always had time for children, hated war, and worked for peaceful uses of atomic energy. Einstein was awarded the Nobel Prize for physics in 1921.

TO THINK ABOUT AND DO

There are many different words that are used to tell about energy. Copy this puzzle on a piece of paper. Use the hints to help you.

1. _____ energy
2. _____ energy
3. _____ energy
4. _____ energy
5. energy _____
6. _____ energy
7. _____ - energy

1. a kind of energy that is used to make things warmer
2. a kind of energy that is used to make a place brighter
3. a kind of energy that is usually transferred through wires
4. a kind of energy that an object has because it can fall and push something
5. energy moving from one place to another
6. the energy present inside the nucleus of atoms
7. energy that can be transferred

WHAT DO YOU REMEMBER?

Copy each sentence on a piece of paper. Write **T** beside the sentences that are true and **F** beside those that are false. Rewrite any sentence that is false to make it true.

1. Energy is needed to do work or to make something move.
2. The amount of energy that comes out is different from the amount that is put in.
3. The force that holds atoms within a molecule together is called a magnetic bond.
4. Energy can be transferred from one form to another.
5. A chemical change in which oxygen is combined with another kind of matter is called oxidation.

200

6. Energy that comes from changes inside the nucleus of an atom is called chemical energy.
7. During both fission and fusion some matter is transformed into energy.
8. Coal, oil, and natural gas are fossil fuels that were formed millions of years ago.
9. Winds, tides, geothermal energy, and solar energy are nonrenewable resources.

ACTIVITY

Here is a way to build a solar heater. You will need two pieces of heavy paper and some masking tape. Also, get a pair of scissors, glue, a large paper cup, and some foil.

Place the two pieces of heavy paper end-to-end and tape them together. Place some foil, shiny side up, over the heavy paper. Glue the foil onto the heavy paper.

When the glue is dry, bend the heavy paper into a cone. The foil should be on the inside. Tape the edges together on the outside.

Cut along the sides of the paper cup so that it is half as tall as before. Line it with foil. Set it in the pointed end of the cone.

Put into the cup something that you want to heat. Tilt your solar heater toward the sun. What happens?

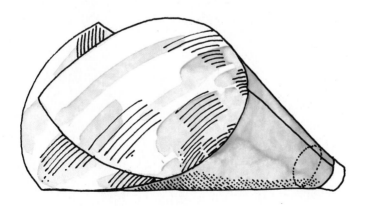

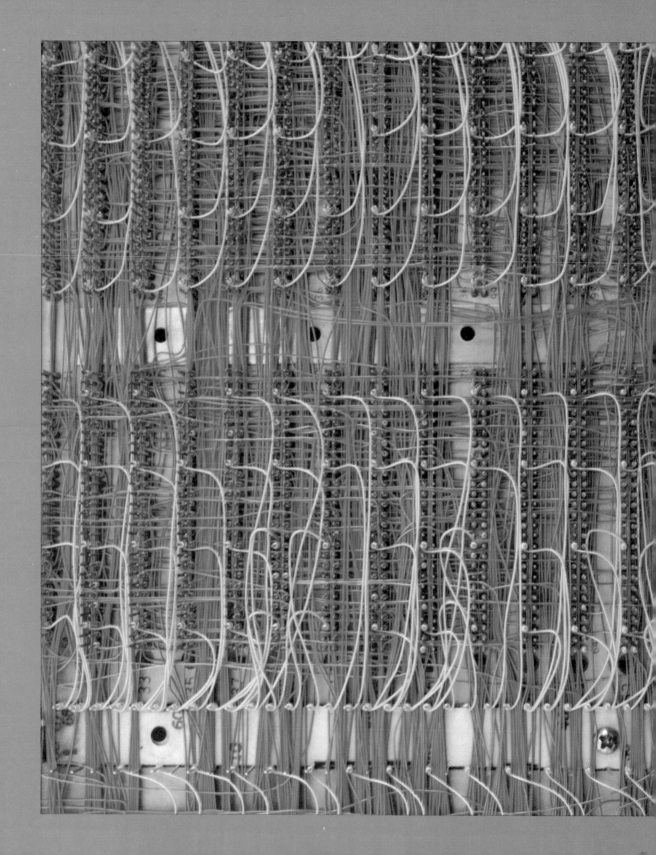

Unit III

Energy and Communications

Properties of Light

8

What can pass through glass or water as well as through millions of kilometers of empty space? What is silent as it passes, yet moves at tremendous speeds? As you may have guessed, the answer is light. You may already know a little about the way light behaves.

Green plants depend on light from the sun to make their food. Without light, then, you would have no food to eat. After all, everything you eat comes from green plants or from animals that eat green plants. Without light you would not even have the fuels you depend on for staying warm.

For more than three hundred years, people have been puzzling over what light really is. Even though many questions are yet to be answered, a great many things have been learned about light. Today we better understand how light behaves and how to use it. Let's find out about some of the things that are known about light.

Where Does Light Come From?

You know that light makes it possible to see things. Some things, such as the sun or a candle, can be seen because they are making their own light. Things that make light of their own are called **sources** of light.

Things that make light of their own may look very different from one another. But they are all alike in one important way. In each of them one form of energy has been changed to another.

The sun is our most important source of light. Even on cloudy days the sun is shining. The sun's energy comes from nuclear reactions deep inside its core.

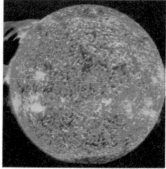

Nuclear reactions on the sun produce tremendous amounts of heat and light.

Erupting Nyiragongo Volcano in Zaire

Have you ever seen a picture of a volcano with lava flowing from it like a river on fire? The lava is so hot that it gives off light of its own.

Whenever something burns, there is a chemical change. In a burning candle chemical energy is changed to heat energy. The heat causes some of the carbon particles on the wick to glow. So light from a candle really comes from two energy changes —chemical to heat and heat to light.

When you turn on a lamp, two energy changes must take place in order for light to be given off. When you turn the switch, the circuit is closed and an electric current begins to flow. This flow causes a thin wire inside the bulb to heat up. The wire becomes so hot that it begins to glow. Electrical energy is changed to heat energy, which is then changed to light energy.

Can you make light inside your body? No, but certain fish and insects can. Chemical changes in the glands of a firefly cause a pale green light to be given off. Chemical energy that is changed to light energy in a living thing is called **bioluminescence** [by-oh-loo-muh-NEHS-ns].

Fireflies displaying bioluminescence

You may have noticed that, in most cases, light is caused by heat energy. Why is heat so often needed to make light?

All matter has some energy. When matter is heated, its atoms get even more energy. This energy causes the atoms' electrons to change to higher energy levels as they move about the nucleus. As the electrons change back to their original energy levels, they give off little bundles of light energy. Each of these bundles is a **photon** [FOH-tahn].

Photons have no mass. They move much like little waves on a pond. In some ways, however, photons act like tiny particles. They move much like bullets shot from a gun. But how can it be that photons behave as both particles and waves?

Waves or Particles?

In 1670, Isaac Newton, a young English scientist, presented an idea about light. He described light as streams of tiny particles. He said that these particles are shot out from the sun and from other things that glow. As soon as the particles bump into something, they bounce off.

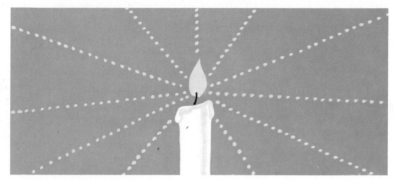

Isaac Newton (*left*) beleived that light behaves as streams of tiny particles.

A few years later, the Dutch astronomer Christian Huygens presented a different idea about the way light behaves. He said that light moves from one place to another in the form of waves.

According to Christian Huygens (*left*), light moves in waves.

But Newton argued that if light moved in waves, it would have to be able to move *around* things. Tests up to that time had showed that light moved only in straight lines.

Let's say that light is made of tiny particles. Suppose we shine two beams of light across each other. Won't these particles bump into each other and scatter when we do this? To find out, you will need two projectors, each with a film in place. You will also need two large pieces of stiff white paper.

Make the room dark. Turn on one of the projectors to shine a picture on one piece of white paper. Look at the picture; then turn off the projector. Do the same with the other projector. Now turn on both projectors, so that the beams of light shine through each other. Look at the picture on each paper. Has it changed?

Do you think that light is made of tiny particles? What should have happened when the particles from one projector bumped into those from the other? What did happen?

When two beams of light shine through each other, the picture that each forms is clear and sharp. But let's say that light is made of particles. Wouldn't they have been scattered as the two beams shined through each other? If this had happened, the pictures on the two screens would not have been clear at all.

ACTIVITY

Let's suppose that light is made of waves. If two sets of waves bump into each other, will they mix and scatter? We can find out by trying this with water waves. You will need a large pan and some water.

Fill the pan with water. After the water is still, dip one of your fingers near one end of the pan. Now remove your finger. How do the water waves move? These water waves are something like the light waves that Huygens described. Dipping the finger into the water is like turning on one projector. Wait until the water is still again. Then dip a finger near the other end. This is like turning on another projector.

Now for the important test! Dip one finger near each end, at the same time. This is like turning on both projectors at the same time. What happens when the waves bump into each other? Do they scatter each other? Or do they pass through each other? Does each wave keep the shape of a circle?

When waves collide, there is no scattering. Instead, the waves just pass through each other. Each wave keeps the shape of a circle as though the other wave were not there. It seems correct, then, to believe Huygens' idea that light moves as waves. There is a problem, however.

Think back to a time when you may have thrown a small rock into a pond. Do you remember seeing the tiny water waves that formed when the rock hit? The water is called the **medium** of these waves. Sound waves also move through a medium. When you speak to someone near you, air is the medium of the sound waves. But what is the medium of light waves?

In Newton's time some people believed that air is the medium of light waves. Now we know there is no air far out in space. Yet light moves even better through empty space than through air. That's how you see the sun and stars, by light that moved through space to you.

How Light Moves

You hear your friends calling you from around the sharp corner of a building. Can sound move around a corner? Or does it always move in a straight line? How do you know?

You may be able to hear your friends from around the corner, but you certainly can't see them. How, then, does light move differently from sound?

Does light move in curved paths or only in straight lines? To find out you will need three 12-by-20-cm white cards, a pair of scissors, and a flashlight. Also get a ruler, a piece of white paper, and some clay.

Cut a notch about 5 cm high and 3 mm wide in the same place in each card. Put one card, notch down, on a piece of white paper. Put pieces of clay under the corners of the card to make it stand up.

In a dark room, have your partner shine the flashlight, about a meter away, at the notch. Does the light that comes through the notch make a straight line on the paper? How can you check this with your ruler?

Stand the other two cards in a straight line about 15 cm from each other. Make sure the light is on the paper as it passes through all three notches. Is the light still making a straight line? Move one card so that its notch no longer lines up with the others. Is the light still on the paper? See if you are right. Does light move in straight lines or curved lines?

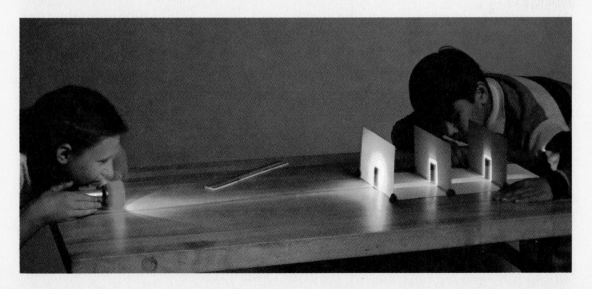

No matter which part of the light you see, it is coming to you in a straight line. This is why you can't see around things.

Just how fast does light move to get to us? If you watch a big thunderstorm, you may get an idea. Look at the lightning move quickly across the sky. Did you hear the crash, bang, and rumble of the thunder? Two things in the storm always happen in the same order. You see the lightning first; then you hear the thunder. If the light and sound happen at the same time, why do we see the lightning first?

To find the answer to this question, suppose that you are an astronaut circling the earth. During each orbit, you go more than 40,000 km in about 90 minutes. But a beam of light can go that far in about a seventh of a second! During one second, light moves 300,000 km. This is equal to more than seven trips around the earth. During that same second, at 20°C, about room temperature, sound would have moved only 344 m. Can you think now why we see light before we hear sound?

One way we can find out about objects in space is by studying the light they give off. Sunlight takes about 8 minutes to reach the earth from the sun, which is about 150 million km away. How long do you think it takes light from the next closest star to reach us?

We know that light moves about 9.5 trillion km in one year. We also know that Alpha Centauri, our nearest star after the sun, is about 38 trillion km away. How long does it take for its light to reach us? How did you find your answer?

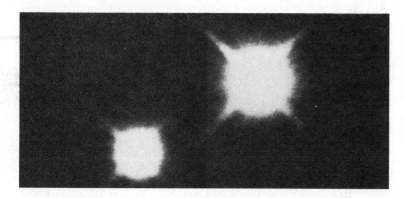

Alpha Centauri in the constellation Centaurus is part of a double star system.

To get an idea of how far light moves in a certain time, let's suppose something. Suppose you stand outside one night and point a flashlight at the sky. You turn it on for one second and then turn it off. The beam of light moves quickly away from the flashlight and keeps going into space. By the morning, the beam may be billions of kilometers away and still going!

The light keeps going as long as it doesn't bump into anything. The earth's atmosphere, however, is filled with gases and bits of dust. And light from a flashlight gives off very little energy. What would happen to the light energy as it hit these bits of matter in the atmosphere?

Getting in the Way of Light

Light moves faster than any other form of energy. As it moves, it meets many different kinds of matter. Some of them slow it down; others do not allow it to pass through them at all.

Some kinds of matter such as glass, water, and air allow light to pass through them. Light passes through in such a way that the things on the other side can be clearly seen. Matter that allows light to pass through in this way is said to be **transparent** [tran-SPEHR-uhnt]. How can you tell by looking at something that it is transparent or not?

When light passes through some kinds of matter, the things on the other side look blurred. The reason is that these kinds of matter scatter light in many different directions as it passes through them. They are said to be **translucent** [tran-SLOO-snt].

Most things do not transmit any light. A piece of wood or a sheet of cardboard will not allow any light to come through. Things that block all light are called **opaque** [oh-PAYK]. Since light moves in a straight line, it cannot move around the wood or the cardboard. Instead, the light stops at the object, leaving a shadow behind it.

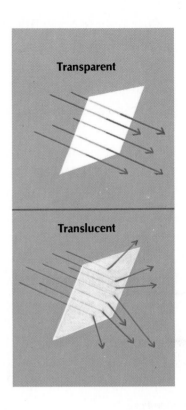

Transparent

Translucent

What happens when light passes through certain kinds of matter? To find out, you will need a 20-liter glass tank, some water, and a cup of milk. You will also need an eyedropper, a projector with a film in place, and a sheet of stiff white paper. Get a partner to help you.

Make a chart like the one you see here. Then pour water into the tank until it is about three-fourths full. Make the room dark. Have your partner hold the paper on one side of the tank as you shine the light through the water. Describe what you see on the paper and record this on your chart. Did the water allow light to pass through?

Now add two drops of milk to the water and stir the mixture. In the second column of your chart, record how the liquid mixture looks now. Project the picture through the liquid in the tank. In the last column of your chart, record what you see on the screen. Why does the picture look blurred this time? Does the mixture of water and milk allow as much light to pass through? Try adding four more drops of milk to the water and stir. What happens to the picture when you project it through the liquid? In your chart, record what you see.

Add the rest of the milk to the liquid in the tank. Is the liquid now transparent, translucent, or opaque? Shine the light through the liquid. What do you see on the paper screen? Does any light pass through the liquid this time?

Amount of Milk	Appearance of Liquid	Image on Screen
0 drops		
2 drops		

The Bouncing of Light

When you combed your hair this morning, did you use a mirror? A mirror is an opaque object that can be used in many different ways. How is each of these mirrors being used?

There are mirrors in most cameras, flashlights, telescopes, cars, trucks, and buses. In fact, mirrors are parts of thousands of things. Each of these things may look very different. But in each of them one or more mirrors is being used to change the direction in which light moves.

We can see stars, candle flames, and the sun because they make their own light. Most things, however, do not make their own light. How can we see them?

We see most things because light bounces off their surfaces. This bouncing of light is called **reflection** [rih-FLEHK-shuhn]. In most cases, matter reflects some light, whether the matter seems to be opaque, transparent, or translucent.

Words such as *shiny, dull,* and *smooth* can be used to describe how well something reflects light. Here is a list of good and poor reflectors. Which things in the list are good reflectors? What makes them different from poor reflectors?

Your body reflects light, just as a mirror does. But people looking at you see *you*—not their own reflections in you. In other words, you are not a good reflector. But a mirror is a very good one. What is it about the surface of your skin, hair, or clothes that reflects light less well than a mirror?

Good Reflectors
Glass
Highly polished metal
Water
Glossy pages of a book

Bad Reflectors
Cork
Blackboard
Towel
Rusty iron

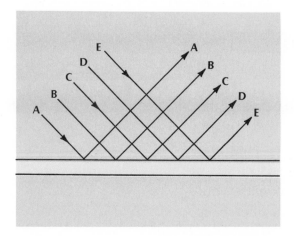

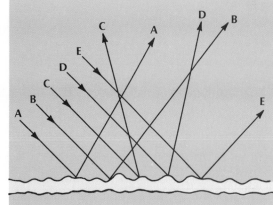

above left: Reflection off a smooth surface; *above right*: Reflection off a rough surface; *below*: Surface of a sheet of paper magnified 175 times

If you could see the surface of a mirror under a microscope, the surface would appear very smooth. If you looked at the surface of a sheet of paper under a microscope, however, you would notice something different. You would find that it is very rough and has many bumps compared to the smooth mirror. How do you think this makes a difference in the way light is reflected? When light hits a smooth surface, all the rays are reflected in one direction. When light hits a rough surface, each of the rough places reflects light in many different directions.

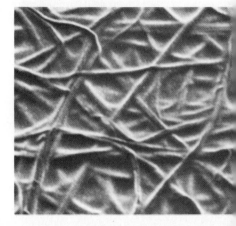

Here is a way to make a mirror. You will need an 8-by-6-cm piece of glass, some smooth foil, a pair of scissors, some tape, and a store-bought mirror.

Cut out a piece of smooth foil the same size as the glass. Lay the shiny side of the foil on top of the glass. Now carefully tape the foil to the glass. Turn it over, and test your mirror.

Can you see your face in the mirror? Compare your mirror to the store-bought one. Are there any differences between the reflections? What do you think causes these differences?

Store-bought mirrors are made by painting one side of a piece of glass with a solution of either aluminum or silver. After this coat dries, a coat of black paint is put on to protect it. The glass allows light to pass through the side that is not painted. When light hits the smooth metal backing, however, the light is reflected out through the glass.

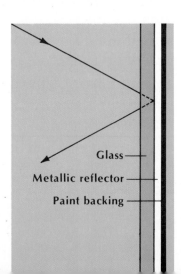

Glass
Metallic reflector
Paint backing

What is the difference between you and your reflection? To find out, you will need a mirror.

Look into the mirror. Do you see yourself? Does it look as if you are behind the mirror? Is there anything different about your reflection?

It is sometimes hard to tell a thing from its reflection. Wink your right eye. Did your reflection wink its right eye? Be careful! Remember that your reflection is facing you. Now move closer to your mirror. Move to one side and then the other. When you move to your right, in which direction does your reflection move?

When you look in a mirror, your reflection appears to be the same distance behind the mirror as you are in front of the mirror. There is one difference, however. Your reflection is reversed. How do you know?

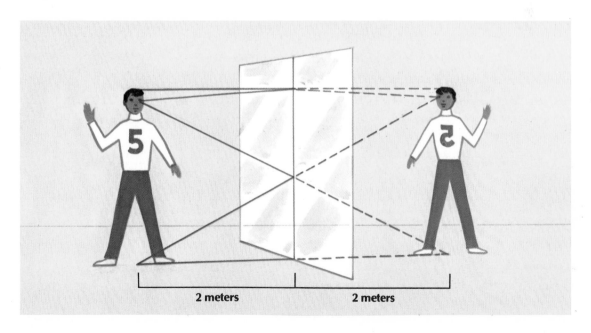

2 meters   2 meters

Have you ever seen your reflection in any of these things? They are good reflectors. Because of their curved surfaces, however, the reflection looks smaller or larger than the thing itself. The funny curved mirrors in amusement parks do the same thing.

Mirrors that curve in like the bowl of a spoon are called **concave** mirrors. They gather light and often make things look larger. Sometimes concave mirrors are mounted on telescopes. The mirrors gather light from space so that pictures can be taken of faint stars. Some hand mirrors are concave. So are automobile headlights and searchlights.

Mirrors that curve out like the back of a spoon are called **convex** [kahn-VEHKS] mirrors. Convex mirrors are sometimes used as rear-view mirrors on cars. These mirrors make things look smaller. They reflect a much larger surface than concave or flat mirrors. How can this be important for the driver?

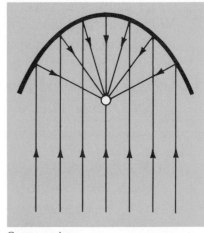

Concave mirror

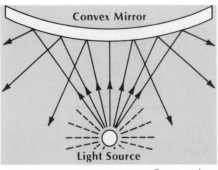

Convex mirror

Bending Light

Have you ever reached for a rock under water? Were you surprised when the rock was not where it appeared to be? Why did this happen? Were your eyes playing a trick on you?

What happens to light when it passes through different kinds of matter? To find the answer, you will need a cup that you can see through, some water, and a pencil. You will also need a piece of paper and a pencil for recording what you see.

Rest the pencil inside the cup. Draw what you see as you look at the pencil from the top and then through the side of the cup.

Now fill two-thirds of the cup with water. Again, draw the pencil as it looks from the top and through the side of the cup. Compare your drawings. How are they different? Take the pencil out of the water. Does its size and shape look the same?

As light moves from one kind of matter to another, its speed changes. The speed may become greater or smaller, depending on the kind of matter through which the light rays pass. When the speed of light changes, another change may also take place. In most cases, light moves in straight lines. If light enters another kind of matter at an angle, however, the change in its speed causes it to bend. This bending of light is called **refraction** [rih-FRAK-shuhn].

An object (turtle) seen under water is really lower than it appears. This is due to the bending of light rays as they move from water to air.

223

Can a coin float in water? To find out, you will need a shiny penny, an opaque cup, and some water. Get a partner to help you.

Put the penny in the cup. Slowly move your head down until you can no longer see the coin.

Now hold your head very still and watch the cup while your partner slowly fills it with water.

What happens to the coin? How can you explain this based on what you know about refraction?

Refraction of light can make some strange things appear to happen. Have you ever looked far down a road on a hot sunny day? You may have seen something that looked like puddles of water. Sometimes, even if it hasn't rained in days, the road looks wet. After walking to where the puddles appeared to be, you find that the road is dry! How can you use the idea of refraction to explain this?

The "puddles" were formed as light moved through different layers of air just above the road. Since the road was hot, the air just above it was warm and less dense than the higher cooler air. Light from the sky was refracted as it moved from the higher to the lower layer of air. Whenever light is refracted in this way, you see a reflection of the sky in the road. It gleams in such a way that it looks much like water.

Below: During a mirage, the warm air near the earth refracts light rays from the sky toward your eyes. This causes you to see an image of the sky, which on ground may appear to be a pool of water.

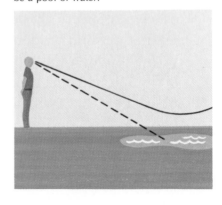

Light and Color

You have seen how light is refracted when it passes from air into water. Drops of water on a leaf in sunlight can refract light, too. This time, however, something different happens.

When light rays pass into the tiny drops of water, a rainbow of colored light appears. This band of colors is called a **spectrum.** Because of their round shape, the drops of water bend the light in a certain way. When this happens, the light is separated into the colors of the spectrum.

It is easier to break up light into its spectrum of colors by using something other than drops of water, however. Isaac Newton used a **prism** to break up light. This is a wedge-shaped piece of glass or other matter that you can see through. When a narrow beam of sunlight passes through a prism, the whole spectrum, from red to violet, appears.

Newton used a prism to produce a spectrum of visible light.

ACTIVITY

You can make the spectrum of colors appear. You will need a glass prism and a sheet of white paper.

Make the room dark except for one window where sunlight shines in. Pull the shade almost all the way down. Only a narrow slit should be left for light to pass through.

Hold the prism in the sunlight. Move it back and forth until the different colors appear on the white paper. Which color is on the top? Which is on the bottom?

Newton tried to break up the spectrum of colors even more by allowing the colors to fall on a second prism. He found, however, that the second prism would not spread out the spectrum into any more colors. Then he thought he would try to place the second prism so that all the colors could be put back together again. It worked! Instead of the spectrum, a slit of white light appeared. Newton had discovered that white light is really made of all the colors of the spectrum mixed together.

below left: When light travels through a prism, it forms a spectrum of colors. *below right*: When light travels through two prisms turned in opposite directions, a beam of white light appears.

When you see a spectrum, you may find it hard to tell where one color stops and another begins. Yet something makes each color different from the other. What is it?

White light is made up of waves of different lengths that all move forward at the same speed. Each of these wavelengths corresponds to a color of the spectrum and has a different amount of energy. Light waves of shorter wavelengths have more energy than light waves of longer wavelengths.

When light moves forward, its wave motion is from side to side. Each time light of a certain color moves a distance that is equal to one of its wavelengths, it completes one side-to-side motion. If two light beams of different colors move the same distance, the one with more energy (shorter wavelength) makes more side-to-side motions. The number of side-to-side motions made by a light beam in one second is its **frequency** [FREE-kwuhn-see].

Whenever you see the spectrum of colors, you will find that they are always arranged in the same order: red, orange, yellow, green, blue, violet.

The color violet represents light of the greatest energy. Violet, then, also has the highest frequency of the colors. Which color has the lowest frequency?

Each drop of water on a leaf acts as a tiny prism, breaking up light into colors. When sunlight shines on drops of water in the air, a rainbow is formed. Sunlight is made up of many wavelengths of light. The drops of water sort them out so that they appear in separate bands of color.

You can see a rainbow only when you face away from the sun. The drops of rain must be in the air somewhere ahead of you. The rays of light are reflected from inside the drops of rain. You can use a fine stream of water from a sprinkler in sunlight to make such a rainbow.

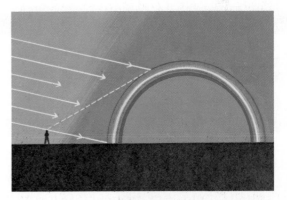

You know that white light is made up of many colors. Sometimes we want to use only one of these colors. The tail light of a car must be red. Yet the electric bulb in the light sends out white light, which is all the colors mixed together. To change the white light to red, we need something that will block out all the colors except red. How do we do this?

The red glass in front of the light bulb absorbs all the colors of the spectrum except red. It doesn't add red; it only takes away all the other colors. What must a green traffic light have in order to appear green?

Maybe you find it hard to believe that colored glass can take away light. Let's find out if it really does. You will need a flashlight and a book. You will also need some circles of different-colored cellophane that are each 6 cm across.

In a dark room, shine the flashlight on the white page of a book. Notice how bright the light is on the page. The page is getting the full light energy from the flashlight.

Now, one at a time, put pieces of different-colored cellophane in front of the flashlight. Hold the flashlight at the same distance, shining the light on the page. What color is the light that falls on the page? What do you think happened to all the other colors of the spectrum? Is the light as bright as it was without the cellophane? How can you explain this?

Some things don't allow any light to pass through them. Yet you can still see them. No light shines through a red apple. Why do these apples look red and not some other color?

Here is a way to show how something that is opaque can be a certain color. You will need a flashlight and three sheets of different-colored paper—red, green, and white.

Make the room dark. Then shine the light on the red paper, keeping the white paper nearby. What color is reflected on to the white paper? Now try the green paper in place of the red paper. What color is reflected this time? Why does each colored paper reflect only its own color of light?

An apple, or any other thing that you cannot see through, reflects only its own color. All the other colors of the spectrum are absorbed. An apple looks red because it reflects the red color and absorbs the other colors. Why does grass look green and white paper look white?

The color of anything that you cannot see through is the color of the light it reflects. If something reflects no color at all, it looks black. Black, then, is really the absence of color.

Look at the colors around you. Do some things reflect more light than others? Why, do you think, should the walls of a classroom be painted a light color? What color would be good to use on the walls of a room with very little sunlight? Color is a very important part of our world, isn't it?

What Did You Learn?

- In every light source one form of energy has been changed to another.
- Newton presented the idea that light is made of tiny particles. Huygens presented the idea that light behaves as waves. Today we describe light in terms of both particles and waves.
- Light moves in straight lines at about 300,000 km each second.
- Light passes through transparent matter. Light is scattered by translucent matter. Light is completely blocked by opaque matter.
- When light bounces off the surface of an object, you can see the object.
- A mirror is a good reflector; its shape makes a difference in the size of a reflection.
- Light moves at different speeds in different kinds of transparent matter.
- When light rays pass from one transparent thing into another at an angle, the rays are bent or refracted.
- Light that passes through a prism is broken up into the spectrum of colors.
- Under certain conditions, a rainbow forms when sunlight shines on drops of rain in the sky.
- Something is a certain color because it absorbs all the colors except the one that it reflects.

Career

Physical Chemist

Photography is something we all enjoy. You look at your baby pictures and wonder how you could have been so little. Moving pictures, television, and satellite photographs from space are other kinds of pictures that people use. We depend on photography to record the events that take place in our lives.

Understanding and making use of the properties of light are needed in making cameras and film. How are pictures printed on film? The likenesses in pictures are a result of light, lenses, and mirrors. The chemicals in photographic materials help to create the pictures on film or special paper.

Regina Caines is a physical chemist with a large film and camera company. She has worked in the film-making part of photography. She helped to produce a color film that makes an instant picture. Her task was to find the kinds of dyes that would work best with the film. It was important to find the dyes that reacted with the reflected light to give bright clear color.

The field of physical chemistry allows a person to work in many areas. Regina Caines is now a manager in her company. Her new job is to make sure that 100 million camera batteries are correctly produced a year.

TO THINK ABOUT AND DO

On a piece of paper copy the following list of substances. Then decide which term—*transparent, translucent,* or *opaque*—best describes each substance and write the term beside it.

1. wood
2. clean air
3. frosted glass
4. brick
5. waxed paper
6. water
7. clear glass
8. steel
9. lampshade

Copy these sentences on a sheet of paper. Write **T** beside the sentences that are true, and **F** beside the sentences that are false. Rewrite any sentence that is false to make it true.

1. In every light source, one form of energy is changed to another.
2. Newton said that light behaves as waves, while Huygens said that light is made of particles.
3. Light moves in straight lines at about 300,000 km each second.
4. Shadows form behind something that is transparent.
5. You can see an object when light bounces off its surface.
6. The shape of a mirror makes a difference in the size of a reflection.
7. The bending of light as it passes from one substance into another is called refraction.
8. When light passes through a prism, it is broken up into the spectrum of colors.

9. A rainbow may form when sunlight shines on drops of rain in the sky.

10. Something is a certain color because it reflects all the colors except the one that it absorbs.

SOMETHING TO THINK ABOUT

1. Find out what a light meter is and how it works.

2. There have been many reports of people seeing objects they call "flying saucers." Explain how what they see could really be reflected light.

ACTIVITY

How does the spectrum of colors make white? To find out, you will need a piece of thick white paper, a pencil, and a ruler. You will also need a pair of scissors, some colored markers, and some string.

From the paper, cut a circle that is 9 cm across. Divide the circle into six equal sections and color them as you see in the picture. In the blue and orange sections, make two small holes about 2 cm apart. Pass a piece of string about a meter long through the holes.

Hold the string on each end. Ask a friend to place the card in the center of the string. Swing the card around until the string is twisted tightly. Pull gently on the loops. Watch the card spin. What happens to the colors on the card?

233

Light and Vision

9

How do most of us learn about the world? Most of us learn more through our sense of sight than through any of our other senses. Through our eyes we learn the difference between night and day, and light and shadow. We use our eyes to tell us that something is near or far away. Our eyes see differences in shades of color and differences in shapes and surfaces. We cannot touch the stars and other things in the sky, but we can look at them with our eyes. The shadows that seem to follow us, the color of leaves in autumn, and the many colors in a rainbow—all these things come to us as sight messages. Our eyes, then, are the sense organs that react to light.

Try to stand on one foot for 30 seconds. Then try to stand on one foot with your eyes closed. What happens? Try to write your name with your eyes closed. What happens? Draw a picture of a house with your eyes open. Then try to draw the same house with your eyes closed. Compare your pictures to those of your classmates.

How Your Eyes Work

Each of your eyes has six muscles attached to the outside of it. The muscles move your eyes so that they can look in different directions.

In order for you to look to the left, the left muscle of each eye pulls the eye toward the left. In the same way, the muscles on the right pull your eyes toward the right. The other ones move your eyes up and down, and even around. Try to move your eyes in different directions. Then watch a classmate try.

Look at the eye in the picture. The **lens** is a clear part near the front of the eye. It is about the size of a small bean. The lens brings together light rays on the **retina** [REHT-n-uh]. In what part of the eye do you find the retina? The lens forms a picture on the retina of what you are looking at. Each lens in your eyes is convex. It is thicker in the center than at the edges.

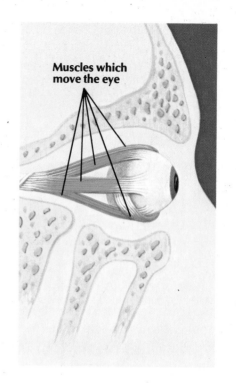

Muscles which move the eye

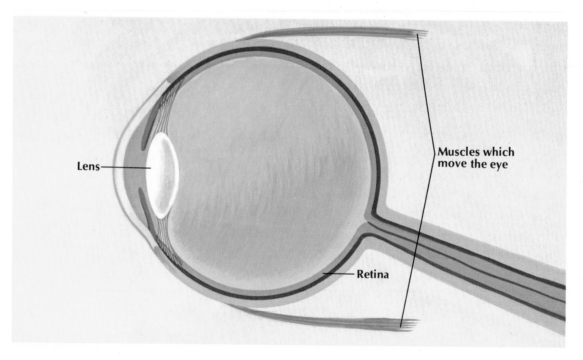

Lens

Retina

Muscles which move the eye

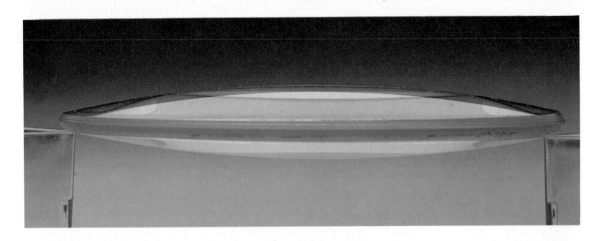

   Look at the magnifying glass. Where is its thickest part? Where is its thinnest part? Is it concave or convex? This kind of lens can form a picture out of the light rays from an object. When it causes light rays from something far away to come together, the picture that forms is small and upside down. The distance from the center of the lens to the picture of the object is called the **picture distance**.

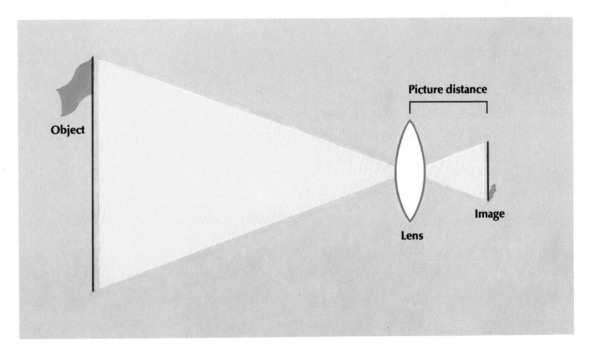

How is a lens used in forming a picture? You will need a magnifying lens, a sheet of white cardboard, a ruler, a sheet of paper, and a pencil.

Make the room dark, except for part of one window. Hold the cardboard behind the lens, as shown in the picture. Move the lens slowly back and forth. Stop when a sharp picture can be seen on the cardboard. Is the picture right side up or upside down?

Measure how far the picture on the paper is from the center of the lens. This is the picture distance. Record it on your paper. Compare your picture distance to the ones that your classmates find.

Object Distance	Picture Distance	Picture Height
1 m		
2 m		
3 m		

Your Living Lenses

The lenses in your eyes are alive. They are made of living cells. And each of these cells has many of the same kinds of parts as other living cells in your body. Yet each cell is as clear as glass. For this reason light can pass through it.

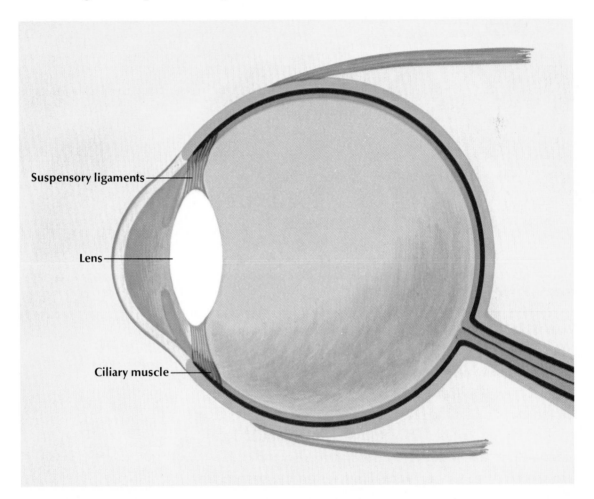

What difference does it make that the cells are alive? Can living cells make a better lens than a lens made of glass? Or is there some difference between the way a glass lens "sees" something and the way the lens in each of your eyes sees it?

What is the difference between the way in which something is "seen" by glass lenses and the way it is seen by the lenses in your eyes? You will need a small lens, a sheet of white paper, a sheet of black paper, and some clear tape. You will also need a small square of clear plastic, a ruler, something that can be used to draw circles, and a pencil.

Find the picture distance of your glass lens, as you did before. From the black paper, cut a circle whose width is the same as the picture distance that you found. Then cut a strip of white paper. Make it a little bit wider than the width of the lens. Cut it long enough so that it goes all the way around the outside of the circle. In the center of the strip cut a hole. Its width should be about 1 cm smaller than the width of the lens.

Tape the strip to the circle. Then fasten the square of clear plastic to the outside of the strip over the hole. To the inside of the paper, fasten a strip of black paper facing the hole. To the inside of the paper, fasten the glass lens against the hole. You now have an "eye."

Stand as far from the window as possible. Hold the "eye" so that the lens brings together a picture of the window frame on the paper "retina." Is the picture very sharp?

Move slowly toward the window. As you move, keep the picture of the window frame on the "retina." What happens to the picture as you come closer and closer to the window? At different distances does the glass lens make a picture that is always sharp? What happens to the size of the picture on the "retina" as you move closer and closer to the window?

Now stand far away from the window. Look at the real window frame. Is the picture that you see with *your* eyes sharp or fuzzy? Walk toward the window and look at the window frame as you walk. Does the sharpness of the frame change? No matter where you stand, you still see it very clearly!

A glass convex lens brings together a clear picture of an object only at a certain distance. Your lenses bring together the light rays from an object so that it can be seen clearly at different distances. What makes the difference?

The lens in your eye is made of tissue that stretches. It is attached to long, tough cords that keep it in place. When you see things close up, muscles in your eye allow the long cords to relax. The lens becomes thicker and more curved. This brings together light rays from closer objects on the retina.

Close object

When you look at things that are far away, the long cords become tighter. The lens becomes thin and flat. This brings together light rays from the faraway objects on the retina.

Far object

The Colored Part of the Eye

When the sunlight in your room is too bright, you pull the shades down. When the light is too dim, you raise the shades. The shades allow you to change the amount of light that comes through the window.

Have you ever walked into a dark room? It takes a minute or two for your eyes to change enough to see the things in the room.

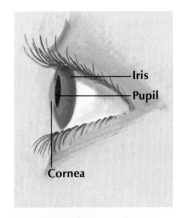

The colored part of your eyes is called the **iris** [EYE-rihs]. It controls the amount of light that can pass through the lens to the retina. The iris is covered by the **cornea** [KAWR-nee-uh]. It is a thin, clear layer over the front of the eye that protects the eye. It also helps to bring together light entering the eye.

Look at the pictures of eyes. Find the dark spot in each. This is the **pupil.** The pupil is the opening in the center of the iris. It looks dark because you are looking into the inside of the eye.

243

Does light make the pupils of your eyes change? To find out, you will need a mirror. Have a partner keep time for you.

Use the mirror to look at your eyes. Look at your irises. What color are they? Now find your pupils and notice their size.

Close your eyes for exactly two minutes. Then open your eyes. Quickly look at the size of your pupils again. What has happened to them?

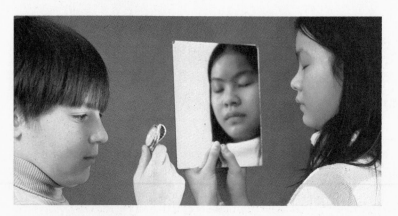

The iris is made of tiny muscles. In bright light, these muscles make the pupil smaller. This allows less light to come in. In dim light, they make the pupil larger. This allows more light to come through.

left: Pupil in dim light; *right*: Pupil in bright light

The Retina

The retina is a thin tissue behind the lens. It forms the innermost layer of the eye. It is here that the pictures of the things you are looking at are brought together. The retina is made of three main layers of cells. The most important layer has nerve cells called **rods** and **cones.** These nerve cells react to light. The rods make it possible for you to see in dim light. The cones allow you to see in bright light and to see color.

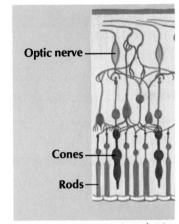

Cross section of retina

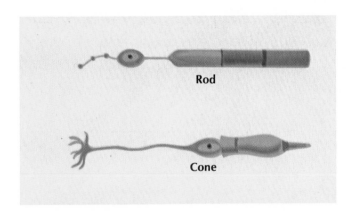

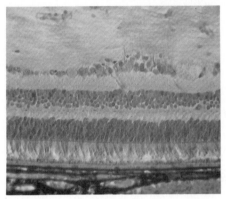

above: Retina enlarged 520 times

In dim light it is hard to tell one color from another. Everything seems to be black, white, or a shade of gray. What kind of nerve cells are working for you at night?

Animals such as dogs and cats always see in black or shades of gray. These animals do not see color at all. Which nerve cells do they have? Which ones don't they have?

Other animals, such as turtles, butterflies, and lizards, can see color. Which kind of nerve cell must be present in their eyes?

Each eye has about 125 million rods and 7 million cones. Why do you think you have more rods than cones?

Each of the rods and cones is separately connected to the brain through the **optic nerve.** Since these nerve cells react to light, they send messages to the brain whenever light falls on them.

When a picture is brought together on the retina, each nerve cell gets a tiny part of the light in the picture. It then sends its own bit of message to the brain. In your brain, these bits of the message are added up into a picture of what you are looking at.

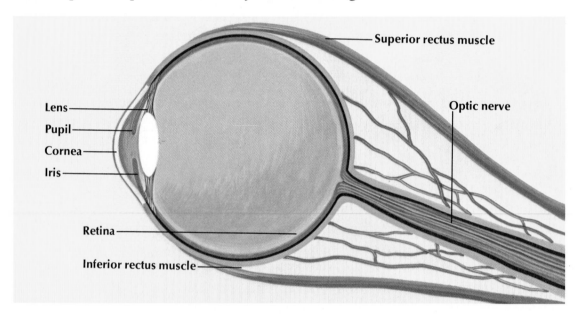

Your brain does three other important jobs that help you see. It turns the picture that was formed upside down on the retina right side up. It controls a group of tiny muscles that can change the shape of the lens in each eye. This change helps you to see both nearby things and things that are far away. The brain also makes sense out of what you see.

Look at the picture of the eye. Notice the point where the nerve fibers come together to form the optic nerve. Since rods and cones are not found at this point, it does not react to light.

What happens when a picture falls at the point on the retina where there are no rods and cones? To find out, you will need a pencil and a sheet of paper.

On a piece of paper, mark an X and a ● about 12 cm apart. Place the ● on the right. Hold the paper at arm's length and close your left eye. Look at the X. Now bring the paper slowly toward you, with your eye still closed. What happens to the ●? Does it seem to go away at a certain point? Bring the paper closer to your opened eye. Do you see the ● again? Why did this happen?

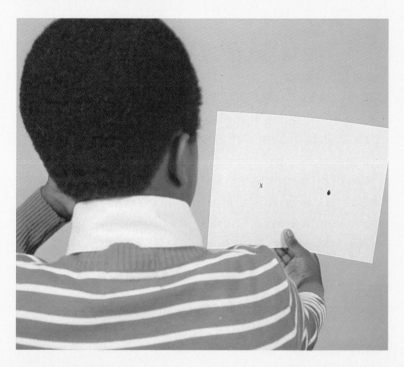

The point on the retina where there are no rods and cones is the blind spot of the eye. If a picture falls on the blind spot, you will not be able to see it. Why don't we notice the blind spot?

Your eyes help you to learn about many different things. But your eyes can also fool you. Let's look at a few of the ways in which they can fool you. You will need a sheet of paper, a pencil, and a metric ruler.

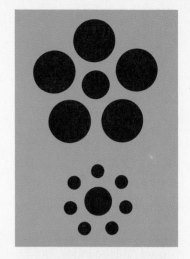

Objects	What You See	Measurements
A. circles		
B. hat		
C. message		
D. people		

Copy the chart on your paper. Look at the circles. Look closely at the circle in the center of each group. Are these circles the same size? Record your answer under the second column in the chart. Then measure and record the width of each circle. How do they compare to what you saw before you measured the circles?

Look at the hat. Is the hat taller than it is wide? Write your answer in the chart. Measure and record how high and wide the hat is. How does what you see compare to what you find when you measure the hat?

Read the message in the triangle to a classmate. Then have a classmate read the message to you. What is wrong with the message? Record what you see.

Look at the two people. Which one do you think is taller? Record your answer in the second column on the chart. Measure and record how tall each person is. What do you find?

Glasses Can Help Some People

If you are like most people, your lenses change their shape in such a way that you see most things clearly. Some of you, however, may have eyes that are a bit too long. Your lenses can bring together a picture of something that is *far away*. However, the picture comes together before it falls on your retina. Things that are not close to you may look fuzzy. But your lenses are able to bring together light from *nearby* objects on the retina. For this reason, you are said to be **nearsighted**.

Some of you may have eyes that are a bit too short. When you look at something *close*, the picture does not come together before it falls on your retina. Things that are close to you look fuzzy. However, you can see things clearly that are *far away*. You are said to be **farsighted**.

top: What a nearsighted eye sees; *above*: What a farsighted eye sees

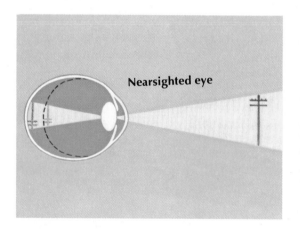

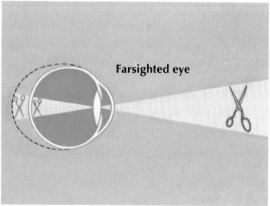

Look at the first picture of the eye. With your finger, trace the path that light takes through the parts of the eye.

In which of the two pictures does the light fall on the retina before it is brought together? Where is the light brought together in front of the retina?

249

Glasses have lenses that change the way light is brought together. They bend light in such a way that it is brought together exactly on the retina.

If you are nearsighted, your eyes are longer than they should be. Because of this, light from faraway things is brought together in front of the retina instead of on it. Your glasses would be made of concave lenses. They are thinner in the middle than at the edges. They will help bring together light from far away objects on the retina.

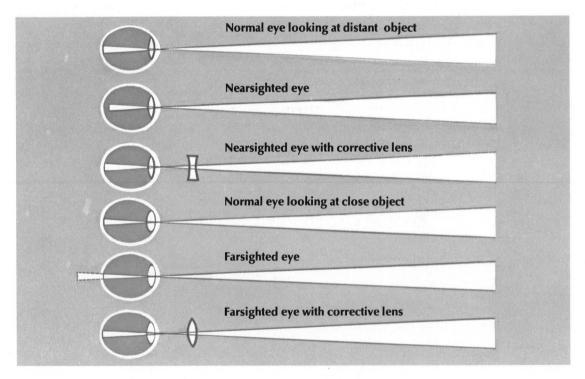

If you are farsighted, your eyes are shorter than they should be. Because of this, the light from nearby objects does not come together completely on the retina. Your glasses would be made of convex lenses. They are thicker in the center than at the edges. They will help bring together light from nearby objects on the retina.

The Care of Your Eyes

It's always easier to do certain things to care for yourself when you understand the reasons for them. Now that you know how your eyes work, you can understand why it is important to take care of them. Here are some ways to care for your eyes.

1. Read and do other close work in good light— not too dim and not too bright. Using too little light at night may strain your eyes. Having too much light, however, may also strain them. Have you ever had trouble seeing on a sunny, sandy beach? Or have you found it hard to read a page of black print on shiny paper? The trouble in each case is caused by bright light that shines, or is reflected, directly into the eyes. This is called **glare.** If it is strong enough, it becomes almost impossible to see. This may happen when a person drives in snow on a very bright sunny day.

When you read under a lamp, you can get rid of some glare by changing the bulb from a clear one to a frosted one. The frosted bulb helps to scatter the light so it doesn't shine directly in your eyes. What can you do to get rid of glare at the beach?

Glare at the beach is caused by sunlight that is reflected directly into the eyes.

251

2. When you watch television or do close work such as reading, raise your eyes once in a while. This gives your eye muscles a chance to change position. This is a sort of "get-up-and-stretch" break for your eyes.

3. Do you squint to see better? Or do you hold your work too close or too far away in order to see clearly? If so, have an eye doctor check your eyes. Getting headaches or seeing double after you have read for a while are other reasons for visiting a doctor.

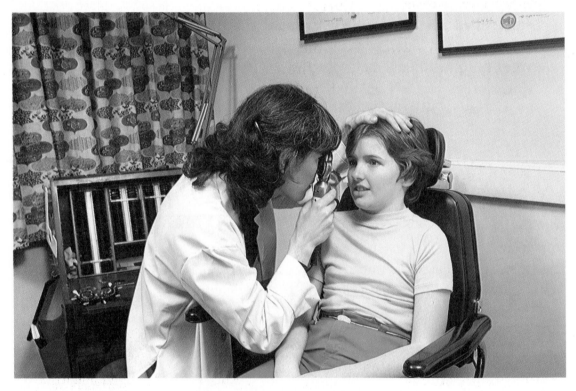

4. Don't read in a moving car or bus. Each time your book moves, your lens muscles must work to change the shape of the lens. Also your iris muscles must keep opening and closing over and over again as the light changes.

5. If something gets into your eyes, don't rub them. Your eyes are made of living cells and can become infected when dirt is rubbed in. Your tears will most likely wash out the dirt. If not, the eye should be washed with water that has been boiled and then cooled. Sometimes lifting the upper lid gently over the lower lid will help. If the dirt remains you should see your doctor.

6. Remember that you have only two eyes. They must serve you for your whole life. Careless play may end in eye injuries that cannot be corrected. For this reason, keep sharp things such as knives away from them. You should stay away from all kinds of fireworks except those that you watch at a public gathering. Never throw sticks, stones, or dirt at anyone.

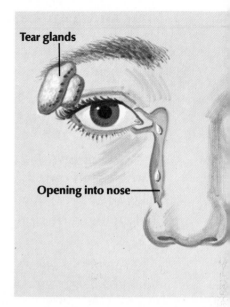

Tear glands

Opening into nose

Can you think of other ways to make sure your eyes don't get hurt?

ACTIVITY

Is there any reason why it is better to have two eyes instead of one? Here is a simple test you can try to find out. You will need a pencil.

Hold one arm in front of you, with your first finger pointing up. Hold the pencil in the other hand. Now shut one eye. Quickly try to touch the pencil to the tip of your finger. Can you do it?

Now open that eye and close the other one. Can you touch the pencil this time? Try the test with both eyes open. Now can you tell one important way in which two eyes are better than one?

What Did You Learn?

- The eyes are the sense organs that react to light. They send sight messages to the brain. They help us learn much about the world.
- A glass lens brings together a clear picture of an object only at a certain distance. Lenses in your eyes bring together light from an object so that it can be seen clearly at different distances.
- The pupil is an opening in the center of the iris. In bright light, it gets smaller. In dim light, it gets bigger.
- The rods and the cones are nerve cells that react to light. They are found in the retina. The rods make it possible to see in dim light. The cones make it possible to see in bright light and to see color.
- The brain helps you to see by turning the picture formed on the retina right side up. It helps you to see by making sense of what you see. The brain also changes the shape of the lenses.
- The blind spot is the point where the nerve fibers of the retina come together. They form the optic nerve that leads to the brain.
- In a nearsighted person, the picture comes together before it falls on the retina. This happens because the eyes are too long. In a farsighted person, the picture does not come together completely before it falls on the retina. This happens because the eyes are too short.
- Glasses are made of lenses that change the way light is brought together.
- It is important to take good care of your eyes. You should try not to overwork them. And you should protect them against injury.

Career

Ophthalmologist

Your eyes are important to you because they help you see many things. It must be hard to tell what something is like when you cannot see.

A doctor who knows about the parts of the eyes, how they work, and how to treat them is called an ophthalmologist (ahf-thal-MAHL-uh-jihst). Dr. Fanny Lowy is an ophthalmologist. For many years, while she raised a family, she treated people from an office in her own home. After her husband died, she closed her office. She then worked as a school doctor for the City of New York until the age of 80.

At the age of 84, Dr. Lowy is still a busy doctor. She helps many people at a home for the aged.

Sometimes, as people grow older, they develop poor eyesight. Some may even become blind. They may sit in the dark and not want to be with other people. Dr. Lowy has planned a special way to help these people. Her plan does not cure blindness, but it helps them deal with loneliness. Dr. Lowy brings these people together in one room and shows them how to move in a special way to music. This allows them to use their other senses.

Dr. Lowy was born in Russia and studied medicine at the University of Vienna. She met her doctor husband there, and they came to America together. In 1978, Dr. Lowy received an award from the Mayor of New York for her work.

TO THINK ABOUT AND DO

WORD FUN

Describe what happens from the time light falls on your eyes until you understand what you are seeing. Copy each sentence on a piece of paper. Then choose the right word or words to complete it.

cones and rods   retina   optic nerve   pupil-
iris   lens   brain   cornea-

1. Light enters the eye through an opening called the _____.
2. The size of this opening is controlled by the _____.
3. The light passes through the _____, which brings the picture together on the _____.
4. The retina has nerve cells called _____.
5. These cells react to light and send messages through the _____ to the _____.

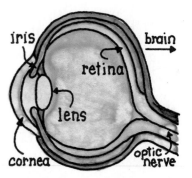

WHAT DO YOU REMEMBER?

Each of these sentences is false. Change a word or two in each to make it true. Write the true sentences on a piece of paper.

1. Cones make it possible for you to see in dim light.
2. In the center of the iris is an opening called the optic nerve.
3. An object can be seen clearly at different distances because the iris in your eye brings together light.
4. The optic nerve helps you to see by turning the picture formed on the retina right side up.
5. The point where the nerve fibers of the retina come together is called the cornea.

256

6. The picture comes together in front of the retina in a farsighted person.

7. Lenses in glasses change the way ~~sound~~ *sight* is brought together.

Can you be sure of what you see? Your eyes and brain work together. Your brain makes sense out of the messages your eyes send to it. You see light and dark patches on paper as objects. It may not seem strange to you because you have been doing it all your life. These pictures may help you understand this.

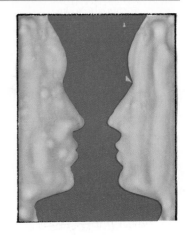

1. Look at the picture. What do you see? _____
Stare a little longer at the picture until something happens. What do you see now? _____
Why? _____

A   B   C   D   E

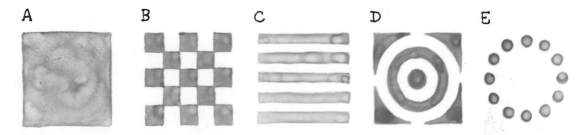

2. What do you see in these drawings? Look at drawings A and B. Do you see these as a plain square and a square of little squares? Your brain arranges them into whole patterns. Now look at drawings C and D. These do not seem to be separate stripes or circles. They seem to belong together. The stripes make a block of stripes and the circles make a target of circles in a square. Look at the dots in drawing E. Do you see a circle? There is no circle, only separate dots. Your brain arranged the dots into a circle for you.

Communications 10

Something exciting has just happened to you! And you can hardly wait to tell someone. You want to share your news—to **communicate.** You may communicate by shouting over the fence to your neighbor or by phoning a friend 3000 km away. Communicating is, in fact, something that everybody does in one form or another. How does a baby let someone know it is hungry? How does a watchdog warn you of danger?

Machines also help you in communicating. Sometimes they even communicate *to* you! Do you get up for school because your alarm clock goes off? Have you ever learned from a news report that school has been called off?

Some forms of communication may seem like magic. You turn a dial and it seems that pictures and voices come out of empty space. In your own home or far from Earth in a spacecraft—you can still be in touch with the rest of the world.

259

The Beginnings of Modern Communication

Whenever you communicate with another person, you must use some kind of language that both of you understand. But this "language" may not be English. It may just be a smile or a wave. The first communication was probably not a spoken word or even a mumbling sound. It is likely, in fact, that early people made up a whole body language before they ever spoke a word.

Sometimes people had to send messages much farther than their voices could be heard. In these cases, many different kinds of signals were used: drum beats, horn blasts, and smoke signals.

There was a problem, however. Once a message was sent, there was no record of it. For this reason, people began drawing pictures in the sand or on the walls of caves. They may have used the pictures for recording the steps leading to a victory. Or they may have made simple drawings to teach the younger people how to hunt.

left: Cave painting, Altamira, Spain;
right: Egyptian hieroglyphics

In time, these pictures became an alphabet of letters that stood for sounds rather than things. The letters were then put together in different ways to form a written language of words.

Books are made of words. This may sound simple. But books can be very important in communicating ideas to many people at the same time. Many copies of a book must be made to reach many people.

Six hundred years ago, there were very few books. Each copy of a book had to be made by hand. In the Middle Ages, some people spent many years of their lives copying a single book letter by letter.

In 1440, however, Johannes Gutenberg made separate pieces of metal type for each letter to be printed. These metal pieces could be used over and over again to print many different books. Now thousands of copies of a book could be printed in less time than one book could be copied by hand! The earliest printing press may have looked quite different from a modern one. But it used the same materials—paper, ink, and type—to make a book.

Before we find out how books are printed, perhaps we should learn something about the paper on which they are printed. The first real paper, made from wood, was invented long ago by the Chinese. But it was not until the early 1700's that the idea of making paper from wood was discovered in Europe. A French scientist got the idea as he watched some insects chewing up wood to make their nests.

top: Page from a book made in the Middle Ages; *above*: Gutenberg's press

left: Paper wasps on nest

261

If you tear a piece of newspaper and hold it against a strong light, you can see the wood fibers sticking out of the torn end. This one page may be made of over eight million such fibers!

Newspaper, magnified

Paper is made from wood that is ground up and mixed with water and other matter. This forms a mixture that looks much like thick soup.

The soupy mixture is poured on to a moving belt made of wire screen. Here the water drips through the holes in the screen. Then the mixture is squeezed through warm rollers that dry and press it into finished, smooth paper.

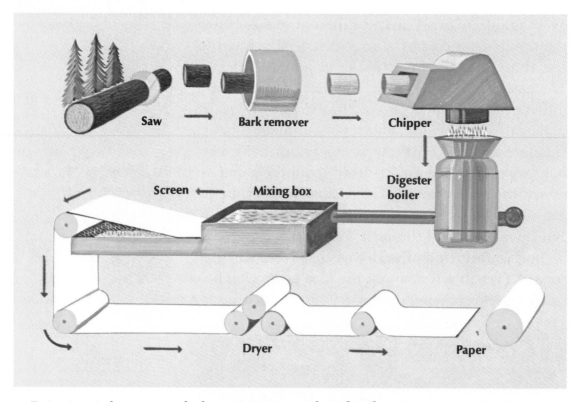

Printing inks are made by mixing powdered coloring matter called **pigments** with certain liquids. This causes a sticky paste to form. For black ink, a pigment called **lampblack** is used.

How is lampblack made? To find out, you will need a glass plate, a candle, a match, and a watercolor brush. Also get some cooking oil, a piece of white paper, a pair of safety glasses, two pot holders, and some water.

Over a candle flame, hold the glass plate by its edges. What happens to the part of the plate nearest the flame? The black soot on the plate is lampblack.

Wet your brush and dip it into the lampblack. On your paper, try to write a message with the brush. Does the lampblack smudge on your paper? Now dip your brush into the oil before you dip it in the lampblack. Try writing a message on your paper now. Does the oil make a difference in your writing?

Lampblack, the fine black soot made by a burning candle, was used by the Chinese people thousands of years ago. Today it is still used in paints and in printing ink.

You can make your own type and print. All you need is a knife, a potato, some ink, a pie tin, and a piece of white paper.

Decide on the letter that you want to print. You will be cutting this letter from the potato to make your printing surface. Since the print will be reversed, you will need to cut the letter backward. You may want to make a drawing of the letter on your paper before you cut the potato.

Now cut the potato in half. Then cut the letter into the potato. Any parts of the potato surface that are not cut out will pick up ink. The cut-away parts will come out white or the color of the paper. After you have prepared your potato, press it into some ink and print with it.

In order to print each of the color pictures in your book, four printing plates were needed. In most cases, the yellow plate is printed first, followed by the red, the blue, and the black. Only tiny dots of a certain color are used to make a plate.

When the picture is printed, the tiny colored dots may fall on top of one another. In this way, shades of color are formed. There are only four printing plates—red, blue, yellow, and black. Then how does green grass get into a picture? Green is formed in places where blue and yellow dots are printed on top of each other.

 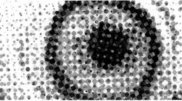

With a hand lens look at one of the colored pictures. Can you see tiny dots of different-colored inks? Together the dots form a picture.

If you could visit a printing plant, you would see several kinds of machines. Folding, cutting, binding, and printing machines are all needed to prepare a book. In one swift movement a printing press can print 64 pages the size of this one! How long do you think it would take a person to write that many pages by hand? If everything were done by hand, books might cost thousands of dollars apiece!

This is the press that printed this book. It can print 32 pages at a time, 32,000 times an hour. How many pages can be printed in an hour?

Transmitting Sound Through Wires

Sound is made whenever something **vibrates** or moves rapidly back and forth. This moving back-and-forth sets up vibrations of the air, or sound waves. Whenever sound waves reach your ear, you hear a noise.

Sound waves allow you to be heard by people who are in the same room. With a public address system you can even be heard by someone who lives several kilometers from your house. But how can you talk with a friend who lives really far away?

You could try talking with your friend over CB radio. Or you could even try using the telegraph, which sends messages based on dots and dashes. But perhaps the easiest way to send a message is by telephone. A telephone can send your words around the world at a speed so great that you do not notice any delay.

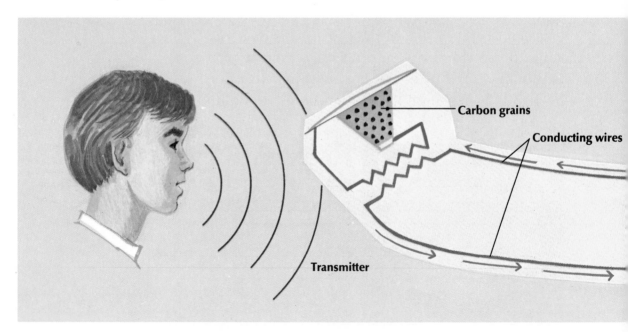

Carbon grains

Conducting wires

Transmitter

When you use the telephone, you say "Hello" into a **transmitter** [tran-SMIHT-uhr], the part that picks up sound waves from your voice and passes them along. Each sound wave from your voice causes a thin metal disk to bend back and forth. As the disk bends backward, it pushes against a box filled with tiny grains of carbon. When these grains are pushed together, they cause an electric current from the telephone company to flow in spurts. Sound energy is being changed to electrical energy.

What happens when you phone one of your friends? Electric current is carried by wires from the phone company to your friend's **receiver.** In the receiver, the current flows through an electromagnet. The electromagnet causes a metal disk just above it to move back and forth. In this way, sound waves are made in your friend's phone. Out comes your "Hello."

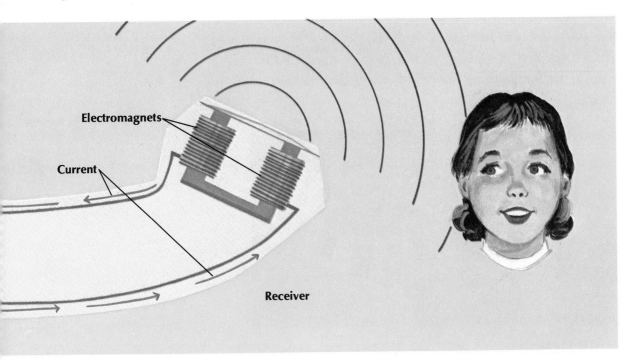

Electromagnets

Current

Receiver

How is electric current changed into sound in a telephone receiver? To find out, you will need a small tin can with both ends removed, a large balloon, a paper clip, a metal file, and a dry cell. You will also need about 2 m of thin wire, a ruler, a pair of scissors, a large nail, some rubber bands, and some tape. Ask a partner to help you.

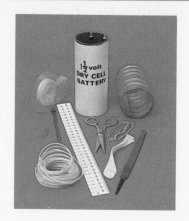

Wrap the wire around the nail. Leave about 30 cm of wire at each end. Then remove about 3 cm of the outside cover from each end of the wire.

Stretch a piece of balloon across one end of the tin can. Fasten it with rubber bands. Tape the paper clip to the center of the stretched balloon.

Now cut a piece of wire about 30 cm long and remove the outside cover from each end. Wrap one end of this wire around the end of the file. Connect the other end to one of the screws on the dry cell.

Ask your partner to hold the open end of the can to one ear. With the free end of the wire that is wrapped around the nail, scrape the file. As you scrape, hold the wire-wrapped nail near the paper clip on the can. What happens?

As the boy in the picture scrapes the wire along the file, he sets up an electric circuit and then breaks it. In this way, short spurts of current are caused to flow through the wire that is wrapped around the nail. With each spurt, the nail becomes magnetized and pulls the paper clip. After each spurt, when no current is flowing, the nail is no longer a magnet. The paper clip snaps back.

The moving paper clip causes the stretched piece of rubber to move. As the piece of rubber moves, the air around it begins to move, as well. In this way, sound waves are set up. When the waves hit a person's eardrum, a sound is heard.

Telephone wires do not carry the sound itself. They carry spurts of electric current that are changed into sound by the receiver. Since your telephone has both a transmitter and a receiver, it is possible for you to talk as well as hear.

What happens when you lift your phone to make a call? First, an electrical signal flashes over the wire that runs from your phone to the telephone office. When you hear the dial tone, you know that this office is ready to handle your call. As you punch or dial the number, each tone or click of your dial sends out a signal. Each of these signals operates a switch in the telephone office to connect your telephone to the phone of the person you are calling.

For calls that are really far away, it would cost a great deal to string wires and cables on telephone poles. In order to make long-distance phoning cheaper, telephone companies use radio relay systems that send calls by radio waves.

Wires inside a telephone switching system

Preserving Sound

Even though we cannot see sound or touch it, we can store the vibrations that cause sound. But how are they stored and then made to "speak" to us? Let's find out by looking at a phonograph record.

If you hold a record close to your ear and listen, what do you hear? Of course, you don't hear anything! But if you look at the surface of the record through a hand lens, you may get a clue about how sound is made from the record.

Through the hand lens you can see some thin, wavy lines. These "lines" are really tiny grooves in the record. Before you can change the grooves into sound several things must take place.

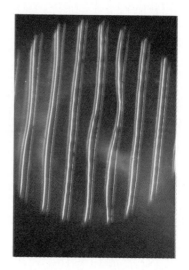

How is sound made from a record? To find out, you will need a sheet of paper, a pin, some tape, a record player, and an old record. Be sure you don't use a record that anyone may want to play again.

Roll the paper into a horn shape and fasten it with tape. Push the pin through the other end of the paper horn. Then cover the head of the pin with tape. Turn on the record player and hold the point of the pin on the turning record. Then listen through the open end of the horn. Do you feel the horn moving rapidly back and forth?

The sound you hear is coming from the paper horn and not from the inside of the record player. What causes the horn to move rapidly back and forth?

270

When you set the needle on a spinning record, the needle follows the grooves in the record's surface. The wavy grooves cause the needle in the pickup cartridge to move rapidly from side to side. The pickup cartridge changes these movements into weak electrical signals, which are then fed into an **amplifier** [AM-pluh-fy-uhr]. In the amplifier, the signals become strong enough to operate the loud-speaker, where they are finally changed into sound.

Thomas Edison and his first phonograph

The phonograph has been improved a great deal since it was made by Thomas Edison in 1877. At first it sounded more like a screechy toy. In fact, the first sounds that Edison recorded were "Mary Had a Little Lamb"!

The way that records are made has changed since Edison's time. When records were first made, a singer would sing as loudly as possible into the wide end of a horn. The loud singing caused a needle at the other end of the horn to move back and forth on a blank record. As a motor turned the record, the point of the moving needle made a wavy groove in its surface.

Today a recording is made on a plastic tape that is coated with tiny grains of a metal oxide. What steps must take place to make a recording?

First, sound waves enter a microphone where they are changed into electrical signals. These signals move through an electromagnet where they cause a change in its magnetic field.

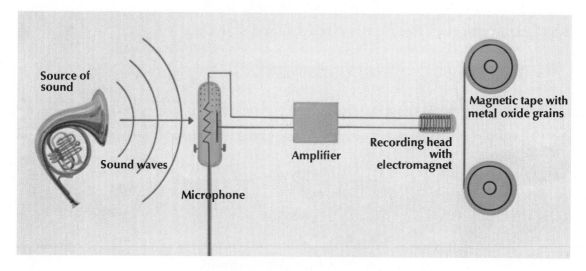

Source of sound

Sound waves

Microphone

Amplifier

Recording head with electromagnet

Magnetic tape with metal oxide grains

As the tape is pulled in front of the electromagnet, the changing field causes a change in the iron oxide grains. The grains become arranged in a different way to make each different kind of sound. A piano sounds like a piano and not like a banjo. A horn sounds like a horn and not like a harp.

Not everybody can visit places around the world. But the recorded sounds of the world can come to you. You can hear the music made by people around the world and the songs of strange birds in the South Seas. Long, long after they have sung or spoken, you can hear the voices of well-known people. You can also hear the sounds of great events. The long ago and far away can become the here and now.

Machines That Use and Store Information

You are living in an exciting time! More information has been gathered by people in the last hundred years than was learned in thousands of years before that. There is so much to know, in fact, that no one person can learn all that is known about a certain subject. A chemist can't learn all there is to know about different kinds of matter. Nor can a geologist learn all that is known about the earth.

Today people must work with huge amounts of information in order to find answers to certain problems. Suppose they had no machines to arrange and store this information. It would take them years to find some of the answers.

A machine was invented to do arithmetic problems in much less time than it would have taken to work out by hand. It was called a **calculator.**

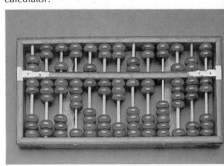

below: The abacus was the first real calculator.

left: This mechanical calculator can add, subtract, multiply, and divide.
right: Simple four-function electronic calculator

The early calculators had one big drawback. They could not store information for later use. Once a set of numbers was added, it was lost. Suppose the same set of numbers was needed for multiplication. Then the numbers had to be put into the calculator again.

The first digital computer

During World War II, a machine called the **digital computer** was made. This machine could do more than add, subtract, multiply, and divide. It could store information inside itself. But the first computers of this kind were huge and cost a great deal to make.

Soon great numbers of these computers began to be made. The new machines could work out problems in a much shorter time than before. They were also smaller and cost less to make. It became possible for many people to use one computer at the same time.

A digital computer can add, subtract, multiply, and divide. But it can also compare two numbers to find whether they are equal or whether one is larger than the other.

For example, the computer can add the numbers 2 and 7, then subtract the number 4 from their sum. The computer can then multiply the result, 5, by another number, 3—all in one continuous operation! In order to do this, the computer must first be told two things. It must be told all the numbers that appear in the problem. Then it must be given a **program** or a set of operations that are going to be done on the numbers.

left: A modern mini-computer

below: Microcircuits are smaller than a paper clip.

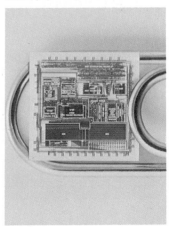

Unlike the early computers, which could store only one kind of program at a time, today's computers can store many programs. And the size of today's computers is very different from the early ones, too.

One thing that led to the changes in computers was the invention of tiny circuits only 1-2 mm wide. These tiny circuits can do the work of much larger systems. Some of the computers that have them are small enough to put in your pocket.

Computers have become a very important part of our lives. They are used to design cars, to translate languages, and to keep rockets on course. You can play games with a computer, just as if it were a person. Many tasks that computers can do in a few seconds would be impossible for one person to do in a year of work!

Beyond the Red and Violet

This girl is holding a sheet of opaque paper between the hot light bulb and the thermometer. Even though she cannot see any rays passing through the paper, the girl notices that the temperature of the thermometer is rising! How can you explain this? Could it be that the paper allows rays that cannot be seen to pass through?

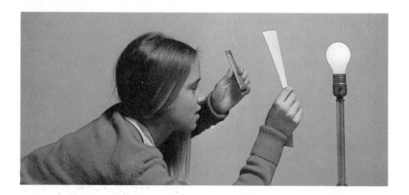

As people studied the spectrum of visible light— red, orange, yellow, green, blue, and violet—they wondered about this question too. They discovered that just beyond red light there are rays of energy that cannot be seen. These rays were called **infrared** [ihn-fruh-REHD]. You yourself give off infrared rays! In fact, everything on the earth gives off these rays.

The electromagnetic spectrum includes rays that can be seen and the shorter and longer rays that cannot be seen.

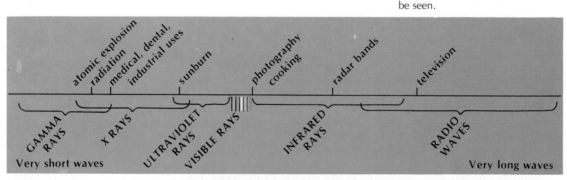

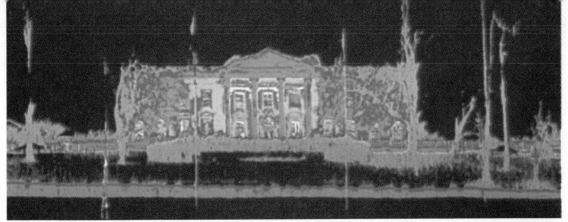

Infrared photo of the White House at night. Why are some areas darker in color?

How can infrared rays be used in communication? Even though the rays cannot be seen, you can take pictures with them. This picture was taken at night with a film that is able to pick up infrared rays.

Some animals, such as snakes, are even better than people at sensing infrared rays. That's how a snake discovers a mouse or a rabbit hiding in the bushes at night. It may be as far away as two or three meters!

Some insects can sense another kind of radiation that cannot be seen by people. Just beyond the deep-violet part of the spectrum of colors is the **ultraviolet** [uhl-truh-VY-uh-liht] band. Ultraviolet rays may change the surface of the skin of some people. Too many of these rays can burn the skin and the covering of the eyes.

The sun radiates ultraviolet light as well as visible light. Plants need the energy from ultraviolet light to make their food. For this reason, special "purple" lights that radiate in the ultraviolet band are used to grow plants indoors.

277

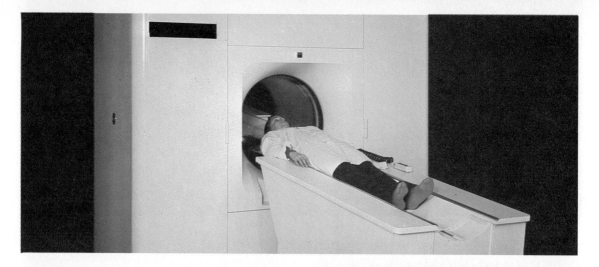

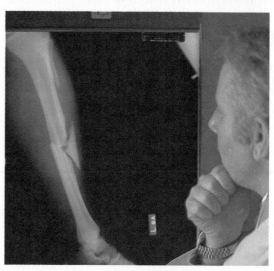

Have you ever had an **X ray** taken? An X ray is another kind of radiation that you cannot see. It is found just beyond the ultraviolet band. X rays have enough energy to pass straight through your skin and make a picture on a certain kind of film.

X rays may be used to search luggage in airports and to check for tooth cavities. X rays have even been used to examine the mummies of ancient Egypt. From X rays scientists can sometimes learn the cause of death of a person who lived over three thousand years ago.

top: The C-T Scanner, a kind of X-ray machine, uses a computer to form a three-dimensional view of the inside of the body; *above left*: X-ray photograph of a computer keyboard; *above right*: Doctor looking at an X-ray photograph of a broken leg

How can you tell exactly where a ship is when you are hundreds of kilometers away? A system called **radar** may be used. Radar uses very short radio waves to "see" something, such as a ship, and measure its distance from a certain point.

Radio waves used in radar bounce off solids instead of passing through them. When these waves hit a plane, a ship, or even a faraway planet, they bounce back like an echo. The "echoes" can then be gathered and displayed on a screen. In this way, people can tell the direction and distance of something. They can also tell the speed at which it is moving.

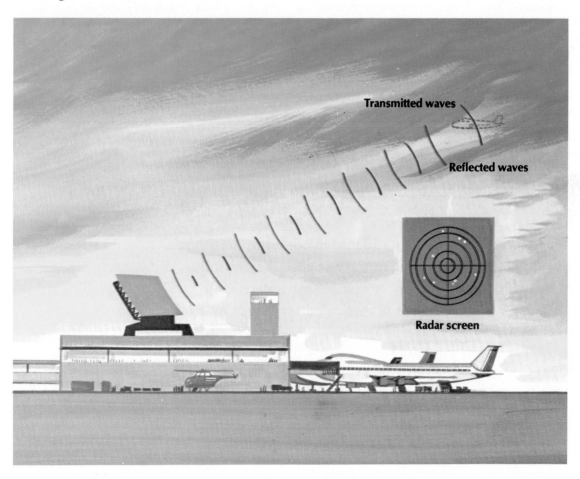

Transmitted waves

Reflected waves

Radar screen

The shortest radio waves, like those used in radar, may be 1 to 30 cm in length. Longer radio waves are used to carry television programs from the station to your home. Even longer radio waves must be used to carry radio broadcasts. These waves may be as long as half a kilometer each.

How do radio waves carry messages? A message that is read or sung over the air "rides" on top of the radio wave. This is the way it works.

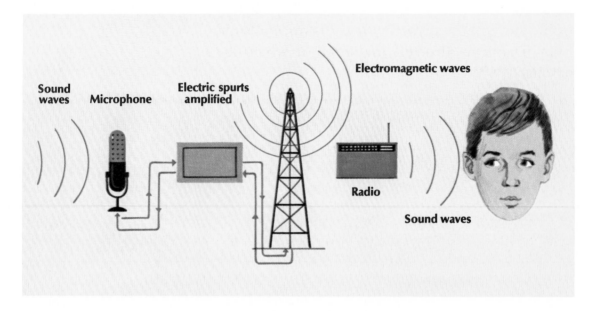

At the station, the announcer speaks into a microphone. The microphone changes the sound waves from the announcer's voice into an electrical current. The current is then made stronger and changed into a radio signal.

At the receiving end, you must select the radio station that you want to hear. Then you turn your knob to the correct frequency for this station. This makes it possible for the radio receiver to select only the signal of your station and to block out all the others.

Now your radio set blocks off the carrier signal in order to separate it from the signal caused by the announcer's voice. The amplifier in your set then makes the voice signal strong enough to operate a loudspeaker.

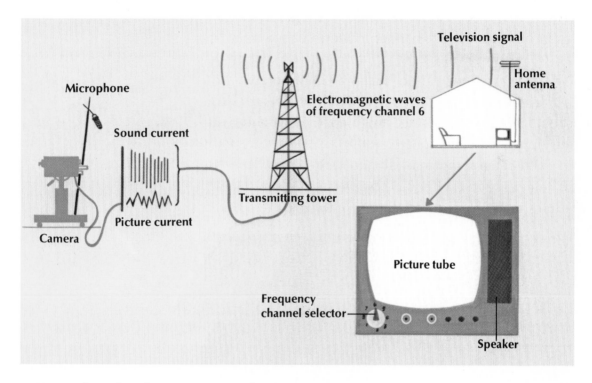

Even though television must have certain equipment to send and receive pictures, it is really a kind of radio. The same kind of equipment that is used for sending and receiving other kinds of radio waves is also used for TV. On waves shorter than those used for AM radio broadcasts, the TV station beams signals from the pictures and sounds. Your set changes these signals back into pictures and sounds.

A camera sends one picture after another—thirty pictures each second. This is so fast that your eyes "blend" them into one picture.

How does a camera "look" at something and change it into waves? And how does your TV set change the waves back into a picture? To find out, you will need a pencil, a marking pen, a metric ruler, and a sheet of paper. The paper should be ruled into squares that are 1 cm on a side. Ask a partner to work with you.

Your partner will be the camera and you will be the TV set. Have your partner make a simple drawing on his or her paper that has been ruled into squares. You should not be able to see this paper. Beginning with the upper left-hand square, ask your partner to point to each square and read all the way across. As your partner points to each square, he or she must say "blank" if the square is white and "mark" if the square is black.

As your partner says "blank" or "mark," you will follow with your marking pen on your paper of blank squares. When your partner says "blank," you do not mark the paper. When your partner says "mark," you color in that square with your pen. When you get down to the last square on the bottom line, you should have the same picture that the "camera," your partner, is seeing.

How does a camera make the pictures that it sends out so quickly? As a camera "looks" at something, a lens inside the camera forms a tiny picture of what it "sees." This happens when light that is gathered on the lens of the camera "draws" a picture in electrons, one line at a time.

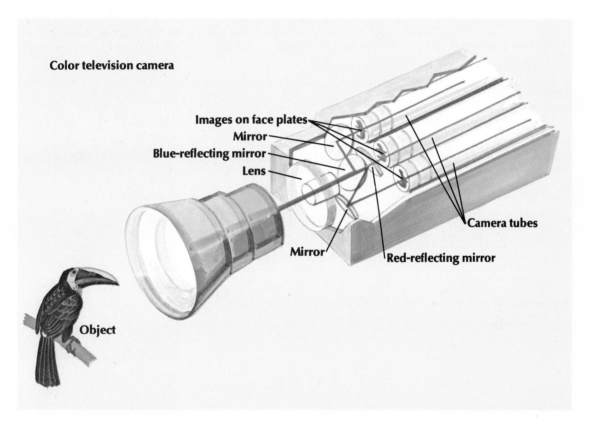

Color television camera

Images on face plates
Mirror
Blue-reflecting mirror
Lens
Camera tubes
Mirror
Red-reflecting mirror
Object

The signals from the camera and the microphone are sent to a powerful television transmitter. Here one signal is made from the separate picture and sound signals. In most cases, this signal is carried by wire to an antenna where it is broadcast.

Television has become one of the most important parts of our communication. Not only can we hear the news while it is news. We can also see the news as it happens.

What Did You Learn?

- Through the ages people have communicated by signaling, speaking, and writing.
- With the printing press, it became possible to communicate written ideas to many people.
- In the transmitter of a telephone, sound energy causes electric current to move from the telephone company. In the receiver, this current is changed back to sound energy.
- In a phonograph, any movements in the record groove create signals that are strengthened in the amplifier and changed to sound in the loudspeaker.
- When a recording is made, a tape coated with grains of a metal oxide is pulled in front of an electromagnet where changes take place in the way the grains are arranged. The rearranged grains cause different kinds of sound when the tape is played.
- When a computer is given a set of numbers and a program, it can carry out several different operations without stopping.
- Beyond the visible spectrum of colors are invisible rays or waves which are useful in today's communications.
- Radar uses short radio waves to find things that are far away and to measure their distance.
- Sound waves can produce an electric current, which is made stronger and changed into a radio signal.
- Television changes light and sound energy into waves, which are then changed to pictures and sound on your set.

Biography

Dr. An Wang (1920–   )

Radios, television, telephones, recordings, and books are some ways people communicate with each other. People also use computers to communicate. There are hundreds of different kinds of computers that store and communicate information. Perhaps you have used a computer to help you with your homework. Maybe you have even played a game on one.

Dr. An Wang is well known for his work with computers. In the early 1950's, he invented what is often called the magnetic memory core. The core memory has remained a basic part of modern computers since that time. It is used for storing information. You can have this information as quickly as the time it takes a finger to touch a button.

Later, he invented a desk-top computer. Dr. Wang set up his own laboratories in 1951 to study and make computers. Each year his company produces new ideas in computers. These machines are being used more and more in business, science, and industry.

Dr. Wang was born in Shangai, China, and went to college there. He completed his studies at Harvard University in applied physics. He has received awards for the work he has done with computers.

TO THINK ABOUT AND DO

WORD FUN

On a piece of paper, copy the numbered spaces and the letters. Then use the clues to complete the spaces with the correct term. Did you form a new term in the box?

1. __ __ __ __ __ __ __ |r|
2.   __ __ | | __ __ m __ __ __ __ __
3. i __ __ __ __ __ __ | |
4.   __ __ t __ | | __ __ __ __ __ __
5. | | __ c __ __ __ __ __ __

Clues

1. With a set of numbers and a program, it can carry out several different operations without stopping.
2. Here sound energy is changed into electrical signals.
3. Anything that is warm enough gives off these invisible rays.
4. These rays can give you a tan.
5. This is the place where current is changed back to sound energy.

WHAT DO YOU REMEMBER?

Copy and complete each of the following sentences on a piece of paper.

1. Through the ages people have _____ by using body motions, signaling, speaking, and writing.
2. Electrical signals are strengthened in the_____ of a phonograph.
3. When a recording is made, a tape coated with grains of metal _____ is pulled in front of an electro-magnet.

4. Radar uses short _____ waves to find things that are far away.

5. The waves from light and sound energy are changed to pictures and sound by a _____ .

SOMETHING TO THINK ABOUT

1. Some highways have signs that read, "Patrolled by Radar." What does this mean and how does the radar work?

2. Find out how each of these people helped to improve communication: Alexander Graham Bell, Gaglielmo Marconi, and Thomas Edison.

ACTIVITY

The Morse Code is another way to communicate. It is a system of dots and dashes that are tapped out on a telegraph set. You can tap out the Morse Code with your fingers, or you can send the code by shining a flashlight.

Look at the Morse Code. To make a dot, tap your finger or flash the light briefly. Use a longer tap or flash to make a dash.

Now write a brief message. Then send it to someone in your class by changing it to dots and dashes.

A •■	H ••••	O •■	V •••■	1 •■ ■■•	8 ■••••
B ■•••	I ••	P ••••	W •■■	2 ••■••	9 ■••■
C •• •	J ■•■•	Q ••■•	X •■••	3 •••■•	0 ■
D ■••	K ■•■	R • ••	Y •• ••	4 ••••■	, •■■•■
E •	L ■	S •••	Z ••••	5 ■■■	. ••■■■••
F •■•	M ■■	T ■	& • •••	6 ••••••	; ••• ••
G ■■•	N ■•	U ••■	$ ••• •■••	7 ■■•••	? ■•••■•

Unit IV

Solar Energy and the Earth

Climates
of the World

11

It's windy, and the temperature of the air is 40°C below zero. Tomorrow it may be even colder. What month could it be, here at the South Pole? Is it December or January or February? No, it's June! What is June weather like where you live? How is it different from June at the South Pole?

In Antarctica the temperature is almost never warm enough to melt snow and ice. Of course, the temperature does change during the year. It changes from cold to very, very cold and then back again. Weather in Antarctica may change from day to day. But most of the time Antarctica is one of the coldest places on the earth.

There are some places where it is very warm most of the time. Why are some places warmer than others? In each place on the earth, we can expect about the same kinds of weather from year to year. Why is this so? To find out, we need to learn more about the earth.

Sunlight and Temperature

The **climate** [KLY-miht] of any one place is its weather over many years. Antarctica has a very cold climate. There, the weather is very cold most of the time, year after year. What is the difference between weather and climate? Here is a saying that may help you. "Weather changes from day to day. The climate we have is here to stay."

On one day it is possible for places with different climates to have the same weather. On a warm summer day, Boston and Miami may have the same weather. However, is it likely that both places would have the same weather in January? Since they have different climates, you can expect that their weather over a year would be different.

upper and lower left: Boston and Miami in June
upper and lower right: Boston and Miami in January

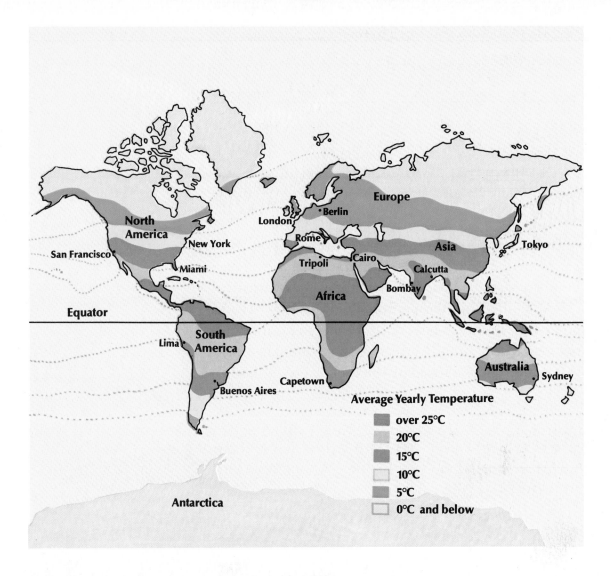

Average Yearly Temperature

- over 25°C
- 20°C
- 15°C
- 10°C
- 5°C
- 0°C and below

What are the temperatures like in different parts of the world each year? Are certain temperatures most often found in certain parts of the world? On the map, find the parts of the world that are most often the hottest. What places are most often the coldest?

Find the **equator** [ih-KWAY-tuhr] on the map. How do temperatures change as you go farther away from the equator?

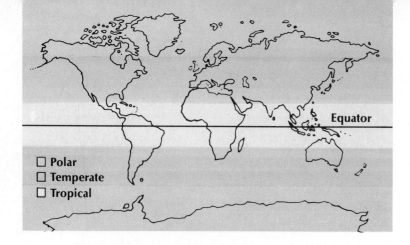

- ☐ Polar
- ☐ Temperate
- ☐ Tropical

Hot, tropical zones are found near the equator. Cold, polar zones are found near the North and South Poles. In between them are the temperate zones

This map shows three temperature **zones** or areas based on distance from the equator. They form large bands across the earth. These bands are **tropical** [TRAHP-uh-kuhl], **temperate** [TEHM-puhr-iht] and **polar** [POH-luhr] zones. Within each zone, the temperatures are mainly alike. Each zone also contains differences caused by the amount of moisture.

The climate of the place depends on both the temperature and the amount of rain or snow that falls.

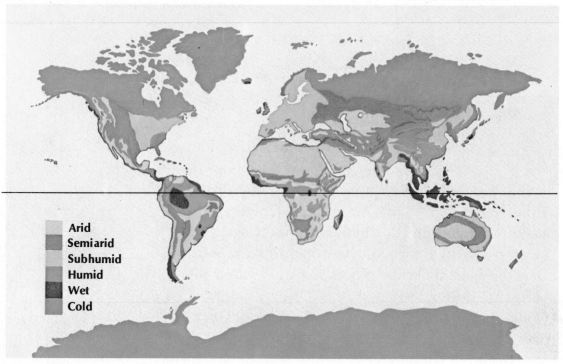

- Arid
- Semiarid
- Subhumid
- Humid
- Wet
- Cold

Most **precipitation** [prih-sihp-uh-TAY-shuhn] falls as rain or snow. The amount of precipitation can vary within each temperature zone. There are six precipitation zones at different places on the earth. These zones are shown on the map below on page 294. The temperature and the precipitation together determine the climate of a certain place. The climate in turn determines what kinds of plants can grow there.

In **wet** climates, lots of rain falls all year around. Notice that most wet climates are found fairly near the equator. In which of the three main climates would you be likely to find a wet climate? With so much rain, forests can grow so thick that little sunlight ever reaches the ground.

Humid [HYOO-mihd] climates have somewhat less precipitation than wet climates and there are not quite so many rainy days each year. Plants that need a lot of water grow well here. Many lakes, rivers, and wetlands can be found.

above: Tropical rain forest, with a wet climate;

left: Florida Everglades, with a humid climate

below: New England forest, with a subhumid climate

Subhumid [suhb-HYOO-mihd] climates have plenty of rainfall during some months and are fairly dry during other months of the year. You could say that they have a medium amount of rainfall. Subhumid areas include both forests and tall grass.

Central California, with a semiarid climate

Semiarid [SEHM-ee-ar-ihd] climates have dry weather most of the year. Grasses that grow here are fairly short. A few trees may be found along streams. The short grasses are used by herds of animals for food.

Arid [AR-ihd] climates or deserts are very dry most of the time. A few rainstorms may come at certain times of the year. Plants that grow there can live without water for long periods of time.

Arizona desert, with an arid climate

Cold climates are found in polar areas or in high mountains. In some places the temperature never rises enough for snow to melt. The snow and ice build up year after year. In some other places the ice and snow melt for a short time during the summer. Many tiny plants grow and bloom quickly before snow comes again.

left: Caribou can live on tiny plants that grow in cold climates. *right*: Polar bears can live in cold climates where the snow never melts.

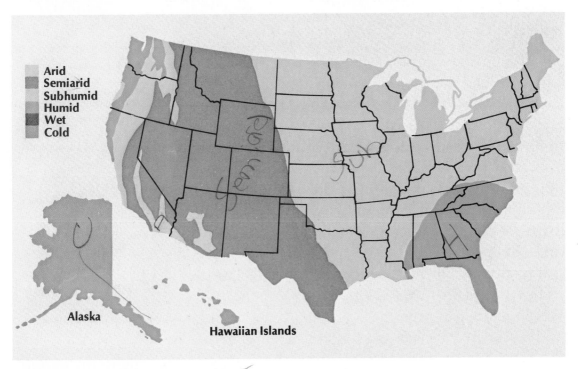

Arid
Semiarid
Subhumid
Humid
Wet
Cold

Alaska

Hawaiian Islands

In most temperate areas there are four seasons. There is a warm summer and a cold winter. Spring and fall have generally cool weather. Most of the United States is in the temperate zone. How many precipitation zones can you find on the map of the United States? What zone do you live in? Remember that one zone does not stop exactly where the next begins. Going from one zone to the next, the change happens slowly.

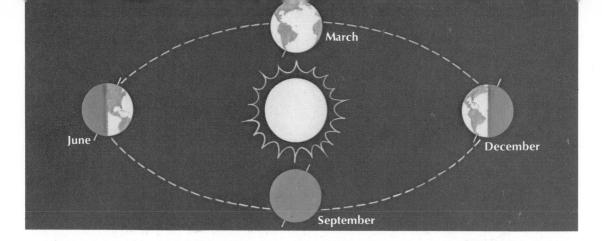

What causes the seasons? Why are seasons different around the world? You know that the earth moves around the sun. The earth takes about $365\frac{1}{4}$ days—a year—to make one trip around the sun. Each day the earth turns once on its axis. (You can think of the axis as a line going through the earth from one pole to the other.) The axis is always tipped in the same direction as the earth moves in its orbit. Because of the tipped axis, places on the earth get different amounts of sunlight at different times of the year.

It is summer north of the equator when the north end of the earth's axis is tipped toward the sun. We get more heat from the sun than at other times of the year. We also get more hours of sunlight. At the same time it is winter south of the equator. Look at the pictures of sunlight on the earth. Can you see why there are some days in the summer when the sun never sets?

When the North Pole is tipped away from the sun, it is winter north of the equator. South of the equator, what season is it? Where we live the sun stays low in the sky. We get fewer hours of sunlight and less warmth from the sun. On the first day of winter, does the sun ever rise at the North Pole?

Where do direct rays from the sun reach the earth in June? Where do they reach the earth in December?

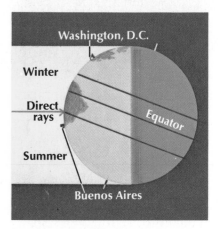

Sunlight and Climates

When it is summer north of the equator, it can be quite hot in the temperate zones. It can be even hotter in the tropics. But it is still quite cold at the North Pole. What is the most important reason for these different temperatures? Each day different parts of the earth get different amounts of energy from the sun.

The number of hours of sunlight in a day are different in different places on the earth. On the first day of summer, we have our longest day. How long is the first day of summer near the North Pole?

At the North Pole on the first day of summer, why is there no sunset?

You can find out why different places on the earth get different amounts of energy from the sun. You will need a globe, a bright lamp, and a partner to work with you. Also get three white cards, a cardboard tube, and some tape.

Tape the three cards on different parts of the globe. Place one card near the North Pole and one on the equator. Tape the third card in between them.

Make the room dark. Place the lamp so that it shines on the whole globe. Ask your partner which card is the most brightly lit.

Next, bring the globe to a sunny window. Hold the cardboard tube as shown. The tube's shadow should be a thin circle around a beam of light. On the card, have your partner draw a line around the beam.

Now hold the tube in front of the middle card. Aim the tube as you did before and have your partner draw a line around the beam. Do the same thing with the card near the North Pole.

Which card was most brightly lit? Were the cards getting the same amount of light each time? On which card was the light spread over a larger part of the card?

Why do different places on the earth get different amounts of the sun's energy? Not all places on the earth are equally lit by the sun. Instead of thinking about all of the sun's light, let's just think about three beams of light. All three beams are the same size and have the same amount of energy.

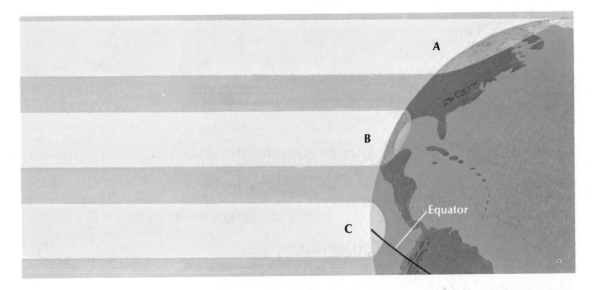

Look at what happens when the beams of light reach the surface of the earth. Beam C shines on a small area at the equator. Beam B spreads over an area that is a little larger. Beam A spreads over an area that is largest of all. Each area gets the same amount of light. But when the light is spread over a larger area, any one place in it gets less light. A piece of land at the Poles gets less sunlight than a piece of land of the same size anywhere else. So there is less brightness at the Poles, even though the sun gives off the same light.

There is a way to compare how beams of light reach different places on the earth. Notice that beams A, B, and C each reach the earth at a different slant or angle.

Let's look at the angles at which sunlight is received at different places on the earth. You will need a globe, some tape, and a metric ruler. Also get two pieces of stiff wire or pipe cleaners that are 10 cm long.

Look back at the picture of the three beams of light. Lay the wire along beam B. Bend 2 cm at the end of the wire so that it fits against the surface of the earth. The bent wire will look something like this. It shows the angle at which sunlight reaches the United States.

Now tape the other wire next to the North Pole. Bend it to fit along the earth's surface. This shows the angle of sunlight at the North Pole.

Each wire is bent to a different angle. The one from the North Pole has a small angle. What does this show you about the slant of the sun's rays in these two places?

Now you are ready to see how the angle of sunlight makes a difference in the heating of the earth. You will need two pieces of thick cardboard, two thermometers, and two pieces of black paper. You will also need the two bent wires from the last activity and some tape.

Place a thermometer on each piece of cardboard. Cover them with black paper. Tape the short end of the wire to each paper. Place each piece of cardboard so that its wire points toward the sun.

The first thermometer receives sunlight at a low angle, as the North Pole does. The second thermometer receives sunlight at the same angle that land in the center of the United States receives it.

Read the temperature of both thermometers every minute for 15 minutes. Record the temperatures on a chart. What did you find out about the angle of the sunlight and the heating of the earth?

The different angles at which sunlight is received cause differences in brightness and in temperature over the earth. When the sun is high in the sky, the sun's rays are most direct. There is a lot of energy in a small area. When the sun is low in the sky, the sun's light is received at a low angle. The same amount of energy is spread over a larger area.

There are several reasons why the angle of sunlight changes. The angle of sunlight changes as you go north or south on the earth. Places at the equator receive sunlight that is more direct than at the poles. The warmest climates are near the equator. As you move farther from the equator, climates get colder.

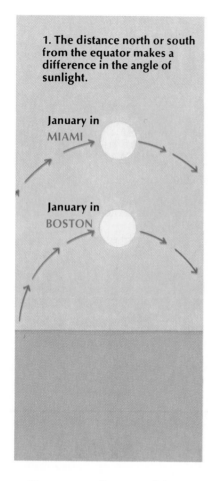

1. The distance north or south from the equator makes a difference in the angle of sunlight.

January in MIAMI

January in BOSTON

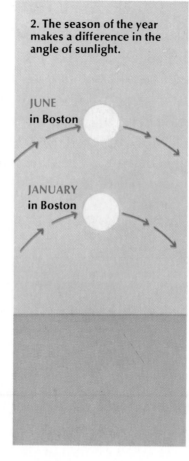

2. The season of the year makes a difference in the angle of sunlight.

JUNE in Boston

JANUARY in Boston

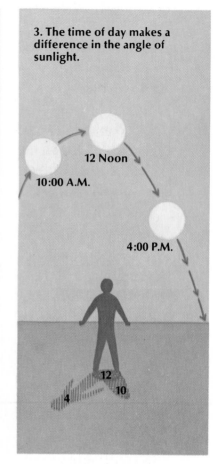

3. The time of day makes a difference in the angle of sunlight.

12 Noon

10:00 A.M.

4:00 P.M.

12

10

4

Because the earth's axis is tipped, the angle of sunlight changes during the seasons. The angle of sunlight is higher in the summer than in the winter.

You may have noticed that the angle of sunlight even changes during the day. You can feel what a difference the angle of sunlight can make in the temperature. The sun is high in the sky at noon. The sun's light is most direct. The sunlight feels warmest at this time of day. The sun is low in the sky at sunrise and sunset. The sun's light is received at a low angle. The sunlight you feel is not nearly as warm as it is at noon.

More Reasons Why Climates Are Different

It is July near the equator and the temperature is hot. Today it is 38°C! But there is snow high on the nearby mountains. Snow forms only in below-freezing temperatures. Why is the temperature so different between the top of the mountain and the plain below? The mountains get about the same amount of sunlight as the plain. The angle of the sun's rays is also about the same.

Mt. Kilimanjaro in Kenya is located almost on the equator. Why is there snow on the top of the mountain?

Sunlight heats the air very little. Most of the sunlight is received at the earth's surface instead. The warmed earth heats the air that is close to it. The higher you go from the earth's surface, the cooler the air is. High mountains are surrounded by very cold air. Also as you go higher, the air pressure is less. When warm air rises, it expands and becomes cooler.

305

Many people choose to live near large lakes or the ocean because of the pleasant temperatures. On warm summer days the land heats up quickly, but the water does not. Cool breezes from the water blow across the warm land. When winter comes, the land cools off quickly, but the water cools more slowly. Now the air over the water is warmer than the air over the land. The warm air over the water mixes with the cold air over the land. This helps to keep temperatures warmer than they might be.

Let's look at a map to see the difference that water can make in the climate. Find the red circle and the green circle on the map. In which place would you expect to find a more even climate? Find the orange and yellow circles. Which do you think has colder winters? Find the blue and green circles. Which do you think has warmer summers? Compare the climates of other places on the map in the same way.

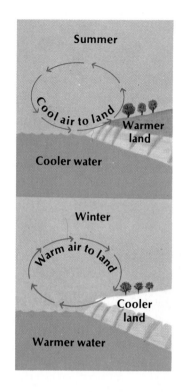

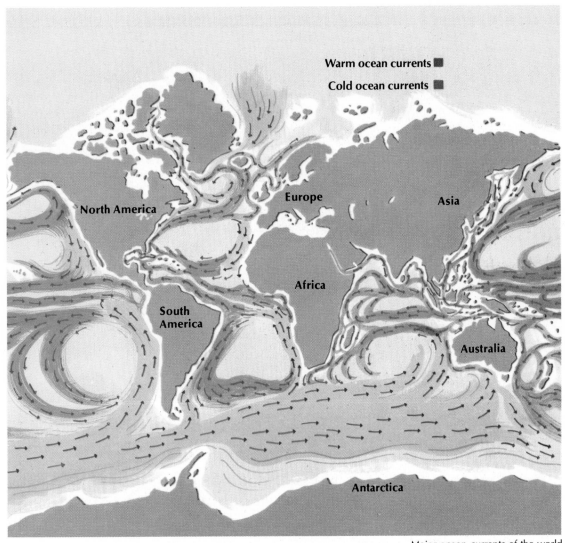

North America

Europe

Asia

Africa

South
America

Australia

Antarctica

Major ocean currents of the world

Ocean currents can also make the climate of an area warmer or colder. Warm ocean currents flow from places near the equator. Cold currents flow from near the poles. Winds blowing over these currents can change the climate of land nearby. How would a cold ocean current change the climate of a warm place in the summer? How would a warm ocean current change the climate of a place in winter?

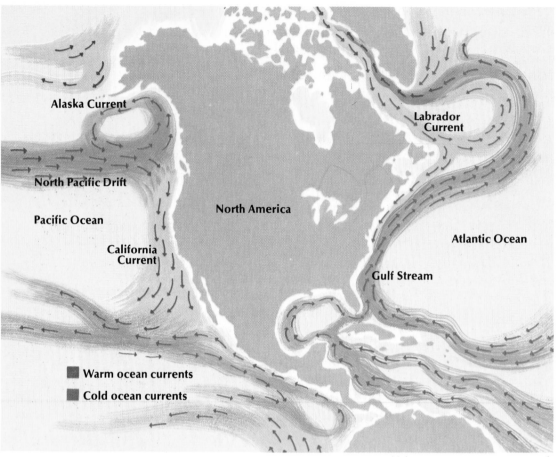

Major ocean currents near North America

A cold ocean current flows just off the coast of San Francisco, California. There, the winds blow over the ocean toward San Francisco. Living near a cold current helps the people to stay cool during the summer months. The average July temperature in San Francisco is only 16°C!

St. Louis, Missouri, is just about as far from the equator as San Francisco is. Winds blow across the country from west to east. But in St. Louis, they do not blow across a cold ocean current. Instead, they blow across the warm land. The average July temperature in St. Louis is a much warmer 28°C.

Warm ocean currents can also make a difference in the climate. The Gulf Stream is a warm ocean current that begins near the equator. It flows to the north along the east coast of the United States. It keeps the land and waters along the coast warmer in winter.

Other things also can change the climate. You know that snow is white. Did you know that a light or dark surface can make a difference in the climate? Some places on Earth are covered with snow and ice for most or all of the year.

Camp near Angmagssalik, Greenland

Does white snow change climates? Would the climate be different if the snow were black? To find out, you will need a sheet of black paper, a sheet of white paper, and two thermometers. Put both sheets in the sunlight. Place a thermometer under each sheet of paper.

Look at the thermometers every minute for five minutes. Keep a record of the temperatures. Which paper becomes warmer? Which paper is more like snow?

Where do you think the air is warmer, above snow-covered places or above dark soil? White snow reflects a lot of the sun's rays. Darker areas of the earth's surface do not reflect nearly as much of the sun's energy. The more rays that are reflected, the fewer rays there are to warm the land. How do large, snow-covered places make a difference in the climate?

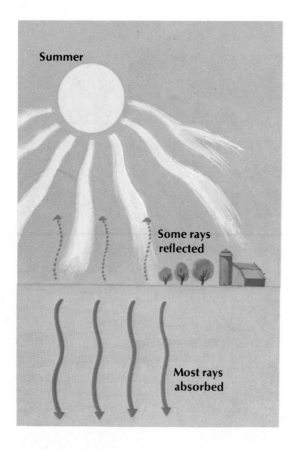

Temperature is very important in shaping our climate. But there is something else that also shapes climate and is different from place to place. Deserts have little of it and some places near oceans have a lot of it. What do you think it could be?

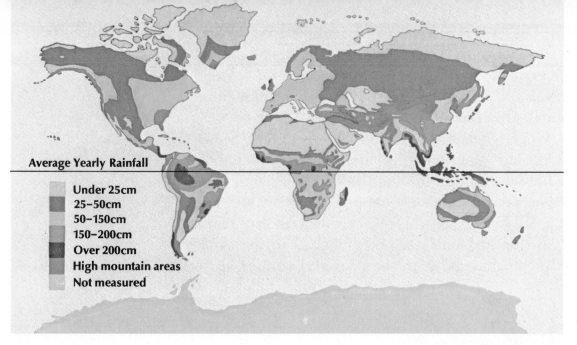

Average Yearly Rainfall

- Under 25cm
- 25–50cm
- 50–150cm
- 150–200cm
- Over 200cm
- High mountain areas
- Not measured

Precipitation

As you know, water also affects the climate. Precipitation falls from the sky as rain, snow, sleet, or hail. Look at the map and its color key. Each color on this map shows how much precipitation falls on that part of the earth. Which places get the most precipitation? Which get the least? Some places get only a few centimeters in a year, while others get over 200 centimeters. Let's find out what causes this great difference.

The location of a place on the earth makes a difference in the amount of precipitation it receives each year. Places where warm, moist air often rises may have a rainy climate. This is true in many places near the equator. There, lots of water evaporates from the warm oceans. Away from the equator there are many places that have cool, dry air. These areas have much less rain. Why would you expect rain to fall where warm, moist air rises?

This rain forest is in Nepal. Here, warm and moist ocean air meets the high Himalaya Mountains. What happens when this air meets the mountains?

Temperature differences over land and ocean cause air to move. Warm air may move into colder areas and make them warmer. Cold air may move into warmer areas and cool them.

When winds meet mountains, precipitation may take place. How does this happen? Hold your hands with one slanting up like the side of a mountain. Place your other hand on top. Blow against the slanted hand. Can you feel the warm, moist breath move up and touch the other hand? In the same way, air may move up the sides of mountains.

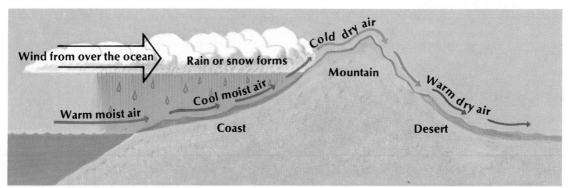

In some places warm, moist winds blow from the ocean toward the mountains. Since the air cannot go through the mountains, it is pushed up. As the air moves higher, it becomes cooler. Clouds begin to form as the water condenses. If there is enough moisture in the air, precipitation will fall on the mountains.

Some desert climates are also caused by mountains. These deserts are found on the opposite side of mountain ranges from the moist winds. Most of the moisture from the winds has already condensed on the ocean side of the mountains. Very dry air flows down the other side. No rain, of course, falls from dry air, and a desert climate is formed.

above: Plenty of rain or snow falls on the ocean side of high mountains, and deserts are formed on the other side. This climate pattern can be found throughout the world.

below: Death Valley, California. On which side of the sierra Nevada Mountains would you expect to find this desert?

The Earth's Climate: Past and Future

What will climates be like in the future? In order to tell what may happen, scientists are studying past climates. All over the earth, things have been found that tell us about climates long ago.

Ocean water changes with climate. If the climate becomes colder, ocean water also becomes colder. Some animals make shells one way in cold water and another way in warm water. When these animals died long ago, their shells sank down onto the ocean floor. Shells in the ocean floor give us a record of climates over 100 million years ago.

We can also learn about past climates from large areas of ice called **glaciers** [GLAY-shuhrz]. The amount of oxygen trapped in the ice is different in different parts of the glacier. The amount depends on the temperature of the air when the glacier formed. Pieces of ice have shown what the climate was in some places for the past 100,000 years.

Some of the best information about past climates comes from trees. Each tree ring shows one year's growth. How much a tree grows each year depends on the climate. By studying how wide the tree rings are, scientists can learn about the climate of a place during the time the trees grew. They can also find out about how old the wood is. Using wood from trees, they have been able to piece together the world's climate to about 4000 years ago. What kinds of climates would cause trees to grow faster or more slowly?

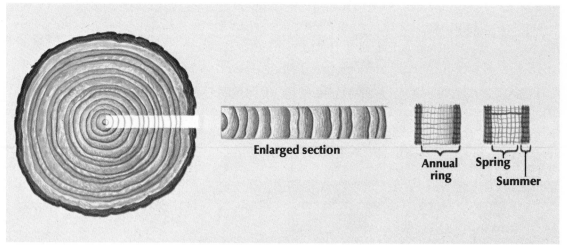

Enlarged section

Annual ring   **Spring**   **Summer**

What is the difference between tree growth in the spring and in the summer?

From what they have learned, scientists think that the earth's climate has changed a great deal. They think the average world temperature at one time millions of years ago was about 23°C. Because of this warm climate, the poles were free of ice! But at other times, climates were much colder than today. Within the last one million years, there were four different ice ages. Ice ages were times when large parts of the world were covered with ice. Ice sheets may have once covered the land where you live.

What is happening right now that may change the earth's climates in the future? For one thing, scientists know that the amount of carbon dioxide in the atmosphere has gone up. This added carbon dioxide comes from the burning of fuels such as oil and coal. Some scientists believe that the larger amount of carbon dioxide will make our climate warmer. Others do not agree. They believe that carbon dioxide will stop some of the sun's energy from reaching the earth's surface in the first place. This would make the atmosphere cooler. If just a little less energy from the sun reaches the earth, another ice age could begin!

The climates of the earth have always changed and will change in the future. What will the climates be like in 50, 100, and 1000 years? Scientists have different ideas of what they think will happen. The answer will come through discovering what causes changes in climates.

above: Los Angeles, California. What do you think the smog does to living things?

left: Here is a picture of the earth from space. How would your home be different if the earth's climate became warmer? If it became colder?

What Did You Learn?

- The climate of any one place is its weather over many years.
- There are three main kinds of temperature zones: tropical, temperate, and polar.
- The temperature and precipitation together determine the climate of a certain place.
- Because of the earth's tipped axis, places on the earth get different amounts of sunlight during the year. This causes the different seasons.
- The different angles at which sunlight is received cause differences in temperature over the earth.
- The higher a place is, the colder its climate is likely to be.
- Temperatures of land that is close to a body of water change less than they would if the water were not there.
- Warm and cold ocean currents can change the climate.
- The lightness or darkness of the earth's surface makes a difference in climate.
- Rainfall, winds, and mountains also make a difference in the climate.
- Scientists have found that the earth's climates have changed many times in the past. They do not agree on how climates may change in the future.

Career

Climatologists

Is winter where you live mostly cold and snowy each year? Maybe you live where winters are mild and wet or hot and humid. Climate in your area is important to people as well as plant and animal life.

Climatologists [kly-muh-TAHL-uh-jihsts] are people who study an area's weather over many years. They look at a number of things that tell about climate. They study the angle and the amount of sunlight a certain place may receive over time. They also study the temperature, precipitation, and wind from one season to another, from one year to the next. They study past weather records. They study the latitude, altitude, and the nearness to bodies of water and land masses. Ocean currents are also part of their study. Climatologists put all their findings together. Then they report and predict what the climate for different areas in the world will be.

Climatologists help people decide the kind of home or factory to build in a particular area of the country. They help people decide if a heating or cooling system is needed. People use information from their reports to decide the kinds and amounts of crops to be planted. Climatologists also study how climates have changed in the past and how they may change in the future.

TO THINK ABOUT AND DO

What are the differences between these climates? Copy the pairs of climates on a piece of paper. Write the differences.

1. between tropical and temperate climates.
2. between polar and temperate climates.
3. between wet and humid climates.
4. between arid and semiarid climates.
5. between subhumid and semiarid climates.

Write these sentences on a piece of paper. Write **T** beside the sentences that are true and **F** beside those that are false. Rewrite any sentence that is false to make it true.

1. The climate of any one place is its weather over a day.
2. Temperature and rainfall make a difference in climate.
3. There are four seasons in both temperate and tropical climates.
4. Because of the tipped axis, places on the earth get different amounts of sunlight at different times of the year.
5. Large bodies of water can change climates.
6. The top of a mountain is usually cooler than the bottom of the mountain.
7. Lighter or darker areas on the ground can make a difference in the climate.
8. The climate of a place has changed over time.

1. When it is summer in North America, what season is it in Australia? Why?
2. Find where your home town or city is on a map. What is the climate where you live? How far would you have to travel to get to a different climate?
3. People make different kinds of clothing and buildings that help them live comfortably in different climates. Find out about clothing and buildings in tropical, temperate, and polar climates.

ACTIVITY

Here is another way to find out whether a lighter or darker area makes a difference in the climate. You will need some charcoal and two dishes of snow. In place of the snow, you can use finely crushed ice cubes.

Break up the charcoal into a fine powder. Sprinkle it evenly over the ice or snow in one dish. Leave the other dish of snow as it is. Place both dishes in bright sunlight or under a heat lamp. Write down the starting time. How long does it take for the snow or ice in each dish to melt completely? Did the black powder make a difference in the melting time?

Energy for Living Things

12

Living things grow, react to things around them, and make more of their own kind. All of these activities take a lot of energy. Where does all this energy come from? The energy that is needed comes from the sun.

And yet only a certain group of living things, the green plants, can use the sun's energy directly. Only green plants can trap and change light energy. They change it into a form that animals and plants that aren't green can use. What would happen to these living things if there were no green plants?

How Do Green Plants Make Food?

Green plants use light to make food out of things that are not food. Out of water from the soil, and out of carbon dioxide from the air, plants can make food. The plants use some of the food they make for their own life activities. When we eat the plants, we use some of the food that the plants have made.

Think of all the different kinds of food we get from green plants. There are sweet plums and sour cherries, yellow corn and purple cabbages. And think of tiny wheat grains and huge pumpkins, juicy tomatoes and hard coconuts. The process of food-making in green plants is called **photosynthesis** [foh-toh-SIHN-thuh-sihs]. Photosynthesis connects things in the world that are living with things that aren't living. Carbon dioxide, water, and the sun's energy are not living. Minerals from the soil that are needed to start photosynthesis are not living as well. Green plants, from the living world, are able to use these materials to make food.

Melastome

Sumac

Maple

American holly

Scrub oak

The green leaf is one of the most important structures for photosynthesis. Green plants that have just one cell and the lower green plants that don't have true leaves carry on photosynthesis, too. In fact, the green plants that have just one cell carry on more photosynthesis than all other plants together! However, here we will look at the leaves of flowering plants only.

Leaves come in many sizes and shapes. Some leaves may be almost one meter in length while others may be smaller than a millimeter. Leaves have different shapes and thicknesses also. Some leaves are thick and round. Others may be thin and shaped like a heart. The edges of leaves do not all look alike, either. Many leaves have smooth edges while others have toothlike edges. We use these differences in leaves to help us tell one flowering plant from another.

The leaves of many flowering plants have two major parts. One is the stalk where the leaf is fastened to the stem of the plant. The other part is the blade of the leaf. It is the thin, flat part of the leaf. The blade often has a broad surface, so most of its cells are able to receive light and air. Thin veins are found in the blade. Each vein is made of special cells. Water and food move through these special cells.

ACTIVITY

Get a few different kinds of leaves and look at them. How are the leaves alike? How are they different? Are they the same size and shape? Which leaf is the longest? The shortest? Find the veins. How are they arranged in each leaf? Make drawings of the leaves and write the names of the different parts on your drawings.

This picture shows how the inside structure of a leaf may look under a microscope. A layer of cells is found on both the top and the bottom of the leaf. This layer makes the leaf strong. It often makes a wax on the outside that keeps water from leaving the leaf too quickly.

The food-making cells are between the upper and lower layers. Notice the small green bits inside the cells. These bits have green chlorophyll inside. It is chlorophyll that traps light energy for photosynthesis.

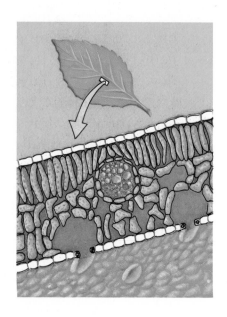

There are many **air spaces** between the food-making cells. The carbon dioxide in air is needed for making food. The air spaces in the leaf must be connected with the outside air so that carbon dioxide can enter. The **pores** in the lower surface of the leaf shown in the picture allow air to enter. A single leaf has thousands of them.

Now try to imagine food-making in the leaf. Sunlight enters the cells and some of its energy is used by the chlorophyll. Water (H_2O) is moved from the roots to the chlorophyll in the leaves. The chlorophyll, with the help of light energy, causes water molecules to break apart into separate hydrogen and oxygen atoms. The hydrogen atoms are kept in the leaf. Most of the oxygen passes into the air spaces and out through the pores of the leaf.

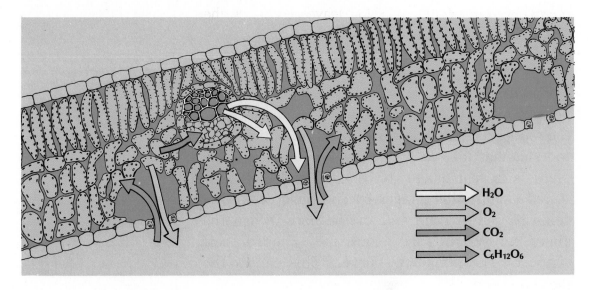

$\Rightarrow$ H_2O
$\Rightarrow$ O_2
$\Rightarrow$ CO_2
$\Rightarrow$ $C_6H_{12}O_6$

The hydrogen meets carbon dioxide (CO_2), that enters through the pores, and a chemical change takes place. A kind of sugar is formed. The formula for this sugar is $C_6H_{12}O_6$. What elements are in the sugar? Where did each one come from?

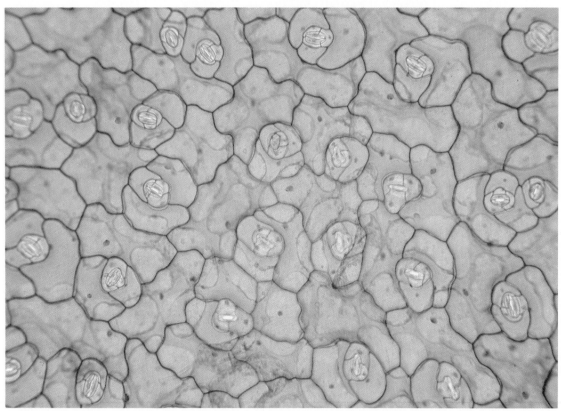

Magnified section of the underside of a leaf, showing pores and guard cells

Water vapor also passes out through the leaf pores. This loss of water is not harmful as long as the roots get enough new water. But sometimes the roots cannot take in water fast enough. Then the plant is in real danger of dying. The leaf is protected against this danger by its **guard cells.** One cell is found at each side of the pore. When the guard cells begin to dry out, they change their shape by becoming less curved. This causes the pores to close so that water doesn't escape. When the guard cells become wet again, they become curved once more. This causes the pores to open so that water can again escape. Guard cells get their name because they guard against too much water loss.

If you have a microscope in your classroom, you can look at the inside parts of a leaf. You will need some outside leaves of a head of lettuce, tweezers, and water. You also will need a glass slide, a cover glass, and a microscope.

In a head of lettuce, the side of the lettuce leaf that faces outside is the underside of the leaf. Gently break the leaf toward the outside. You will find that the thin outside layer of the leaf hangs from the broken edge. It looks like very thin paper. With tweezers, pull off a very small piece of this layer. Place it in the center of the glass slide. Put a drop of water on it and cover it with the cover glass.

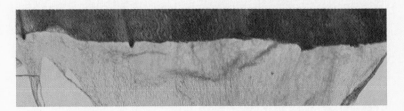

Look at the leaf piece under the microscope. Find the guard cells and describe their shapes. Are the pores open or closed? How can you tell? Make a drawing of what you see.

Somewhere in your leaf piece you may find a branch vein. What does it do? Now look at the food-making cells. The green bits that have chlorophyll inside may be moving inside the cells. Since they are part of the living matter inside the cells, the green bits move along with it. Why are the food-making cells packed closer together in the upper part of the leaf than in the lower part? Think about the parts that you find only on the lower surface of the leaf.

How Do Living Things Get the Energy Stored in Food?

During photosynthesis green plants make sugar and give off oxygen. Plants, like all living things, must use some of the food stored in their cells. They use energy in food to grow and to react to different things around them. Plants also use energy to make more of their own kind. But plants can't use the energy while it is stored in food. The food in the plant cells must join with oxygen before the energy can be used. When this happens, carbon dioxide gas is given off. This is called **respiration** [rehs-puh-RAY-shuhn].

Photosynthesis: Energy + Carbon dioxide + Water → Sugar + Oxygen

Respiration: Oxygen + Sugar → Carbon dioxide + Water + Energy

How does the activity in this plant change from day to night?

You will notice that photosynthesis is just the opposite of respiration. Photosynthesis builds up sugar. Respiration breaks it down. Photosynthesis uses carbon dioxide and gives off oxygen. Respiration uses oxygen and gives off carbon dioxide. Photosynthesis gives the plant sugar for its cells. Remember that sugar gives both energy and building materials.

A green plant carries on both photosynthesis and respiration. Extra sugar is most often stored in plants in the form of starch. It may also be changed into other kinds of sugar.

328

What may become of the carbon dioxide breathed out by these people?

Animals, including you, and plants that aren't green cannot make sugar. They must get it from green plants. Animals and plants that aren't green carry on respiration, but not photosynthesis. During respiration both animals and plants give off carbon dioxide. This carbon dioxide goes into the air and also into the water. From the air, land plants get their carbon dioxide to make sugar. Water plants get it directly from the water. You can see that the same carbon atoms that are now part of you have been used many times before. You are made of matter that has been used before! The carbon dioxide you are breathing out right now will be used by plants to make food again. Then it will become part of other living things.

Photosynthesis and respiration happen everywhere in the world where there are plants and animals. You can make a tiny world of plants and animals. In it you can see how they live together, as long as there is the right amount of plants for the animals. You will need a small clear bag, some tape, and water from a fish tank, enough to fill the bag ¾ full. Also get two or three small water snails, a few pieces of water plants such as the elodea, and a liter jar.

Put the snails and plants into the bag of water. Twist the top of the bag again and again, sealing it with tape. Place the bag in a jar to hold it up. Leave the jar in a place where it can get light, but not direct sunlight.

You have made a place where certain plants and animals can live together. No water or air can get into the clear bag. Only energy can pass through. What form of energy? How long do your plants and animals live together? Why are they able to live together in this tiny world?

How does your body exchange carbon dioxide for oxygen? When you breathe in, air enters your nose and passes into an air tube. At its lower end the tube divides, sending one branch to each lung. In the lungs, these branches divide again and again. They divide until all parts of the lungs are reached by the branching air tubes.

The smallest branches of the air tubes open into a bunch of tiny **air sacs.** The air sacs are lined with a single layer of cells. Around cells are very thin blood vessels.

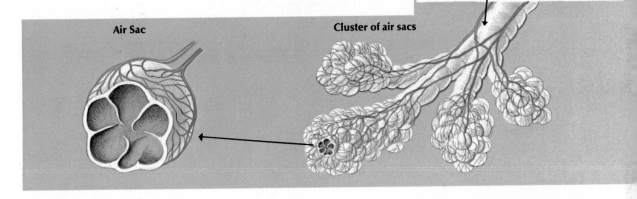

Air Sac

Cluster of air sacs

Oxygen from the air that you breathe in passes through the walls of the air sacs and into the blood vessels. The oxygen in the blood is carried to all the body cells. When it joins with food in the cells and energy is released, carbon dioxide is given off. The carbon dioxide passes out of the cells and into the blood. When the blood reaches the air sacs, the carbon dioxide passes out of the blood vessels and into the air sacs. It leaves your body when you breathe out. The air we breathe in is about 20% oxygen and just a trace of carbon dioxide. The air we breathe out is 16% oxygen and 4% carbon dioxide. In other words, with each breath, we trade some carbon dioxide for some oxygen.

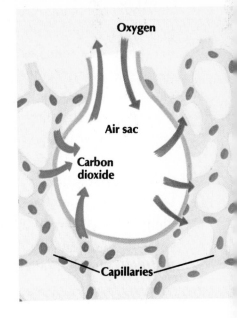

While reading this sentence you have probably breathed in and out once. How often do you exchange carbon dioxide for oxygen in one minute? Here's a way to find out.

Put the inside of your hand in front of your nose. Every time you feel the rush of air on your hand, count it as breathing out once. Ask your partner to keep track of the time. Your partner will tell you when to begin counting the number of times you breathe out. After one minute has passed, your partner will tell you to stop counting. How many times did you breathe out in one minute? You take in half a liter of air each time you breathe in. How much air did you breathe out in one minute?

Now, jump on one foot for a minute. When you are finished, have your partner time you for one minute while you count the number of times you breathe out. How many breaths did you breathe out this time? Why do you exchange carbon dioxide for oxygen more often during and right after jumping than when you are resting?

From Sugar to Other Compounds

Green plants make a lot of sugar. Then why don't all plants taste sweet?

A green leaf doesn't taste sweet, and neither does a piece of bark or root. Parts of some plants do taste sweet because they have large amounts of stored sugar. That's why many fruits taste sweet. That's why we can remove sugar from stems of sugar cane, roots of sugar beets, and the sap of sugar-maple trees.

left: The greenish-white roots of sugar beets like this one are placed in machines that spin off the beets' dark syrup, leaving white sugar crystals. *right*: Between 30 L (about 7 gal.) and 40 L (about 10 gal.) of the sap from a sugar maple tree are needed to make only 1 L (about 1 qt.) of maple syrup.

All plants, however, change some of their sugar into other compounds. In fact, every plant is made of compounds that began as sugar! Rough bark, soft petals, wax on leaves, even the odor of the flower—all began as sugar made by photosynthesis. The sugar was then changed into these other compounds.

These foods are all rich in starch. Which ones get their starch from wheat flour or other cereals?

Have you ever tasted freshly picked peas or corn? They have a sweet taste. In a few days, or even in a few hours, they taste starchy. What happens is that their sugar is changed into starch. This starch is the kind you eat in potatoes, cereals, breads, and other foods.

All plants change some of their sugar to fat. You don't notice the fat in plants because most parts of a plant don't have much fat in them. Some plants, however, store a great deal of fat in certain parts. Peanuts, beans, and nuts all have a great deal of stored fat. Liquid fats from plants are called vegetable oils.

These foods are all rich in fats. Which ones contain vegetable oils?

Sugars, starches, and fats are the fuels that give energy to your body. But your body itself is made mostly of another kind of compound called protein. Your skin, your blood, your hair, your muscles are made mostly of protein. Every single cell in your body has protein in it.

All the protein in your body came from plants! You got some of it by eating plants. You got the rest by eating food from animals that ate plants. The beginning of every protein is in a plant, just as the beginning of every kind of food is in a plant.

Which of these protein foods came directly from plants, and which came from animals that ate plants?

There are many different kinds of proteins. All of them are alike in certain ways:

1. All protein molecules are made of long chains of smaller molecules fastened together.
2. The smaller molecules are called **amino acids.** [uh-MEE-noh AS-ihds].
3. Most protein foods have many of the different amino acids.

When you eat proteins, the molecules are broken up into separate amino acid molecules. Once inside your body cells, these molecules join together again. They make the proteins that form many parts of your body.

Beginning with sugar, a plant growing in sunlight can make vitamins. They are needed for good health. Although you need only tiny amounts of each vitamin, each one is very necessary. They play an important part in keeping your body in good running order, and in your general good health.

Do you know the names of some vitamins or minerals that we get from these foods?

Minerals are also needed for good health. Calcium and phosphorous are important for growing bone. Iron is needed for making the red blood cells that carry oxygen to all the parts of your body.

Here again, you can thank green plants. Through their roots, plants take in minerals from the soil. You can get them by eating plants in almost any form, or from animals that eat plants.

Flow of Energy

Green grass under your feet, green tree leaves overhead, green fields of crops, green algae floating on the ocean—all green plants are changing the sun's energy into a form that can be used. Much of the energy is used by plants in their own life activities. But some of the energy becomes the energy upon which animals and plants that aren't green depend. Green plants are known as **producers.**

Since animals and plants that aren't green get their energy from green plants, these living things are known as **consumers.** Plant-eating animals, the **first-level consumers,** directly depend on green plants. They depend for their energy on stems, leaves, roots, flowers, seeds, or fruits of green plants which they use for food. Some plant-eating animals are birds, deer, rabbits, some insects, squirrels, cows, sheep, some fish, and other sea animals. What body parts do these animals have for eating plants?

below: Ground squirrel; *lower left*: Land iguana; *lower right*: Bohemian waxwing. What kinds of food are these animals eating?

337

The kinds and number of insects are so great that there are several groups of animals that live on them. These groups—along with all consumers that eat any foods other than plants—are called **second-level consumers.** You probably think mostly of meat-eating animals when you think of second-level consumers. They may eat one another, they may feed on mostly first-level consumers, or they may eat both. Birds, spiders, and bats eat insects. What other animals can you name that eat insects? Some meat-eating consumers are foxes, lions, cats, hawks, eagles, and owls.

left to right: Horn bill; Corn snake; Barn owl. What kinds of food are these animals eating?

In every community of living things that you are part of, you are a consumer. You are a first-level consumer because you eat plants and foods made from plants. You are also a second-level consumer when you eat meat and other foods made from or by animals, like milk and eggs. Make a list of some of the foods that you eat. Can you see why you are called a variety eater? Bears and skunks also eat both plants and animals. They will eat fruit, eggs, insects, or flesh.

Decomposers [dee-kuhm-POHZ-uhrz], such as fungi and the bacteria of decay, are another kind of consumer. They get their food from breaking down the remains of plants and animals or their wastes. Decomposers help return their matter to the soil, water, and air. Green plants can then use this matter again for photosynthesis.

Here is a way to see what happens when fungi and decay bacteria feed on plant matter. You will need a small clay pot and some soil. Also get a small, clean bottle and stopper, and four washed grapes.

Place two grapes into the bottle, and put in the stopper. Place the other two grapes into some soil in the pot. Sprinkle a little more soil over the grapes, and then water the soil.

Put the pot and the bottle near a window and leave them for at least a week. After digging up the grapes in the pot, describe what you see. Compare these grapes with those in the bottle. How are they different? What made the difference?

The flow of energy from producers to consumers in a community can be shown in a **food chain.** The arrows show how the energy is moved from one population to another. Start with a green plant, such as a bush. It will take in carbon dioxide from the air and water and minerals from the soil. Together with the energy of sunlight and the minerals needed to start photosynthesis, the green plant makes sugar. The plant's sap may be eaten by an insect. The insect may be eaten by a spider, which is then food for a snake. The snake may be eaten by a water bird. A fox may feed on this bird. After the fox dies, bacteria of decay will return the matter of the fox's body to the soil. Name the producer, first-level consumer, second-level consumers, and the decomposer.

You can draw a food chain for a marsh community. You will need to use library books to find out where to place each of these populations in your food chain. You will also need a large piece of paper and colored pencils or crayons.

Dragonfly

Hibiscus

Butterfly

Water snake

Bullfrog

Hawk

In order to show the energy flow through the marsh community, what else besides the populations do you need in your food chain?

Many Related Food Chains

This picture appears to be a simple food chain in which cows, the consumers, feed on grass plants, the producers. What other populations might there be on a farm such as this? What might their food chains be?

The cows are eating clover and other plants on the farm. You get milk from the cows. Bees make honey from clover, and you may use honey on your toast. Grasshoppers may feed on clover and birds may eat the grasshoppers. Rabbits may eat the clover, and you may eat rabbits. Can you think of other ways in which the food chains might be related to one another? This chart shows many different food chains in the farm community. Notice that the chart looks more like a web than a chain. In fact, the food chains of the populations in a community are together known as a **food web.**

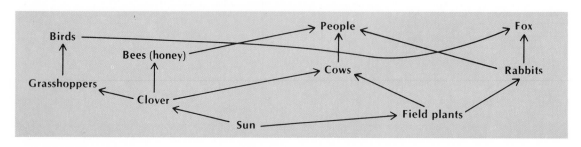

The populations in the picture can be arranged into what is called a **pyramid** [PIHR-uh-mihd] of mass. The pyramid shows the total mass of living things at each level in the food web. At the bottom are the producers, whose total mass is very large. First-level consumers, with a smaller total mass, feed upon the producers. Then second-level consumers, with a smaller total mass, are followed by final consumers, with an even smaller total mass.

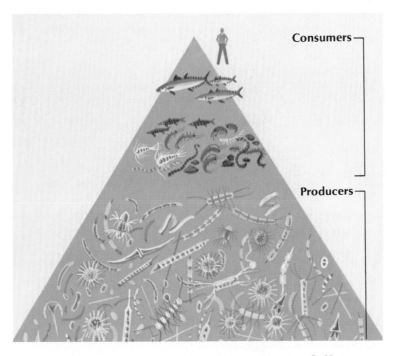

Here is a food pyramid for an ocean community. What might a food pyramid for a land community have at each level?

For this ocean community to support a full-grown person's gain of 0.45 kg, the sea must make 450 kg of living matter. Notice that the person at the top of the pyramid is the final consumer in the ocean food web. With each transfer of matter, there is about a 10-to-1 loss in mass. So 450 kg of ocean plants produce 45 kg of small plant-eating animals. The animals, in turn, produce 4.5 kg of fish—the amount needed by the person to gain 0.45 kg.

343

Besides the pyramid of mass, there is also a pyramid of energy in a food web. From the bottom of the pyramid, where there is a large amount of energy for the producers, the energy is used up steadily. In the final consumer at the top, the energy is stored in very small amounts. This loss of energy in the pyramid is in the form of heat and work done by living things in the course of their activities. Notice that energy is not returned to the community. How is it added again?

At what level in the pyramid is the stored energy most abundant?

344

A Community and Where It Lives

You have seen how the consumers in a community depend on the producers for food. You have also seen how living things depend on nonliving matter such as light, water, minerals, and certain gases. When you study how living things in a community **interact** with each other and the nonliving matter around them, you are studying an **ecosystem** [EHK-oh-sihs-tuhm].

There are many different kinds of ecosystems—ocean, forest, jungle, desert, tundra, and grassland. Changes are going on in ecosystems everywhere in the world. In order to understand how these changes take place, we will follow the changes in just one ecosystem.

This land was used for many years for farming. Before that, the land had been a forest ecosystem. Once a farmer cut trees and cleared and plowed the land, the forest community was destroyed. Many different kinds of crops were grown on the land. As the minerals in the soil were used up and crops were not so good, people finally decided to quit farming the land. What do you think happened then? Would the forest ecosystem ever return? Changes would begin to take place on the land, but such changes do not take place overnight. They take many, many years.

Grasses and other small plants such as weeds start to grow on the land. You can now see the beginnings of a field. These first new plants are called **pioneers.** Why do you think this is a good name for them? How do these plants start to grow here? Where do they come from? Maybe wind blows their seeds from another place to the field. As animals feed on the grasses, the seeds they carry on their bodies may fall onto the field.

What changes can you see in this ecosystem compared to the picture above?

In time many small plants cover the field. Insects and birds come to the field to feed on the plants. After a while, these plants and small animals die. As their bodies are broken down, their matter is returned to the soil. This matter enables the soil to hold water and the minerals that are in it. Because tall grasses grow well in this soil, they replace the short grasses and weeds. Other animals such as ground squirrels and woodchucks begin to return to live in these grasses. When they die, the matter in their bodies is returned to the soil.

As more matter is added to the soil for many years, bushes and trees are able to grow. These plants replace the tall grasses. Bushes and trees provide more shelter and food for many different kinds of animals. Finally, larger trees grow and develop. The conditions are again just right for a forest ecosystem. What kinds of animals would you now expect to find here?

How long may it take for farm land to return to a forest ecosystem like this one?

The community in the plowed field went through several different stages. Notice that there was a change in most of the living things that made it up. New plants and animals appeared. They brought about changes where they lived. These changes made it possible for new living things to replace them. The community kept changing until the conditions were just right for certain kinds of trees and their seedlings. The changes that took place in the farmer's land took many, many years. The several stages of change are called **succession** [suhk-SEHSH-uhn]. Succession takes place in all ecosystems and may take hundreds of years.

348

These pictures show the succession of a pond to a forest. Compare the pictures with those of the succession of the plowed land to the forest. How are the stages alike? How are they different?

What Did You Learn?

- Living things need the sun's energy to grow, to react to different things around them, and to make more of their own kind.
- During photosynthesis, green plants use the chlorophyll in their cells to convert the energy in sunlight to the energy stored in sugar.
- The leaf is the main structure for photosynthesis in flowering plants. In sunlight, the chlorophyll within the food-making cells in the leaf produces sugar. Minerals taken in by the roots start the process. The sugar is made from water also taken in by the roots and carbon dioxide that entered the leaf through its pores.
- The guard cells around the pores in green leaves stop the plant from losing too much water.
- Cells of most living things get energy from food by using oxygen and giving off carbon dioxide. This is called respiration.
- Plants provide us with sugar, starches, fats, proteins, vitamins, and minerals.
- Since animals and plants that aren't green depend on green plants for their energy, they are called consumers.
- The flow of energy from producers to consumers is called a food chain.
- Since each consumer uses energy during its life activities, the energy in the consumer at the top of a pyramid is stored in very small amounts.
- An ecosystem is a community of living things interacting with each other and with nonliving matter.
- The several stages of change that a community goes through are called succession.

Biography

Joseph Priestley (1733–1804)

Sometime during the 1600's, an English scientist discovered that something in the air was needed for life. In 1774, Joseph Priestley found out what it was. Priestley discovered oxygen while heating a chemical. He called this gas the "perfect air."

The study of air and other gases was among the chief interests of Joseph Priestley. He did several kinds of tests with oxygen. Once he filled a jar with the gas and put a mouse into it. The mouse became very active. Another time he placed a candle in the gas and found that it burned more brightly than in air. The gas was given the name oxygen by another famous scientist.

Joseph Priestley was a minister and a teacher. His work in science began as a hobby. He was born in England and did most of his work there. In 1794, he and his wife moved to America, where he kept up his writing, testing, and preaching until he died.

Priestley discovered other gases and new laboratory tools. He wrote many books about these discoveries.

TO THINK ABOUT AND DO

WORD FUN

Number a piece of paper 1 through 6. Next to each number write the word from Column B that matches the group of words that describes it in Column A.

Column **A**

Column **B**

1. stops a plant from losing too much water
2. food-making in green plants
3. make the proteins that form many parts of your body
4. green matter inside the food-making cells of a leaf
5. getting energy from food by using oxygen and giving off carbon dioxide
6. open spaces in the lower surface of a leaf that allow air to enter

chlorophyll
pores
guard cell
photosynthesis
amino acids
respiration

WHAT DO YOU REMEMBER?

This picture shows a food chain in a pond community. On a sheet of paper, list the name of each plant or animal that you see. Beside the name of each animal write the name of the animal or plant that it eats. Then identify each living thing in your list by telling whether it is a producer or a first- or second-level consumer.

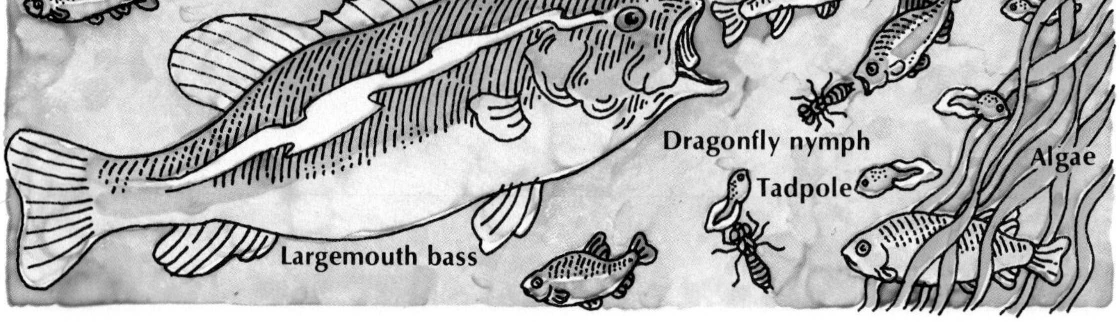

Golden shiner

Redfin shiner

Dragonfly nymph

Tadpole

Algae

Largemouth bass

Each sentence below describes a change that takes place in the succession of a pond to a marsh or a swamp. Copy the sentences. Then write the letter A next to the sentence that tells what happened first. Write the letter B next to the sentence that tells what happened next, and so on.

1. Trees and other larger plants grow around the pond and reduce its size.
2. The pond fills with waste from decomposing organisms and becomes more shallow.
3. The pond becomes a marsh or a swamp, or it may dry up completely.
4. Fish and simple plants like algae do not have enough water to live in the pond.

ACTIVITY

Here's a way to find out whether plants grow better in one color light than another.

You will need four bean seedlings, a grease pencil, and pieces of red, green, blue, and clear plastic.

Number the seedling jars 1 through 4. Make a tent out of the clear plastic and place it over jar 1. In the same way, cover jar 2 with the red plastic, jar 3 with the green plastic, and jar 4 with the blue plastic. Put all the jars in a place where they will receive the same amount of light daily. Be sure to water the seedlings when needed.

Look at the plants every day during the next few weeks and write down what you see. What happens to the plants? In which light does a green plant grow best?

Heath Science provides pronunciation for many unfamiliar words. In the pronunciation the words are divided into syllables and respelled according to the way each syllable sounds. The syllable that bears the greatest emphasis when the word is spoken appears in capital letters.

The key below is used with permission from *The World Book Encyclopedia*. The key shows how common word sounds are indicated by diacritical marks and by respelling. The key also shows examples of the **schwa,** or unaccented vowel sound, as represented by ə.

Letter or Mark	As in	Respelling	Example	
a	h*a*t, m*a*p	a	ANIMAL	AN-uh-muhl
ā	*a*ge, f*a*ce	ay	SPACE	spays
â	c*a*re, *ai*r	ai	HAIR	hair
ä	f*a*ther, f*a*r	ah	LARGE	lahrj
ch	*ch*ild, mu*ch*	ch	CHEW	choo
e	l*e*t, b*e*st	eh	ENERGY	EHN-ur-gee
ē	*e*qual, s*ee* machine, city	ee	LEAF	leef
ėr	t*er*m, l*ear*n, s*ir*, w*or*k	ur	EARTHWORMS	URTH-wurmz
i	*i*t, p*i*n	ih	SYSTEM	SIHS-tuhm
ī	*i*ce, f*i*ve	eye	IODINE	EYE-uh-dyn
k	*c*oat, loo*k*	k	CORN	kawrn
o	h*o*t, r*o*ck	ah	ROCK	rahk
ō	*o*pen, g*o* grow	oh	MOLDS	mohldz
ô	*o*rder, *a*ll	aw	FALL	fawl
oi	*oi*l, v*oi*ce	oy	POISON	POY-zuhn
ou	h*ou*se, *ou*t	ow	FOUNTAIN	FOWN-tuhn
s	*s*ay, ni*c*e	s	SOIL	soyl
sh	*sh*e, aboli*ti*on	sh	MOTION	MOH-shuhn
u	c*u*p, b*u*tter, fl*oo*d	uh	BULB / BLOOD	buhlb / bluhd
ů	f*u*ll, p*u*t, w*oo*d	u	WOOL	wul
ü	r*u*le, m*o*ve, f*oo*d	oo	DEW	doo
zh	plea*s*ure	zh	EROSION	ih-ROH-zhuhn
ə	*a*bout, *a*meba	uh	LAVA	LAH-vuh
	tak*e*n, purpl*e*	uh	FIDDLE	FIHD-uhl
	penc*i*l	uh	CYCLE	SY-kuhl
	lem*o*n	uh	CARBON	KAHR-buhn
	circ*u*s	uh	MUSCLES	MUHS-uhlz
	curt*ai*n	uh	MOUNTAIN	MOWN-tuhn
	sec*ti*on	uh	DIGESTION	dy-JEHS-chuhn

Bacteria [bak-TIHR-ee-uh]: tiny one-celled protists, 46–47, 339; in food chain, 340; kinds of, 47; reproduction of, 91

Base: any substance that turns red litmus paper blue, 135

Basket stars, 40

Bass, 10

Batfish, 10

Batteries [BAT-uh-reez]: a group of cells; inside each of these cells there are chemicals that can produce an electric current, 156, 168; solar, 156

Beans, 58

Bear, 22

Beetle, 32

Bioluminescence [by-oh-loo-muh-NEHS-ns]: chemical energy that is changed to light energy in a living thing, 207

Birds: warm-blooded animals that breathe air, have feathers, and hatch from eggs; most of them can fly, 18–21, 26; bills of, 21; breathing of, 19; classification of, 9; feet of, 21; flying of, 20; in food chain, 340

Blind spot, 247, 254

Budding: a way of reproducing in which a small swelling from certain plant or animal cells grows into a new plant or animal and breaks away from the old one, 93, 108

Burning, energy used in, 179, 206

Butterfly, life cycle of, 87

Calculator: a machine that does addition, subtraction, multiplication, and division very quickly, 273

Camera, how it works, 282–283

Carbon dioxide, and climate, 315; in food chain, 7, 340; in respiration, 331

Car engine, 183

Caterpillar, 87

Cave paintings, 260

Cedar tree, 65

Cell division [sehl duh-VIHZH-uhn]: the division of one cell into two new cells that are exactly the same, 89, 108; chromosomes during, 90; meiosis, 98; in one-celled plants and animals, 91–92

Cells: the basic parts of living matter, 5; animal, 7; food-making, 324, 327; in lens of eye, 239; plant, 7; in retina of eye, 245, 254

Centipede, 33

Charge: the result, positive or negative, of inequality of the number of protons and electrons in an atom, 144; attracting, 148; moving, 147–151; repelling, 147

Chemical bonds: forces that hold together atoms within a molecule, 180

Chemical cell, 155

Chemical change: the change of one kind of matter to a completely different kind, 128, 138, 180; kinds of, 129; oxidation, 182

Chemical energy: energy produced when certain kinds of matter are brought together and a chemical change takes place, 174, 179; in light, 206

Chemical formula: a way of writing what a compound is made up of; the symbols for elements are used, 127, 138

Chemical reaction: chemical change in which at least one new substance is formed, 130; iron oxide, 181

Chemicals, and electricity, 155–156; testing, 133–137

Chemical sentences, 131–132

Chemist: a person who studies the chemical and physical properties of matter, 133, 134

Chicken, egg of, 98–99

Chlorophyll [KLAWR-uh-fihl]: the green coloring matter in plant cells; involved in photosynthesis, 70, 324, 327

Chromosomes [KROH-muh-sohms]: parts of the nucleus in every living cell that control the growth and activities of the cell, 90, 108; during meiosis, 98

Cilia, of one-celled animals, 45

Circuit [SUR-kiht]: a path over which electrons can move, 157; closed, 157; short, 163

Circuit breaker: a safety device with a special switch that automatically interrupts the circuit when the current becomes too strong, 164, 168

Circuit tester, how to make, 161

Clam, 37; breathing of, 38

Classification: putting things into groups with other things like them, 3; of animals, 8–9; of living things, 4–6; of mollusks, 37; of plants, 53, 62, 79; of seeds, 57–59

Climate [KLY-miht]: the weather of any one place over many years, 292, 316; changing, 313–315, 316; desert, 312; kinds of, 294–295; and ocean currents, 307–309, 316; seasons in, 297; and snow, 309–310; sunlight and, 299–304; around the world, 294

Closed circuit: path over which electric current can flow continuously, 157, 168

Coal, 183, 198

Coccus bacteria: round-shaped bacteria, 47

Coelacanth, 15

Color, 225–229, 230; and animals' eyes, 245; importance of, 229; printing plates for, 264–265

Communicate: to share information, 259

Communication, early kinds of, 260; invisible, 276–283; printing, 261–265; radio, 280–281; recordings, 270–273, 284; storing information for, 273–275; telephone, 266–269; television, 281–283, 284

Community: producers and consumers that live together and interact, 345–349

Compound [KAHM-pownd]: matter made from two or more elements joined chemically, 126, 138; formation of, 131; kinds of, 127; making new ones, 137; separation into parts of, 132; from sugar, 333–336

Computer, digital, See Digital computer

Concave mirrors: mirrors that curve in like the bowl of a spoon, 222

Conductor: anything that allows electrons to move smoothly through it, 160; good, 160, 168; poor, 162, 168

Cones, of the eye: nerve cells in the retina, 245, 254

Cones, of a tree, 64–65

Conifers [KAHN-uh-fuhrz]: plants that make seeds in cones, 64, 79, 80; kinds of, 65

Consumers: those living things that get their energy from green plants or from animals that eat green plants, 337, 350; first-level, 337–338; second level, 338

Convex [kahn-VEHKS] mirrors: mirrors that curve out like the back of a spoon, 222

Copper, 124; an electrical conductor, 160

Corals, 42

Corn, 59

Cornea [KAWR-nee-uh]: a thin clear layer over the front of the eye that protects it, 243

Cotyledon [kaht-1-EED-n]: the part of the seed where food is stored for the growing young plant, 57, 58, 80

Crabs, regeneration in, 95

Crocodiles, 16

Crustaceans, water, 33

Daphnia [DAF-nee-uh]: a genus of water flea, 34, 35

Decomposers [dee-kuhm-POHZ-ehrz]: living things that get their food from breaking down the remains of plants and animals or their wastes, 339

Desert, 295, 345

Desert climates, 312

Dicots, 57, 80; flowers of, 61, 63; leaves of, 60; stems of, 61

Dicotyledons [dy-kaht-1-EED-nz]: seeds with two food parts; they are also called dicots, 57, 60, 61, 63, 80

Digital computer: a machine that can do arithmetic problems very quickly and can store information within itself, 274, 275, 284

Direct current: electric current that moves in only one direction, 167, 168

Dissolve [dih-ZAHLV]: to break up solid particles among the molecules of a liquid matter so they become part of the solution, 123

Dolphins, 22

Ducks, 8

Dynamite explosion, 182

Earthworms, 8, 41; regeneration of, 94

Earwig, 32

Echinoderms [ih-KY-nuh-durmz]: invertebrates which have spiny skins and live in the sea, 39, 48; kinds of, 40

Ecosystem [EHK-oh-sihs-tuhm]: the total system within which the members of a community interact with each other and the nonliving matter around them, 345, 350; kinds of, 345; succession in, 347–349

Eel, 8, 10

Eggs, of birds, 20; of chickens, 98–99; of fish, 13; of frogs, 96, 97; of mammals, 24; of reptiles, 17

Einstein, Albert, 186

Electric current: the flow of a charge between two points, 149, 157, 168; even flow of, 151; for machines, 151; fuses for, 164; in lightning, 150; making, 153; paths for, 157; switches for, 158; in telephone, 267

Electricity, conductors of, 160; energy from, 165–167; in lightning, 150; from magnets, 152–154; movement of charges in, 147–151; negative charge, 144; positive charge, 144; at rest, 144–146; safe use of, 163–164; static, 146, 149; water-generated, 190

Electric switches, kinds of, 158; thermostat-controlled, 159

Electric wires, frayed, 163; insulation for, 162; material for, 160

Electromagnet [ih-lehk-troh-MAG-niht]: a bar of soft iron with wire wrapped around it; this core of iron becomes magnetized whenever the current flows, 165, 168

Electrons [ih-LEHK-trahnz]: negatively charged parts of an atom that move around its nucleus, 117, 138, 168

Element [EHL-uh-muhnt]: any matter that is made of only one kind of atom, 124, 138; in compounds, 126

Energy: the ability to do work, 174, 198; chemical, 174, 179; from electricity, 165, 174; geothermal, 192, 198; heat, 179, 181, 183, 206; law of conservation of, 177–179; light, 174, 179; matter and, 180–184; mechanical, 174; kinetic, 174; nuclear, 185–188; from plants, 205; potential, 174; from rivers, 190–191; solar, 193, 198, 301, 302, 321; sources of, 189; using, 173, 189; from water, 190–191; from wind, 191

Energy transfer: the movement of energy whenever something happens, 175, 198

Equator [ih-KWAY-tuhr]: an imaginary line, on the surface of the earth, drawn around its center, halfway between the North and South Poles; it divides the earth into Northern and Southern Hemispheres, 293

Euglena, 45, 46

Geothermal, 192

Geyser, 192

Gills: breathing parts of animals that live in the water; in fish, 11, 12; in frogs, 15; of mollusks, 38

Glaciers [GLAY-shuhrz]: large areas of moving ice, 313

Glare: bright light that shines, or is reflected, directly into the eyes, 251

Gold, 126; as conductor of electricity, 160

Gopher, 25

Grasshoppers, life cycle of, 87

Grassland, 345

Greenhouse effect: the trapping of heat when sunlight passes through glass and heats the air inside, 195, 196

Green plants, 321, 337; in food chain, 340; food made by, 322–327, 350

Group tests, 133–134, 138

Growth, of living things, 5, 89

Guard cells: cells around the pores of leaves which help them not to dry out, 326, 350

Gulf Stream, 309

Gutenberg, Johannes, 261

Hair, electricity in, 144–145; growth of, 89; of mammals, 22

Heat, electricity from, 156

Heat energy, 179; in car engine, 183; and iron oxide, 181; in light, 206

Horses, 25

Hot spots, 192

Humid [HYOO-mihd] climates: climates that have somewhat less precipitation than wet climates, 294, 295

Huygens, Christian, 208, 230

Ice cap, 296

Indicators [IHN-duh-kay-tuhrz]: substances used to test chemicals and indicate their properties, 135

Information, using and storing, 273–275

Infrared [ihn-fruh-REHD]: rays of energy which cannot be seen, just beyond red light on the spectrum of colors, 276

Inheritance, in plants, 102

Inherited traits: traits that are passed on from parents to young, 101

Ink, making, 262

Insects: arthropods, all of whom have a jointed body and jointed legs, 36; in food chain, 340; life cycles of, 87

Insulators [IHN-suh-lay-tuhrz]: poor conductors of electricity, 162, 168

Interact: to act upon another thing and be acted upon by it, 345

Invertebrates [ihn-VUR-tuh-brayts]: animals without backbones, 9, 26, 31, 48; one-celled, 44–47; soft-bodied, 37–38; spiny-skinned, 39–40; sponges, 43; stinging-celled, 42; worms, 41

Iris [EYE-rihs]: the colored part of your eyes, 243

Iron, 124

Iron oxide, 180–181

Iron sulfide [EYE-uhrn SUHL-fyd]: a compound made of iron and sulfur, 131

Jellyfish, 42

Jungle, 345

Kangaroo, 24

Kinetic energy [kih-NEHT-ihk EHN-uhr-jee]: the energy of motion, 174

Lakes, temperatures near, 306, 316

Lampblack: a kind of pigment, 262, 263

Lamprey, 12

Larva: a stage in the life cycle of an insect, 87

Law of conservation of energy, 177–179

Law of conservation of mass-energy, 188, 198

Monocotyledons [mahn-uh-kaht-l-EED-nz]: seeds with only one food part; they are also called monocots for short, 57, 80

Mosses, 68–69, 79, 80; kinds of, 69

Motor, electric, 167; solar, 195

Mountains, and precipitation, 312; temperatures on, 305, 316

Movement, of birds, 20–21; energy of, 174; of living things, 5–6; of plants, 7

Mushrooms, 73; kinds of, 74; spores of, 73

Nails, growth of, 89

Nearsightedness: a defect of vision causing faraway objects to look fuzzy, 249–250, 254

Negative charge: the charge carried by the electrons in an atom, 144, 168

Nests, of birds, 20

Neutral [NOO-truhl]: neither acid nor base, 135

Neutrons [NOO-trahnz]: particles that have no charge and are found in the nucleus of an atom, 117, 138, 168

Newton, Isaac, 208, 230

Newts, 14

Nonrenewable resources, 189

Noon, sun at, 304

Nuclear energy: the energy inside the nucleus of an atom, 185–188

Nuclear reactors: special places where energy from the nucleus is obtained and controlled, 186

Nucleus [NOO-klee-uhs] of living things: the control center of every living cell, 90

Nucleus in matter: the central part of an atom containing protons and neutrons, 117

Nuts, 58

Nymph: the wingless stage in the life cycle of certain insects, between the egg and adult stages, 87

Ocean currents, and climate, 307–309, 316

Oceans, 345; temperatures near, 306, 316

Octopus, 37

Oersted, Hans Christian, 152

Oil, 183, 198

Oil spill, 190

Opaque [oh-PAYK]: blocking the passage of all light, 216, 230

Opossum, 24

Optic nerve: the nerve that connects the eye to the brain, 246

Orbit of the earth, and seasons, 298

Ovary [OH-vuhr-ee]: the oval-shaped part of the pistil of a flowering plant where seeds are made, 55, 56

Ovules [OH-vyoolz]: parts of flowering plants which will become seeds if they are fertilized, found inside the ovary of the plant, 55

Oxidation [ahk-suh-DAY-shuhn]: a chemical change in which oxygen is combined with another element to form one or more new compounds, 182, 198

Oxygen, discovery of, 132; for living things, 5; in respiration, 331, 350; symbol for, 131

Oyster, 37

Paper, early kinds of, 261; making, 262

Paramecium, 45, 46

Particles, of light, 208, 209

Peanuts, 58

Peas, 58

Penicillin mold, 77

Periodic chart, 125

Phonograph, 270–272, 284

Photon [FOH-tahn]: a tiny bundle of light energy that moves as a unit with the speed of light, 207

Photosynthesis [FOH-toh-SIHN-thuh-sihs]: the process of food-making in green plants, 322, 325; and respiration, 328–331; sugar in, 329, 350

Radiation, of nuclear power plants, 187

Radiotelescope, 258

Radio waves, messages carried by, 280–281, 284; in radar systems, 279; for telephone calls, 269

Rainbow, 227, 239

Reaction [ree-AK-shuhn]: a chemical change, 130; iron sulfide, 131

Receiver: the part of the telephone that receives the sound waves that have been carried along by wires, 267, 284

Recordings, how they work, 270–272, 284

Redwood trees, 65

Reflection [rih-FLEHK-shuhn]: the bouncing of light, 218, 230; in mirror, 220; reverse in, 221

Reflectors, 219

Refraction [rih-FRAK-shuhn]: the bending of light, 223, 230

Regeneration [ree-jehn-uh-RAY-shuhn]: the growth of missing parts from the remaining body cells, 94; of planarian, 95

Repel [rih-PEHL]: to push away from; like charges repel each other, 148, 168

Reproduce [ree-pruh-DOOS]: to make more of own kind, 86; by budding, 93; by cell division, 91–92

Reptiles: cold-blooded animals that breathe air and are hatched from eggs, 16–17, 26; breathing of, 17; classification of, 9

Resources: nonrenewable, 189, 197; renewable, 197

Respiration [rehs-puh-RAY-shuhn]: the use of oxygen to release the energy stored in food and the giving off of carbon dioxide by living things, 328

Retina [REHT-n-uh]: the part of the eye that receives the picture formed by the lens; it is connected with the brain by the optic nerve, 236, 245–248

Rice, 59

Rivers, energy from, 190–191

Rods: nerve cells in the retina of the eye, 245, 254

Roots, 53; of ferns, 66

Roundworms, 41

Salamanders, 14, 16

Sand dollars, 40

Scales: small, hard plates that cover and protect the fish, 10–11

Scorpion, 36

Sea anemones, 42

Sea cucumbers, 40

Sea fans, 40

Sea horse, 10

Seasons, causes of, 298, 316; in temperate climates, 297

Sea urchins, 40

Seeds, in cones, 64–65; parts of, 57

Semiarid [SEHM-ee-ar-ihd] climates: climates that have dry weather during most of the year, 295, 296

Sharks, 13

Sheep, 22

Shells, animals with, 37–39

Short circuit, 163, 168

Silicon, 125

Silver, 124, 126; as an electrical conductor, 160

Skeletons, amphibian, 9; bird, 9, 19; exoskeleton, 32; fish, 9, 10, 11, 12, 13; mammal, 9, 25; reptile, 9; sponge, 43

Snail, water, 38

Snake, in food chain, 340

Snow, and climates, 309–310

Sodium, 125

Solar cell: a device that changes the sun's energy directly into electrical current, 156, 193

Solar collectors, 197

Solar energy, 183, 193, 198, 301, 302

Solar motor, 195

Solid: the state of matter in which the molecules are held very tightly by forces between them, 118, 138

Solution [suh-LOO-shuhn]: the mixture that is formed when a solid is dissolved into a liquid, 123

Sound, preserving, 270–273; transmitting through wires, 266–269

Sound waves, 266; medium for, 211; movement of, 212; speed of, 214

Spectrum: a band of colors that occurs when light is bent in a certain way, 225, 226, 230

Spider, 37; in food chain, 340

Spirillum **bacteria:** spiral-shaped bacteria, 47

Sponges, 43, 48

Spores: plant parts that make sperm and egg cells, 67; of molds, 75; of mosses, 68; of mushrooms, 73

Spruce tree, 65

Squid, 37

Stages: parts of a life cycle, 87

Stamens [STAY-muhnz]: the thin plant stems that contain the pollen, found around the pistil of a flowering plant, 55, 80

Starch, in foods, 334, 350

Starfish, 39, 40; regeneration of, 94

Static electricity: isolated charge that occurs when there is an unequal number of electrons and protons; an excess of electrons produces a negative charge and an excess of protons produces a positive charge, 145, 146, 149, 168

Stem, 53; classification of plants by, 57, 61; of ferns, 66

Structure [STRUK-chuhr]: an arrangement of parts, 8; of plants, 53

Subhumid [suhb-HYOO-mihd] climates: climates that have a few months of rainy weather and a few months of dry weather, 294, 295

Succession [suhk-SEHSH-uhn]: changes that occur in an ecosystem in which new populations may replace the original inhabitants, 348, 350

Sugar, in photosynthesis, 329, 350; in plants, 333, 350; in respiration, 329, 350

Sulfur, 125

Sun, energy from, 193, 198, 301, 302, 321; light from, 206; and seasons, 298

Sunlight, angle of, 303, 304, 316; and climates, 299–304

Sunrise, 304

Sunset, 304

Sweeteners, 137

Switches, for electric current, 158, 168

Symbol [SIHM-buhl]: a letter or pair of letters that can be used to stand for an element, 125; in chemical sentences, 131

Tadpoles, 97; life cycle of, 15; regeneration of, 94

Telephone, 266–269, 284; how it works, 269; parts of, 267

Television, 281–283, 284

Temperate [TEHM-puhr-iht] climates: climates found in between the tropical climates and the polar climates, 294

Temperatures, changing, 314; and climates, 292–298; on mountaintops, 305, 316; and precipitation, 311–312

Temperature zones, of world, 293

Thermostats [THUR-muh-stats]: electric switches that are controlled by changes in temperature, 159

Tick, 36

Tides, energy from, 191, 198

Tin, 124

Toads, 14

Traits: differences in how living things look and behave that are passed on from parents to children, 100, 108; inheritance of, 102, 103; measurement of, 104; variations in, 105, 106

Transfer, energy, 175, 198

Translucent [tran-SLOO-snt]: scattering light as the light passes through a material, 216, 230

Transmitter [tran-SMIHT-uhr]: device that picks up sound or light waves and changes them into electrical spurts which can be sent by wire or radio waves to a receiver, 267

Transparent [tran-SPEHR-uhnt]: letting light through so that the things on the other side can be clearly seen, 216, 230

Tree rings, 314

Trees, 61; conifers, 64–65

Tropical [TRAHP-uh-kuhl] climates: hot climates found near the equator, 294, 316

Tundra, 296, 345

Turtles, 16

Twins, identical, 106

Ultraviolet [uhl-truh-VY-uh-liht] band: rays of energy, just beyond the deep violet part of the spectrum of colors, that cannot be seen, 277

United States, different climates in, 308

Uranium [yuh-RAY-nee-uhm], 185

Variations [vehr-ee-AY-shuhns]: differences in traits among living things, 105–108; kinds of, 106

Vertebrates [VUR-tuh-brayts]: animals with backbones, 9, 26; kinds of, 2

Vibrate: to move rapidly back and forth, 266

Vitamins, 336

Volcano, energy from, 206

Vorticella, 45

Wastes, nuclear, 187

Water, energy from, 190–191

Waves, light, 210–215; ocean, 191; sound, 211, 212, 214

Weather, 297; in Antarctica, 291

Wet climates: climates where lots of rain falls all year, 294, 295

Whales, 3, 25

Wheat, 59

Whelk, 37

White light, 226, 227

Wind, energy from, 191, 198

Windmills, 191

Wood, 61

World, climates of, 294; ocean currents of, 307; rainfall in, 311; temperature zones of, 293

Worms: invertebrates with elongated, soft bodies, 41, 48; earthworms, 8, 41, 94; flatworms, 41; planarians, 95; roundworms, 41

X ray: a kind of radiation beyond the ultraviolet band; you cannot see it, 278

Yeast: a kind of fungus, 76–77

CREDITS

Photography © Russell Abraham, Jeroboam, Inc.: 86 left / © T. E. Adams, Peter Arnold, Inc.: 41 upper right, 45 lower right, 74 bottom, 76 top / Em Ahart, Tom Stack and Associates: 37 upper middle / © American Museum of Natural History: 175 top / American Science and Engineering: 278 top / William H. Amos, Bruce Coleman Inc.: 72 bottom / Erik Anderson: 317 / Peter Arnold, Peter Arnold, Inc.: 192 / Robert J. Ashwood, NAS, Photo Researchers: 323 upper middle / Lionel Atwill, Peter Arnold, Inc.: 229 lower middle / Philip Jon Bailey, Taurus Photos: 177 upper right / Bell Laboratories: 275 right / Lester V. Bergman and Associates, Inc.: 77 middle right / The Bettmann Archive, Inc.: 271 / Alan Blank, Bruce Coleman, Inc.: vi / Dieter Blum, Peter Arnold, Inc.: 16 lower right / Carl W. Bollwinkel, Hungerford and Associates: 77 upper right / Björn Bölstad, Peter Arnold, Inc.: 78 right, 229 lower right / Animals Animals © Tom Brakefield: 21 middle left / Jane Burton, Bruce Coleman, Inc.: 96 middle and lower right / Bill Byrne: 21 upper right and middle far right, 340 lower left and lower middle left / Regina Caines, Polaroid Corporation: 231 / A. James Casner, III: 106 top left, 114, 137, 227 bottom / George Mars Cassidy, Van Cleve Photography: 182 / The Cerro Tololo Inter-American Observatory: 215 left / Richard Choy, Peter Arnold, Inc.: 70 left / © Alfred Cooper, Photo Researchers: 16 lower top / Gene Cox, Bruce Coleman, Inc.: 44 lower right / Culver Pictures, Inc.: 261 lower right / Bill Curtsinger, Photo Researchers: 21 bottom / Daedalus Enterprise, Inc., Life © Time Inc. 1980: 277 top / Dr. E. R. Degginger: 8 left, 13 bottom, 34 top, 87 top series, 99 upper right, lower left, middle right, 100 top, 106 bottom, 176 right, 180 left, 190 bottom / Dr. E. R. Degginger, Bruce Coleman, Inc.: 10 upper right / Peter Del Tredici: 74 lower middle / Phil A. Dotson, NAS, Photo Researchers: 337 lower right / Frank Dukepoo: 109 / Robert B. Evans, Peter Arnold, Inc.: 37 lower middle, 40 lower left and lower right / Richard E. Ferguson, Nature Photography: 78 left / © Dr. William E. Ferguson, Nature Photography: 59 left, 77 upper left, 337 upper right and left, 340 upper series / Jeff Foott, Bruce Coleman, Inc.: 21 left, 37 lower right / Ford Motor Company: 275 lower left / David C. Fritts: 345 lower left / Craig Fusaro, Tom Stack and Associates: 40 upper left / Gamma/Liaison: 190 middle / Warren Garst, Van Cleve Photography: 24 middle and lower right / Keith Gillett, Tom Stack and Associates: 42 bottom / Sal Giordano, IV: 99 upper left / © Rube Goldberg, permission granted by King Features Syndicate, Inc.: 175 bottom / © Eric V. Grave, Photo Researchers: 45 left / Farrell Grehan, The Image Bank: 172 / Al Grotell, Peter Arnold, Inc.: 42 middle left, 43 left / Groffman, FPG: 54 / Gerhard Gscheidle, Peter Arnold, Inc.: 229 lower left / C. Haagner, Bruce Coleman, Inc.: 2 / Dirck Halstead, Liaison: 49 / Phillip A. Harrington, Peter Arnold, Inc.: 46 left / George H. Harrison from Grant Heilman: 22 lower right, 33 middle left, 251 bottom / Hal H. Harrison from Grant Heilman: 33 middle right / Grant Heilman: 37 upper right, 59 middle and upper right, 66 lower right, 67, 95, 122 top, 174 bottom, 180 lower right, 214, 227 left, 324, 326, 333 middle, 342, 345 upper right / Vance Henry, Taurus Photos: 25 left / Robert

372

147, 148 top, 178, 179 top, 212, 222 top left, 252 bottom / Steve Paulson, Tom Stack and Associates: 142 / Barbara Pfeffer, Peter Arnold, Inc.: 86 middle / Pfizer, Inc.: 77 lower middle / © Hans Pfletschinger, Peter Arnold, Inc.: 15 top, 17, 32 upper right, 36 upper left, upper middle left, 38, 87 lower right series, 96 top and left, 177 lower left, 207 right, 261 bottom / Alan Pitcairn from Grant Heilman: 183 left, 345 lower middle / G. D. Plage, Bruce Coleman, Inc.: 206 middle / © Dr. Robert H. Potts, Jr., Photo Researchers: 8 bottom right / Allan Power, Photo Researchers: 10 lower right, 37 middle right / Carl Purcell, Photo Researchers: 222 top right / S. Rannels from Grant Heilman: 66 upper right / Raytheon Company: 202 / Animals Animals © Michael and Barbara Reed: 22 middle / Hans Reinhard, Bruce Coleman, Inc.: 21 middle right / Kent Reno, Jeroboam, Inc.: 20 left / Ed Robinson, Tom Stack and Associates: 10 lower left / Martin M. Rotker, Taurus Photos: 41 lower right / Jeffrey Rotman: 33 lower left, 40 lower middle, 42 left, 94 top series / Leonard Lee Rue, III, NAS, Photo Researchers: 8 middle right / Leonard Lee Rue, III, Van Cleve Photography: 24 lower left / Runk/Rannels from Grant Heilman: 98 / Runk/Schoenberger from Grant Heilman: 7 left, 11, 12, 30, 34 bottom, 37 left, 39 top, 43 middle left and middle right, 45 upper right, 47 upper right, 52, 92 lower right, 93 upper right / Joseph S. Rychetnik, Photo Researchers: 86 lower right / SEF/EPA: 260 left / Scala/EPA: 261 upper right / © David Scharf, Peter Arnold, Inc.: 219 / Charles Schmidt, Taurus Photos: 216 / Peter Schweitzer: 320 / Shostal Associates: 309 / Rhoda Sidney, Monkmeyer Press: 278 lower right / Slidemakers: 129 lower left, 270 top / Camilla Smith, Rainbow: 177 upper left / Clyde H. Smith, Peter Arnold, Inc.: 297, 329 / Wayne Springer: 18 bottom, 46 top, 72 top, 75 bottom, 92 left, 120 bottom left, 122 bottom, 146, 196, 223, 224, 241, 264, 270 bottom, 282, 300, 302, 303, 309 bottom / Tom Stack, Tom Stack and Associates: 22 top, 23 upper right, 40 upper right, 42 middle far right, 43 right, 295 left, 338 left, 340 top, 345 lower right / Deidra Delano Stead: 58, 62, 76 bottom, 93 bottom, 104 bottom, 105, 194, 210, 221, 225 bottom, 238, 247, 251 top, 252 top, 253, 312 top, 328, 332, 339 / Ken Stepnell, Taurus Photos: 24 upper right / David M. Stone: 16 upper top, 22 left, 69 upper right, 74 upper middle / Erika Stone, Peter Arnold, Inc.: 106 right / John E. Swedberg: 74 upper left, upper right, lower left, lower right, 204 / Taurus Photos: 174 top, 191 left, 312 lower right / Kim Taylor, Bruce Coleman, Inc.: 99 middle / Margaret K. Tenney: 296 top / William A. Tenney: 23 lower right, 73 middle, 99 bottom, 116 top, 167, 190 top, 195 right, 295 upper right and lower right / F. A. Thornhill, NAS, Photo Researchers: 338 middle / Norman Owen Tomalin, Bruce Coleman, Inc.: 323 lower right / © Ron Trimarchi, Taurus Photos: 174 middle right / John Urban: 153, 154, 157, 159, 161, 163, 165 top, 209, 213, 217, 228 top, middle, 229 top, 276 / V-DIA/EPA: 260 lower right / Peter Vandermark: 165 / R. S. Virdee from Grant Heilman: 305 / Carole Vogel: 234 / Wang Corporation: 375 upper left, 285 / D. Waugh, Peter Arnold, Inc.: 290 / © Carroll H. Weiss, RBP,

1980, Camera M. D. Studios, Inc.: 61 lower right, 245 / Richard Weiss, Peter Arnold, Inc.: 16 middle right / Harry Wilks, Stock, Boston: 189 / Myron Wood, Photo Researchers: 323 middle right / C. M. Wright, Tom Stack and Associates: 313 left / G. Ziesler, Peter Arnold, Inc.: 20 middle right, 36 lower middle / Zoiner, Peter Arnold, Inc.: 183 right / Nikolay Žurek, Jeroboam, Inc.: 278 lower left

Special thanks are extended to the following schools which were helpful in the production of photographs: Coolidge Elementary School, Watertown, Massachusetts; Our Lady of Lourdes Parish School, Jamaica Plain, Massachusetts; Cambridge Alternative Public School, Cambridge, Massachusetts; Cathedral Grammar School, Boston, Massachusetts; Blessed Sacrament School, Cambridge, Massachusetts

5 6 7 8 9 0